THE ULTIMATE CANON OF KNOWLEDGE

Dr. Alvin Boyd Kuhn

THE BOOK TREE
San Diego, California

Originally published
1963 by the author
© 1963
Alvin Boyd Kuhn

New material, layout & revisions
© 2024
The Book Tree
All rights reserved

ISBN 978-1-58509-463-9

Front cover design
© Shaiith

Interior layout & design
Paul Tice

Published by
The Book Tree
San Diego, CA
www.thebooktree.com

We provide fascinating and educational products to help awaken the public to new ideas and information that would not be available otherwise.
Call 1 (800) 700-8733 for our FREE BOOK TREE CATALOG.

CONTENTS

Chapter One
Echoes of Past Wisdom..5

Chapter Two
Mind and Supermind..16

Chapter Three
Reality and Appearance..23

Chapter Four
Theism—Deism—Pantheism...34

Chapter Five
Kinship of Mind with Nature..42

Chapter Six
The Natural Revelation...54

Chapter Seven
Mind's Source in Nature...66

Chapter Eight
The Wisdom of Aurobindo...77

Chapter Nine
The Insights of Carl Jung...88

Chapter Ten
The Heart of Nature..96

Chapter Eleven
God and Nature...*104*

Chapter Twelve
Finding Truth Without Science...115

Chapter Thirteen
The War of Opposites..130

Chapter Fourteen
Cosmic Mind Made Manifest...142

Chapter Fifteen
Understanding the Mind of God...154

Chapter Sixteen
Structure of the Archetypes..170

Chapter Seventeen
The Four Powers of Creation...179

Chapter Eighteen
Experiencing the Divine Fire...193

Chapter Nineteen
The Rules of Nature Connected to Man.....................................205

Chapter Twenty
Spiritual Truths in Nature...215

Chapter Twenty-One
Reading the Stars..222

Chapter Twenty-Two
The Limits of Consciousness..230

CHAPTER ONE

ECHOES OF PAST WISDOM

Ever since man has found himself in this particular world and possessed of an order of consciousness that dowered him with the power to think about his situation, he has also recognized that he is ineluctably driven to wonder about his existence in such a universe. From the start of his self-awareness, he has been persistently haunted by the desire to know the what, the how, and, ultimately, the why of it all. With the dawn of sentience there arose first the questions about his environment, this amazing world in which he finds himself cradled, its components earth and water, air and fire and all their interrelations, those stars that glitter in the upper firmament, and all the phenomena attending the cycling round of day and night and the seasons, sun and moon, lightning, thunder, rainbow, aurora borealis, ice, steam, hail, cold, heat, color, life and death of vegetation, and the endless forms and movements of things.

Then, as this wondrous gift of consciousness develops its astonishing powers, he finds that it introduces him into a world that lies not outside, but inside, himself, so that he must balance himself, as it were, between two worlds of being. He finds he must study both of these worlds, as his exercise of the powers of the one within gives him understanding and control of the one without. Finally when usage has sharpened the faculties of consciousness to great acuteness, his genius drives him to seek answers to the question of how these two worlds may be related to each other. He thus becomes a philosopher seeking that inner satisfaction of his thinking power which he calls meaning. Vaguely at first, then more clearly, he finds that his experience leads him to believe that this precious core of meaning is involved in the relation between the two realms of his being. All through his history he has wavered between two positions, at times being convinced that the keys to meaning are to be found entirely in the outer world, but again being persuaded that they are better to be discovered within the area of his reflecting consciousness. So his philosophy has oscillated between naturalism and idealism, and it cannot yet be said that the human mind has arrived at an understanding of precisely how the two areas of his experience, his two worlds, are related to each other. The quest for a more lucid insight into this problem and a sounder understanding of its total import is the theme of the present work.

The evolutionary development of man's powers of consciousness, deepening and exalting his intelligence, commits him inevitably to an ever-intensifying search for knowledge and the satisfactions and delights of understanding. The scriptures of antiquity which he has cherished as his greatest treasures of light and truth admonish him that understanding and wisdom are the most precious things he can discover in life. He feels within him an insatiable curiosity, a veritable hunger and thirst for the truths and realities of his existence. He is still Ajax crying for the light. For all too largely his life is a groping amid shadows, a wandering in strange and uncertain courses, a stumbling progress not without falls and injury. Ignorance, breeding doubt and fear, still darkens his vision and makes his advance precarious, perilous. In want of clear knowledge of his road, evils ambush his path among unknown ways, accidents befall him, catastrophe strikes him suddenly and he writhes too often in misery and suffering.

So his quest for the understanding that brings wisdom and security still persists and grows more exciting as his continuing effort brings him new rewards that enlighten and cheer him and entice him on to further pursuit of his high goal. Thus goaded and lured, driven by pressures and elated by fresh delights, he presses on toward some distant goal, which a more or less blind instinct seems to tell him lies ahead for his attainment.

The world and his experience with it confront him with the staggering fact of the endless diversity and multiplicity of the phenomena of life. He is constantly challenged, first with the meaning of particular events, then with the meaning of the total ensemble of world existence. Deepening reflection seems to convince him that the solution of problems posited by the flow of immediate and particular events can be found only in a comprehensive understanding of the ultimate meaning of the whole. The quest for this consummate insight has led him to formulate the principles of what he calls the science of total being, *ontology*. After centuries of effort to reach determinations as to this crowning interrogatory, he seems forced to fall back on the recognition that life and the universe are gigantic mysteries which overtax his present powers of full comprehension. However they give evidence all along of embodying the mighty secrets of their nature and being, prodding man's undying curiosity to delve into them. When he presses for an answer to the inevitable question as to *what* the world is, he sees that it is virtually impossible for him to frame anything but a tentative answer and never a final one. For if he settles upon some conceived or postulated primary essence as the substrate and core of all being and names it, he is at once faced with the question of *what* that original essence is. The ultimate thing that is the what of existence is beyond his ken.

If Thales thought this basic constituent of being is water, Anaximander, air, Heraclitus fire, and Democritus atoms, and modern science finds that it is indeed atoms, yet the search for *what* they are must still go on. Centuries of the profoundest reflection of the Hindu mind have been crowned with the simple realization that the universe of life exists and that man himself is an integral part of its substance and its mystery. The inner and the outer worlds of his dual existence find, and will increasingly find, themselves convergent and unified in his own experience.

The brooding mind of the German Emmanuel Kant assured us that we can never know the objective world, that anything is in itself. But if man and the universe are identical in ultimate essence, there is the cheering possibility that man will come to know the universe as he comes to know himself in the heights and depths of his own nature. In fact it was the Greeks who urged man to know himself first of all, and he would progressively know all things. Much futile effort, especially in the domain of religion, has been put forth over the centuries to discover the nature of man entirely apart from his relation to the objective world that extended outside his interior world of consciousness. In fact this move was motivated by the supposition that his true nature could best be introspected when he detached his consciousness and interests as far as possible from the concrete world and concentrated intently upon the world within. Much philosophical persuasion of the sort still drives religious and cultural endeavor in the groove of this belief. It will be a primary objective of this essay to uncover the supreme falsity of this conviction. The effort will be to establish beyond dispute that the highest and most blessed attainments of wisdom and understanding open to man's consciousness will accrue to him through the exercise of his faculties of intelligence by which he will be able to relate his life most harmoniously and benignantly to the objective world outside himself.

It is the record of a lugubrious history that, particularly in the area of our Western world, the aberrations of the human mind under the spell of subjective religious misconceptions cut off the life of society from wholesome conceptual relation to the external physical world. The whole bent was to abstract the soul of the individual as far as possible from absorption in the interests of the flesh and its place in the outside world. This motive sprang from the persuasion, fostered by ecclesiastical pietism, that interest in the life of the senses detracted from the primary interests of the soul, that a hearty indulgence in the natural impulses of the body were hostile to the life of the soul, and that therefore the lure of the world was to be resisted and destroyed.

It needs no dissertation to elaborate and certify what the record of history reveals as to this portent obsession of the dour religious consciousness over the centuries. It has left its lamentable record in the tale of corruption, banality, superstition, bigotry and general moral and mental blight that overspread the area of Christian Europe over the middle period which has come to be known as the Dark Ages. The liberalization of the Medieval mind that came with the Italian Renaissance of the fourteenth century turned attention to some extent back to the world of nature, and salutary results were manifested. It was the force that possibly led most directly to the first real investigation of the natural world that came with the seventeenth century and has now burgeoned into the prodigious marvel of modern science. The benefits and blessings accruing to humanity from the relatively few years of this late focusing of the powers of the human mind upon the life of nature have at last administered the just and stern rebuke to the follies of pietistic religionism which arrant fatuity in that field had so fully deserved. The blight of evil character was lifted off the field of nature, and the moment man sought her companionship and her secrets, she rushed forward to reward him with an infinitude of blessings. This has been mostly, however, on the side of physical easements and comforts for his bodily existence. The question to be discussed here is whether man has yet gained from nature anything like a full measure of her power to illuminate his consciousness with the light of infinite knowledge, wisdom and understanding. Wonderfully as she has demonstrated her ability to contribute to our physical well-being, is it possible that she has still untapped resources to enlighten his intellect and beatify his spiritual life? The essay will aim to make clear her marvelous potentiality to ennoble the character and elevate the position of man's cultural status in his life on the planet.

The modern world is not at all cognizant of the splendid achievement of the ancient civilizations of two lands at least, namely Egypt and Greece, in so relating their minds to the order of nature that their life in general flowered out in a state of health and wholesomeness that has hardly been matched in the history of the world since. History discloses that the daily life of the Egyptian citizen was one lived in close and intimate relation with the life of nature. No one can study the life of the Greek people of two to three millennia ago without recognizing the tremendous part that what they called *physis,* or nature, played in their modus of living both at the physical and the intellectual level. Their philosophy, which is still regarded as the heyday of the human achievement in that field, was solidly based on the foundations of all conceptuality found in the order of the natural world. Man and the meaning of his life were not envisaged as detached from the material world, but as of kindred nature with it and in its higher ranges an efflorescence from it. Man was considered as a blossom or flower on the highest branch of the tree of nature. Man was the highest product, the ripest fruit on the tree of the world. His life therefore inevitably stood in close correlation with the life of nature. The truth of nature could be truth for him.

And significantly enough, the genius of Greece's two most inspired thinkers, Plato and Aristotle, essayed to place man in proper and salutary relation to the two worlds of man's life, the ideal and the physical. Plato strove to place the foundations of human life in the domain of the ideal; equally Aristotle sought to establish them in the domain of the physical. It must be conceded that it was Aristotle who achieved a more satisfactory amalgamation of the two phases of our existence in the union of the noumenal and the phenomenal worlds. The Stagirite did not discount the ideal basis of our life, but he emphasized the utility of its unfoldment to beauty and its ultimate divinization.

But since the days of ancient Greece and Egypt, the mental attitude toward nature has floundered about in a sort of semi-darkness only dimly lighted at times by a more competent insight. A special kind of introspective envisioning of nature, which the Greeks had developed to a state of fair acuity seems to have been lost with that general decay of philosophical acumen that all too quickly followed on the age of Plato and Aristotle, and that left the near-Eastern world conditioned for the message of Christianity, which offered the vistas of heavenly consolation and bliss when sturdy effort to achieve the good life on earth seemed to have collapsed.

We should never forget or minimize the importance of the recognition of the historic phenomena which the philosophical life of the ancient Greeks presents as challenge to our intelligence. Greek thought rose to its highest summit of lucid envisioning of truth when it was still invigorated by the conviction that the world of external nature was permeated and animated by the spirit of the divine mind. The benignant force of the great God Pan was present in every tree, brook, hill and woodland nook. If nature could be so enlivened, beautified and sanctified by the deific principle, it was reasonable to assume that the life of man might equally beneficently partake of the universal largesse of felicity. If the historic record can be taken as confirmation of the soundness of the philosophy that generated its special outcome, it must be a judgment in the case that Greek pantheism produced an elevation of the human mind that still commands the unbounded admiration of mankind. It somehow committed the civilization of the epoch to the thesis that man's life with nature afforded him the most propitious opportunity for the attainment of the supreme values. The benignant and felicitous aims of life might be achieved here on earth if one lived in harmony with the soul of nature. If such was the source-spring of the élan that exalted the Greek mind to the heights, we are challenged to review this bright episode to recover the dynamic principles involved in it. For with the coming of Christianity no one longer listened with enchantment to the shrill piping of the goat-footed god in sylvan dell, as the piety-drunk zealots of the new faith shouted in riotous exultation, "Great Pan is dead." We shall never perhaps know how crucial was this crisis in human thinking, for the issues of two thousand years of tragic history were weighing man's mind in the balance. An obviously high intelligence had inspired ancient civilization to place its faith in nature, and for a moment it brought a splendid flare of human genius that has enlightened culture ever since. Why the brilliant light was so quickly extinguished is one of the most intriguing puzzles of world history. It is hoped that the present work may offer something in the way of a solution of this mystery, so fateful for all later development in the West. If a wholesome faith in the beneficence of nature somehow deceived, betrayed or failed the human spirit at this crucial juncture, it is of infinite importance that the causes of this tragic debacle should be discovered. Sir Gilbert Murray has characterized it by his famous phrase, the "failure of nerve." But if the Greek genius failed to sustain human confidence that supreme values were to be found in nature and the life of earth, does history, on the other side, certify beyond question that Christianity's contempt for the world and nature and its flaunting of the banner of salvation through Christ have exalted human life above the level to which paganism had raised it in the Platonic era?

What is obvious of course is that the exaltation of man is to be achieved, not by the dominance of either of the two elements of culture over the other, but by the fusion of both phases of influence in the life of the race. It is probably a quite adequate statement of the general truth of things in the realm of religion and philosophy that the aberration and error that has pervaded these areas of human ideation have sprung from failure to keep the two sources of dynamic influence, the objective nature outside man's consciousness and the spiritual forces within it, in complete and harmonious accord with each other. To open human life to the sweeping forces of the one, while closing it against the other, has at all times brought debacle and wreckage.

Since the human being stands at the point of balance between the two areas of his being, the physical and the spiritual--the astute Egyptians of old said that he stood on the horizon line between the heaven of spirit and the earth of matter--it is undoubtedly the supreme task of his existence that he master the consummate art of maintaining himself in as steady a balance between the claims and the forces of his dual life as possible. All religion, along with philosophy, has exhorted him to the cultivation of the interests and potentialities of his spirit conceived as divine. Perhaps paganism fell before Christianity because, in spite of its confidence in the beneficent offices of nature, it had not adequately discerned the principles and divined the technique of the truly harmonious adjustment of human life to the natural world. The human child is born into the very lap of nature, his nurturing mother, and he accepts her fostering ministrations gratuitously. His relation to her is instinctive and spontaneous, and most intimate. But when with maturity and the emergence of intellect and reflection, the matter of maintaining his salutary relation to his benignant mother becomes an obligation demanding the exercise of a phase of his genius which is little known to average humanity and is developed only by the highest culture of his psycho-spiritual capability. It was never enough simply that he dwelt with nature as a chick under her wings, that he partook of her lavish gifts for his sustenance, that he accommodated himself harmoniously to her requirements, or even that he received her bounty with gratitude and delight. For the ultimate exaltation of his being from his cradling in her lap there is demanded a refinement of his aesthetic and intellectual faculties that is beyond the attainment of common humanity and has been rarely achieved by exceptionally evolved souls.

It was a revelation of immense significance to the world when Kant brought thought to face the stern fact that the external world of nature was, so to say, opaque to man's cognition until he himself supplied the lens of vision through which her features took form and began to have meaning for him in every way. Just ahead of him, Berkeley had elaborated the conception that the world of nature was in fact not external to man, but existed only within the area of his own consciousness. It had no existence until human faculty created it by his perception. Kant went with this formula to the point of admitting that the objective world was in existence *for us* only as far as and such as we could interpret it to our cognition, but held to the conclusion that our translation or reproduction of it was not at all what the world was in itself. Knowledge of its true being was beyond our reach. Whatever it was in itself, we beheld it draped in the mantle woven of our own conceptual faculty. And this veil was so dense and impenetrable that seldom could the vision of man catch more than the dimmest outlines of nature's beauteous forms. There was needed, but seldom provided, the development of an intellectual-intuitional lens of vision powerful enough to refute Kant's interdiction of our knowledge potential and to give us glimpses of nature's real being.

Through the voice of the personified Isis, nature has so far declared that no man has lifted her robe of mystery to disclose her real being, which was the inner essence of the light of the suns. But now modern nuclear science has so thinned the texture of that robe that at least the mechanism of her infinite power is in part observable. This still is not enough. The canon of knowledge of the thing which nature is in itself will be available to man when, with science trembling on the verge of discovery that matter is not only energy, but the energy of infinite mind, he can so align his mind with that which the cosmos essentially is, that his knowledge of nature will match her own intelligence.

At any rate it has been generally recognized that whatever the world might be in reality, if it was to be lived with to best advantage by us, its children, the whole enterprise in living with it had to be engineered and managed under the terms imposed by our own faculties and resources. Only as man came to know its procedures and habitudes could he cope with it successfully. The matter of first importance for him was to learn to utilize the available resources of his own intelligence to acquire a mastery of the energies and materials which nature placed in his hands. This committed him to a study of his experience with her forces, a problem of quite an empirical nature. Yet so infinite and varied were the elements of this experience that his mind was challenged to rationalize the vast multitude of facets and nuances which the business of living in the milieu of nature presented to him. Thus he was led to departmentalize his quests and his knowledge into the separate sciences dealing with the subjective side of his nature, in distinction from those that were concerned with the world which he naively persisted in thinking lay objectively outside his own consciousness. So he formulated the study of the various phases of his own inner phenomena, such as religion, philosophy, psychology, ethics, logic, epistemology and their corollaries.

But, dowered as he was by nature with an irrepressible yen for knowledge, the more familiar he became with the ways and habits of the world about him, the more insatiable became his demand to know the *why* of the total scheme of things. For, whatever wonderful things were revealed to him in his effort to accommodate his life to that of nature, he still remained in ignorance of what a perfect science of living demanded for his highest happiness until he had some clearer vision of the ultimate end and goal toward which he should orient the direction of his total effort. His knowledge of the *what* and the *how* of the universal order could instruct him how to adapt his life, by sheer empirical outcome of his constant tentative, to the interests of his security and his well-being. Still every deliberate choice of action in daily living had to be grounded on *some* reason, however vaguely formulated, and that reason had to bear some relation to a larger context of meaning which by regression brought thought back to some total and ultimate motivation for the existence of man and the world. The little ill-defined reasons which at times seemed no more than idle whimsicalities, dimly perceived and often demonstrably erroneous and even harmful, had to have some integral place and function in a universal scheme and synthesis of the total meaning of life. Hence was born the mental enterprise which is known as philosophy, regarded by reflective minds as the noblest engagement of man's interest in his life in the world. It sprang from the necessity of his knowing how best to order his life in its relation to the cosmos as a whole. The issues of pleasure and satisfaction following certain modes of his activity, and the issues of pain and suffering ensuing upon certain other modes of behavior, bred in his consciousness the concept of meaning. By trial and error, if by no other route, things, events, actions came to have meaning; but the meaning of small immediate events had in turn to find itself validated in the context of a larger vista, in fact only partially spoke its piece and rendered its verdict unless it could hint at some significance for the wider range of values. As mind power developed and expanded, this perception of meaning, generated by smaller eventualities, seemed to demand for their rational justification an extension of their reference and pertinence to some final synthesis of all possible knowledge. The view of a tiny area of experience always seemed to necessitate for understanding a fully synoptic, all-embracing perspective.

This effort, in fact, is the gist of the highest endeavor of man's mental faculty. The bent, the drive, the inappeasable hunger of his mind for consummative intelligence must be recognized as the supreme and incontrovertible evidence that the indefeasible fire of a divine nature glows within the depths of his organic being. It is the certification of his membership in an order of being transcending the level of existence to which he is attached by means of his animal body. This was categorically stated by Plato, who declared that "through body man is an animal; through intellect, he is a god." Plato's predecessor in philosophical excogitation, Heraclitus, had put it in terms conveying the same affirmation: "Man is a portion of cosmic fire imprisoned in a body of earth and water." This understanding was one of the prime canons of pristine spiritual wisdom of antiquity, out of which came the various revered "scriptures" of the world.

The quest of philosophy, the term significantly meaning the "*love* of wisdom," and not, except indirectly, the science of wisdom, has thus been the loftiest incitement of the human spirit toward its fuller grasp of essential and ultimate verity. It inspires his endeavor to know more thoroughly the nature of the forces that breed, enfold, nourish and sustain his existence. The quest engages the exercise of his faculties of cognition at their highest degree of clear vision and piercing insight. It is believed that he rises to the expression of his divinest potential when this quest most enthusiastically absorbs his interest. The smoldering embers of his Promethean fire are fanned to brightest flame when the winds of his purest intellectual understanding blow across the field of his spirit. The ancient seer-psalmist did not miss the mark when he adjured the human to seek wisdom and understanding, rating them above all other things deemed precious. Indeed he postulated them as the essential bases of any true happiness. They are the well-spring of blessedness; those who neglect them become the victims of ignorance and calamity.

Down through the ages, then, the human mind has grappled with the facts of his experience, the data of history, the world of nature and has striven to distill out of the melange the priceless essence of comprehension and knowledge, the better to guide his way. As nature takes the water in the soil and by passing it through the fiber of a grape-vine converts it into the life-giving substance of wine, so the genius of the human strains the raw matter of his experience through the alembic of his thought faculty and distills out of the composite the essence of knowledge and enlightenment. Mind, so to say, compresses out of the crude elements of earthly experience the ichor, the wine and nectar of a semi-intoxication of consciousness that yield intimations of divinity. Philosophy thus inspires the most exalted delights of which the human genius is capable. "Sweeter than honey and the honeycomb," exults the Psalmist.

Since this quest is the noblest interest of mankind, the picture which world history paints as to the fortunes of the great effort to pursue it is fairly disenchanting, even distressing. To a depressing extent it is a record of failure, of blindness and confusion, of mental darkness, rather than the glow of the sacred fire on the hearth of the human temple. The sad reflection about it is that this diviner flame of the human spirit appears to have flared out for want of adequate fuel since that "ancient" epoch. The flame was bright enough to enlighten the mentality that produced those "sacred scriptures" which are still revered as the core of divine truth, the actual "Word of God." That glorious flare-up left us the Hermetic wisdom of Egypt, the epic of creation and divine ordinance of the Hebrew Old Testament, the lofty mysticism and profound rationalism of early Greece, the legacy of Zoroaster, of the Buddha, Sankaracharya, Krishna, Confucius and Orpheus. But then, after a last outflaming in Neoplatonism in the first three Christian centuries, the light dimmed, and nothing can be recorded but faint stirrings and flickering among the ashes and embers ever since, giving fitful flashes at various times. And as zest for keeping the divine flame aglow on the human hearth diminished, the hopes of a bewildered humanity turned toward heaven in yearning for new lightnings from the empyrean. The candle light of the human mind, after one brilliant flash, appeared to be too feeble to sustain itself. Overwhelmed with despair of attaining the good life through human wisdom, men fell back on the age-old tradition of the coming of Messiah, who would fill the world with the radiance of his celestial glory. The road to blessedness ran not though the terrain of divine philosophy, as the Neoplatonists had endeavored to convince the darkening world, but through the frenzied zeal and pious faith of a belief in the advent of Messiah.

The obsession of the general mind with this expectation, entailing as it did the end of the world in the apocalyptic crash, suffocated all hope of resuscitation from the esoteric message of man's own divine potential that had come down from ancient Egypt. Down plunged the soul of the West into the abyss of the Medieval Dark Ages, as Justinian at last closed the Platonic academies, the fanatical mob burned the great Alexandrian library in the fires of their hatred of philosophy and learning and Hypatia was slaughtered at the altar. Even Jerome was forced to recant his former joyous declarations of his love of the classic literature of Greece and Rome. "What," shrieked Tertullian, "have Homer and Virgil to do with Jesus and the Gospels?" The celestial radiance of the embodied Son of God had dimmed to near extinction the brightest flame of pagan wisdom. All history converged in the person of Jesus and all salvation was henceforth provided by the supernuclear dynamic concentrated in the essence of his shed blood. All previous pretension to wisdom was rendered irrelevant by the Savior's death and resurrection. Man's best wisdom is blatant folly compared with God's revelation of his nature in his Son.

Hence the humanistic sagacity of a primeval arcane science of the soul was crushed into nescience and oblivion for all the ensuing centuries. Yes, now and again sporadic efforts were made by intelligent individuals or groups to bring to the surface the submerged heritage of wisdom, but such attempts to restore the light were forced to remain subterranean to escape the watchful surveillance of the all-powerful Church. Finally after the Italian Renaissance and the Protestant Reformation had to a degree emancipated the mind of Europe from the strangling tyranny of ecclesiasticism, the quest for light and truth could be resumed at its ancient humanistic level. Whatever the voice of God in divine revelation might proclaim of truth and wisdom for humanity, it could now be complemented and reinforced by his voice made articulate in nature. And it could be a festal day for all the race if perchance it were found that the divine voice spoken through nature is more authentic than that uttered through assumed revelation.

CHAPTER TWO

MIND AND SUPERMIND

But even with the freedom to follow truth to its hidden lairs in all fields, and with the energy of modern intellectuality assiduously in pursuit of essential knowledge in every area of discovery, the cultivation of philosophy has not been adequate to the task of recapturing the full light of the lost heritage. Philosophy has become too largely the dry bones of a once lush and dynamic corpus of living truth. It has become the jejune and desiccated husk of its former meaty substance and has withered away into something called in dilettante fashion the "speculative enterprise." It is hardly expected anymore to go beyond speculation; any serious effort to find and establish truth with any degree of finality is regarded as rash presumption. If the cause of this default of wisdom and certitude be sought, it is as likely as not to be found in the faulty way in which man's intelligence has been utilized to determine truth. It has been exercised too largely *in vacuo,* that is, in logical processes that are rendered inane and irrelevant by too complete abstraction, in which truth is contorted into amorphous forms by the indeterminate connotation of the words used to express it. The search has been too largely confined to the purely subjective and ideological milieu and reference. Mind has tried to find its way to truth through jungles of the filmiest concepts whose outlines are blurred by the hazy and wavering definitions given to the words utilized for description.

Truth is being sought in the too rarefied atmosphere of pure logic and the thinnest abstrusities of thought. The effort at this level severs thought from life and reality. However god-like the faculty of reason, its operation is rendered futile and treacherous if it be detached too completely from the basic grounds of reality where alone its initial premises can be established with certitude. It will lose its way in the criss-cross of twists and turns in a pathless woods of abstractions if it does not hold itself in firm anchorage to the realities of the universal order. Given concepts embodied in language, which itself often gives misshapen form to ideas, he uses logic to weave a tangled skein of ratiocination that leaves him with nothing substantial in his hands. It is an effort to rationalize the principles of logic, when the aim should be to rationalize the real world.

He attempts to construct a fabric of concepts of gossamer thinness, assuming that it must necessarily match the pattern of the objective order, but finds in the end that it is a gross caricature of the world. How often it has been found that the status of things in the actual arena of natural event belies the conclusions of abstract logic!

A homely illustration of what is affirmed here may be cited to show the possibility of the miscarriage of logic which can miss the mark of truth and fact. Pure abstract logic would certify the truth in the following proposition: If an apple a day keeps a doctor away, two apples a day would keep two doctors away, and half an apple would keep half a doctor away! In the thin air of abstraction, the logic is impeccable. It may be objected that it is unfair to introduce mathematical considerations into it; that this presumes a comparison between two elements that are incommensurable. This is admitted, but it demonstrates how readily logic can be twisted awry of truth by just such matching of incommensurables. The premises for syllogistic reasoning must ever remain grounded in the concrete world. If the mind soars too far aloft, it loses sight of landmarks and may become lost in the void.

Thus so much of the effort of the human mind to ratiocinate the living world by formal logic has rendered the house of philosophy a ghost-like domain of dry-as-dust concept juggling and dialectical hair-splitting. It has become a battle of formal concepts, one being used to test another, and out of the jostling and confusion have come much incongruity and contradiction. In the attempt to explain such of the categories as substance, essence, subsistence, existence, space, time, dimension, succession, duration, contiguity, continuity, division, wholes, parts, unity, plurality, quality, change and a lot more, argument runs into such twists and turns that often a proposition can be shown to negate itself or stand stripped of all possible meaning. Mind can think of the common supposititious case of the irresistible force meeting an immovable object, yet knows that it could not occur in reality. Thought can claim that no object can be so small that it can not be further cut in two, yet factually the claim is belied. If space is to be filled with some substance, are the particles composing it continuous with each other, or must there be interstices filled with air or with nothing?

The quantities and qualities hypostatized as the data and tools for the work of pure science are never factually existent in the objective world. The theoretical "point" whose movements generate the dimensions of geometry has no factual existence. The concrete belies the abstract; the objective phenomenon balks when the subjective harness is thrown upon it. Living matter at many a turn controverts the formal principles of thought. When logicians argue profoundly whether there can be a vacuum; whether an extended object can occupy space;

whether a thing can legitimately be said to be in a "place;" whether it is possible to conceive of a thing changing in any way; whether the man who was the boy twenty years ago is the same person; is growth a real possibility?; is form the same thing as shape?; is space real or imaginary?; can a thing be one when it is composed of parts?; and finally whether it can be proved that a thing is identical with itself; it can be seen that human thought can follow the abstract principles of "pure" ideation into all quirks and oddities of fancied logic. In one case it has been contended that it is impossible to determine the meaning of the preposition "in." Zeno "proved" by incontestable "logic" that Achilles could not overtake the tortoise and the flying arrow could never reach its target, because it had to stop to "be" somewhere at each moment.

When one has tried to follow the processes of this sort of reasoning, one turns with mental relief to the actualities of the concrete world with the firm conviction that the mind can never apprehend the deepest truth of the living experience. The conclusion from all this must be that thinking which does not start from and continue in close relation to its foundations in the physical universe must lead to falsity.

Facing this general realization that naive reflection could hardly miss, the philosophical reaction could move in two directions to find a way out. Since mind in its own domain and relying on its own resources could not be trusted to encompass truth, might it not be possible that consciousness could use some other faculty than sheer reason to attain the truth objective? The other alternative was the instinctive supposition that truth could be learned by direct observation of the world of life as it lay naked under man's eye. The first line led to the predication of the existence of a "higher" faculty in the psychic nature of man than reason or even mind itself, to which the name of *intuition* was given. The second line led to the study of natural science, or what the Greeks had first called *natural philosophy*. The Greek word for nature was *physis,* but it embraced a wider field than is commonly subsumed under the modern term *physics*. The Greek conception so closely linked the possibility of the discovery of truth by the mind with the world of nature that all philosophical study would have to be nature study. All philosophy would have to be natural philosophy.

But with the decay of the Greek brilliance after the Platonic period, the perception of the indissoluble kinship between mind and nature faded out; and religion, exulting in the cry that Great Pan was dead, swung the pivot of thought clear off the pedestal of nature and strove to ground it on sources of intelligence emanating miraculously when tapped by the power of faith, from some fount of revelation transcending the range of all intellectual faculty. Since the mind alone seemed to disqualify itself by its own illogicality, the idea that mind, steadied and guided by reference to the truth irrefutably established in nature, might still find the road to understanding and wisdom, did not occur to religionists swept impetuously up to the heights of mystical afflation and straining feverishly for effluxions of divine unction. Nature's silent voice could not be heard by zealots filled with wild expectation of Pentecostal inspiration and Messianic eschatologies. If the world is shortly to be dissolved with the "fervent heat" of the Apocalypse, one could hardly look to it for salvation. So the alternative possibility that intellect, working in close harmony with the living world, might enlighten the human mind with true knowledge leading to wisdom and the highest blessedness possible to humanity, was occluded from the philosophical purview for many doleful centuries. The historical outcome was the unrestrained revel of religious zealotry in wild extravaganzas of faith and pietism which stretched through the European Medieval period till the age of modern science. Under Christian influence, the focus of philosophical reflection retreated from the physical world into the metaphysical. The truth that was only to be gleaned from the study of outer objectivity was sought in the recesses of inner subjectivity. Thought cut itself loose from earth and sought its answers in the misty void assumed to be bathed in celestial omniscience. Pious imagination, under the spur of exuberant faith, was free to sweep and scar amid the beatific creations of its own inspiration. Of a surety there was much here to engage the soul in the delights of mystical revel, as the unctuous recital of such experience from the long line of Medieval Christian mystics abundantly testifies.

The human mind is bound at times to exult in its sense of freedom to fly at will through the upper regions of thought and feeling. As antidote to the suffocating thralldom of dull and commonplace existence, it can be thrilling and transporting. It is a legitimate exercise of the powers of consciousness, one of the modes of expression of the natural force of the life principle itself in its effort to relate itself harmoniously with the conditions of its existence on earth. But the whole issue of sanity or dementia, happiness or wreckage, hinges upon its being exercised in a balanced relation to the actualities of physical existence and the instruction that is to be in the end gained from the observation and intelligence of nature alone.

But always the adventure into the world of transcendentalism, the reaching out into the unknown for mystical rhapsodies, is beset by difficulties and is rendered precarious by lack of any charts of the terrain or directions for finding one's way. Even India has supplied no Baedecker for planned tourism in this region where consciousness is expected to be ravished with divine enchantment. There are no road signs marking the turns and crossroads. The soul traversing this fancy-land must really create the scenery he enjoys, for what objectivity the adventure seems to have must be the product of his own fabrication. If imagination is not sufficiently productive, the sense will be frightened at the emptiness, the blankness and the hollowness of the dismal abyss. There is nothing to put bounds to the forms created by the vagaries of wayward thought. There is nothing substantial for thought to take hold of. Fancy can run riot to its wildest fling, but it all can be a chaos of senseless chimerical hallucination, lacking all coherence or vital meaning. Catalogued now in the terms of modern psychology as the region of the unconscious, it can be found as likely haunted by the demons of guilt, the monsters of fear, as by the cherubim and seraphim of divine ecstasy.

The thesis presented here does not concede for an instant that the use of the intellectual genius of man in its exercise of pure reason is a fruitless enterprise. The function of the reason is to test the principia of truth and the concepts of the understanding by logical processes. This mental faculty must be the ultimate arbiter of what will pass the judgment as truth. It is the instrumentality by which decisions can be determined as right or wrong. It is man's guide to safe walking on the pathway of life.

The contention of mystics that the mind, sheer intellect, is incapable of giving man the vision of truth or the experience of reality, and that for these he must develop the function of a higher faculty known as spiritual intuition, is erroneous because it is expecting and demanding that the mind, as intellect, should exercise a function and render consciousness a service which is not at all within its province. In thus depreciating the mind as inadequate, they are judging it on the ground of its failure to furnish the *content* of exalted experience, when its proper service is to pass judgment as to the truth or falsity, the right or wrong, of experience furnished by life itself, the content of experience furnished by the other modes of perception, mainly sensation, feeling and reflection. They demand that intellect weave the warp and woof of experience, when its prerogative and duty only require that it pass judgment on the character and value of the experience undergone by the total organism. They ask it to render heroic service beyond the line of duty and outside the range of its capability.

Moreover, in disdaining the use of the intellect in their groping for rapturous adventure in the transcendental void "above the mind," they run the risk of losing balance and suffering psychic damage in consequence. For the maintenance of this psychic equilibrium, an essential of stability and happiness at all times, even the most divine entrancements of the feelings must be in the end checked and evaluated for their good or evil influence by the cold judgment of the intellect. It marks a significant epoch in the history of Hindu mystical philosophies that India's most eminent and brilliant philosopher, Sri Aurobindo, has in categorical terms declared that the most enchanting afflations of the soul in mystical union with the divine must in the end be submitted to and passed upon by the logic of the mind. The mind is thus the court of last resort in determining the value of experience in any area of consciousness. It is the umpire in the game of life.

Furthermore the mystics base the claim for the superiority of this alleged "higher" faculty of intuition on a distinction between two phases of the activity of mind which in truth are not to be thus set apart. They arbitrarily take one mode of the mind's activity, which is its normal activity when functioning at its highest and best, extrude it outside the province of mind itself, classify it as a separate and distinct faculty and locate it "above" mind, when it is in reality the most perfect functioning of the mind itself. Aurobindo has been at pains to correct and rebuke this unwarranted and false differentiation between mind and its own supreme form of brilliant operation. The intuition so lauded and exalted "above" the intellect is only that intellect itself sharpened and developed to almost magical competence by long and exacting training in logical processes. Insights and determinations that in the initial stages of mental development were reached only by the slow steps of discursive reasoning, at a later stage of proficiency are caught in lightning flashes of vision and understanding, darting so rapidly into the field of cognition as to seem like the operation of a higher faculty. It is comparable to the brilliant and spontaneous execution of a Beethoven or a Paderewski at the piano, in contrast to the slow, tedious and laborious efforts of their first childhood practices. This thing called intuition is simply mind functioning like the geni that it is, at the incredible height of its magical power. Intuition may be said to be the attic of the house of mind, but it is still beneath the roof, not above it. It is the marvelous flower of the mind. It is still "intellectual." A vast confusion could be avoided and a great simplification of the principles of epistemology achieved if this false distinction was obliterated.

Emmanuel Kant has contributed much to the matter of seeking the principia of truth and the grounds of reality in the realm of the transcendental and the abstract stretching into the upper regions of thought. He has concluded that in that airy domain lie the categories by which all judgments are gauged. Mind itself supplies the forms and molds into which the content of experience must be poured to take shape and meaning. These are native to the Overmind of the universe itself and emerge into the area of human consciousness from that source. They come to man along with the power of mind itself. But he is doubtful of the practical value of the "abstract universals" discerned by the mind by the processes of "transcendental logic." He goes so far as to call them "shams." He regards them rather as the ghosts of truth, not the actuality. He affirms in his *Dialectics* that in its highest efforts to conceptualize truth, reason endeavors to scar beyond experience, and that such speculation has never added to our knowledge. These wraiths of thought essence can give us no authentic certain knowledge of the reality of the soul, God and the world. Still he concedes that as far as they are clear determinations arrived at by correct logical courses they perform some useful service as "regulative ideas," tending to keep mystical ideation from running out of bounds.

It is a matter of incidental, but great curious interest to a deep student of philosophy to note, however, that Kant's position on this item, the comparative valuelessness of the transcendental ideas, puts him in direct opposition to Plato, who made these "abstract universals" the very gist and essence of truth and reality, calling them God's "archetypal ideas." He constituted them as the basic architectural framework of the universe, the patterns over which all things were made. And--also very curiously, but naturally enough--as Kant's position reversed Plato's stand as to the content and value of the noumenal world, so also it exactly reversed the Greek philosopher's characterization of the phenomenal world. Plato considered the objective world of sensual experience to be but an imperfect, shadowy, dim blur of the real world of the divine ideation, rather an obscuration than a revelation of it. Kant thought that, in spite of the fact that we can not know the things in themselves, they yet did a fair job of representing their true nature and import to our cognition. But it was we who put our own stamp of recognition upon them. It is certainly true that we objectify them through the lens of our own cognitive powers.

In the light of the thesis to be adduced in this work, it is likely that Plato comes close to truth in affirming that the archetypal creative ideas are vaguely, if at all, perceived by the generality of mankind. All too universally the phenomena of the physical world speak no message beyond their crass objectivity. Mortals see their physicality, but not their ideality. Poets, artists, philosophers and idealists strain to catch something of noumenal import in the phantasmagoria of the scene. But to most the show remains opaque, never becomes translucent. The magic power to transform a concrete object or phenomenon into a divine idea demands a refinement of intellectual genius that is potential in our endowment but as yet not extensively developed. These "forms" of true being, as Plato called them, as yet hover over the human scene and haunt more sensitive minds with a half-spectral ghostlike appearance. The mind-magic that will enable reflection to bring them clearly within the focus of observation is the talisman that will open our blind eyes to the presence and their beauty.

CHAPTER THREE

REALITY AND APPEARANCE

Plato has charmed the fancy of thinking men since his day with the fascinating idea that the soul in its celestial state before descent to earth and body beheld these noumenal archetypes in their somehow objectified ethereality, but lost cognition of them when plunged into the coarser life of the flesh. To redeem her life to felicity it was her incarnational task to recover the memory of these forms and the method was a clarification of her vision by contemplation of the beauty of their earthly phenomenal representation. The soul must achieve a clear "reminiscence" of the divine ideas through a study of "divine philosophy."

But Plato's academic pupil and successor, the great Aristotle, ventured to assign the category of reality to these forms in their physical objectivity here on earth. The objects and phenomena in nature were, he averred, precisely these noumenal structures crystallized in matter. God's creative fiat had projected his divine thoughts into space and stamped them upon matter in its plastic state and they had hardened in substantial form. The question of their reality hinged on whether this category was to be attributed to them in their first or noumenal state or in their second or phenomenal state. Are things real when they subsisted as thought energizations of divine mind, or when they have concreted in material substance? Thus was the great debate launched on the world, and it has raged down the centuries; materialism versus idealism. No voice has as yet been strong enough to command the rating of authority to hand down a verdict as to which side holds the truth. Man lives in two worlds, one of physical objectivity, the other of consciousness: is his life in the objective world more real than his life in consciousness? As a thing would not exist for him at all if it was not existent in his consciousness, the noumenal form of the thing would seem to constitute its reality. However, if things were to exist for him only in their noumenal form, he himself could have no existence among them. Certainly they would seem to be most real in that form in which they sustain his own existence.

But is not this eternal debate in the end gratuitous and inane? Who shall say that a house is more real when it exists as a mental picture in the mind of the prospective architect or builder than when finally it stands in wood or brick on its site? All argument is certain to fall wide of the mark of specific reference if the terms used to define the matters at issue are not themselves rigidly defined. And who has ever laid down the precise definition of reality, or when has such an absolute definition been unanimously accepted? Fact is that the whole controversy is over this very point: What constitutes reality? If we had a categorical definition of reality, that itself would decide whether it was subjectively noumenal or objectively concrete. And since man must juggle the concept between the two worlds of his experience with it, true in one world and equally true in the other, and the ambivalence being irresolvable in favor of neither side, does not common sense dictate the final conclusion that things are equally real in both worlds? Or that the category of the reality of things is hypostatized when it is seen to be the product of the interrelation of both mind and matter in experience? Reality comes into being as the child of the dual parentage of ideality and objectivity.

Ancient Egyptian sagacity affirmed that man lived his life on the horizon line between the heaven of subjectivity and the earth of objectivity. The profound truth expressed by this symbolism should long ago have enlightened the human mind with the knowledge that all questions and problems whether of thought or of practical living find their resolution in the balance between ideality and factuality. Plato announced this principle in his doctrine of the golden mean, where truth stands at the point of equilibration between the two scales of the balance. What the present essay will attempt to demonstrate is the weight which the competent envisagement of nature can contribute to maintain the proper balance.

The failure to achieve this equilibration consistently in both the ideologies and the practical policies of men and nations throughout the course of history has stamped that history with the impress of abnormality and disaster. Tragedy of one degree or another ensued whenever the balance was too far shifted to one pan of the scales or to the other. St. Paul expressed it forcefully when he said that the interests of the flesh meant death; the interests of the spirit meant life and peace. To immerse dominant and unremitting concern in the flow of outward events with no deeper aim than to reap the harvest of sensual excitation, is to let the spirit languish and droop in virtual starvation. On the other hand, to withdraw the spirit as far as possible from its vital attachment to the world and the flesh is to deprive both elements of the human compound of their mutually salutary influences. Of the two aberrant tendencies it would almost seem as if the persuasion that the soul would receive extreme benefit from the farthest possible detachment from linkage with the body would be the most flagrantly injurious. But it is evident that both parties, the idealists, the monists, the absolutists and spiritualists on the one side, and the materialists and the positivists and naturalists on the other, have never approached the question from the standpoint of a reflection that the most naive reasoning should have propounded at all times. On their side, the naturalists remained stupidly blind and logically impervious to the need of an answer to the question why, with what adequate objective, the consciousness of a cosmocrator would wish to give itself the purely sensuous experience involved in the incarnation of its multiple fragmented elements in matter; and on their side the idealists with equal caecity never thought to demand an explanation as to why, if felicity was at the command of infinite deific being in the higher levels of existence, this power obviously chose to involve itself in the inertia, the darkness and the deadness of material embodiment. These considerations, which must be the backdrop for a clearer outlining of the primal motivation of the incarnational strategy, have not been envisaged in the philosophical purview at least since the ancient day. This default of knowledge has left the entire debate floundering in barren deserts and dangerous morasses over the intellectual and religious landscape. That loss of nerve, that failure of philosophy, that retreat of the spirit from hope of earth to refuge in heaven that supervened on the Platonic era has cast its fatal blight over the life of the Western world for all succeeding centuries. The obscuration of the light of ancient Egypt's arcane wisdom has left the philosophical mind groping in the shadows and apparitions of truth ever since the early time.

If a final word is ever to be said on the subject of reality versus appearance, it will no doubt be the assertion of what might be called plain common sense, the simple naive reaction of common thought. If a thing exists at all, it must be conceded to have vindicated its title to reality. Anything that yields us experience must have demonstrated its reality. Its fief on the title is established if it simply remains what it asserts itself to be and does not masquerade as something else. Doubt as to its reality arises only when it does not match some characterization of it that we have conceived for it. As a thing in itself, it must have reality in simply being what it is, as Kant conceded. If it chances to fail to fulfill some categorization of it to which we have assigned it, we accuse it of cheating. It can claim its own reality, but may miss the reality we have demanded of it.

Then as to the issue of reality versus illusion, or mere appearance. Here again even if the nebulous thing called illusion can be clearly entified, the judgment of unreality is not thereby postulated. As said above, a thing need only be what it claims to be or admittedly is, to vindicate its title to reality. Well then, an illusion is something definitely meeting the requirements of its description or definition, so that if it is truly an illusion, it is a real illusion. Our denunciation of it as illusory has only specious truth because we have demanded that, to win our verdict of reality, it be something other than it is, an illusion. As long as it remains true to its actual nature and being, we can not challenge its reality.

A somewhat different situation is met with in the issue of reality versus appearance. Infinite confusion has crept in here because this word *appearance* is susceptible of carrying two quite divergent connotations. There can be the appearance to our vision of something that does not prove to be identical with what we expected or demanded it to be, and we denote this as a false appearance, in the sense of an apparition and not the veridical substance of it. Then--and this is the point at which philosophy has failed--there is the appearance to our vision of something that was not in the range or focus of vision before. A thing not seen before now comes into view makes its appearance, as we say an actor emerging onto the stage from behind the wings makes his appearance. In the first connotation there is the question as to the reality of what appears; in the second there is no such question. Something as to which there is no question of reality or unreality, that was not in view before, now comes into view. Something wholly real appears to our view.

It is contended here that this is a point of utmost significance in the whole philosophical polemic over the questions under discussion. It hits directly the matter at issue between Plato and Aristotle, the battle between idealism and realism. Plato and his wing of idealists assert that the appearance of the divine ideas in the world of matter and form lacks reality and is false appearance; realists and positivists on the other hand claim that it is not a false, but a true, appearance. That is the issue in its most "realistic" form of statement.

A divine idea that before lurked unseen in the depths of cosmic mind, having been projected into a world of physical existences, now makes its appearance. The divine fiat projected it from out of the world of invisibility into the world of visible existences. In the simplest possible terms, it was unseen before, but is now seen. The only question that leaves the matter of its reality at stake is whether the thing that thus objectively appeared *is* the same thing that before its visible manifestation in our world was the divine idea. If it was such then, it must be the same thing now that it has appeared. God has simply clothed his divine idea in physical garb and brought it out from behind the wings of the cosmic theater and so it has made its appearance to us. If it is the same idea that the creative mind held as a noumenon, there can nevermore be a question as to its reality as a phenomenon. Certainly as a thought-form it was real to God, as our thoughts are real to us. If he wished us, his children, to know his thoughts, and took into account that we have no clairvoyance to visualize his mental pictures, he took the pains to objectify his ideas in such concrete substance as would make them visible to our sensory faculty. If Plato was quite right about this, it must be concluded that God perpetrated a poor, a muddled, job in converting the images of his thought into material objectivity. His negative did not bring out the form and outlines with sharp distinctness. Kant thought that they were sufficiently clear; Aristotle contended that they were true to the original archetypes. It can be admitted that they are virtually opaque to merely sensual perception. Something keener than mere eye vision is required in the way of a lens. Almost the main purpose of this study is to elaborate and illuminate what kind of vision it is that man must develop in order to read God's thoughts after him.

Idealists have betrayed the weakness of their contentions throughout the interminable debate by their insistent use of two words in the presentation of their case. These are the adjective *mere* and the adverb *only*. Invariably they have spoken of their alleged false appearance of phenomena as "*mere* appearance," or "*only* an appearance." In the name of common logic, how can any appearance of objectivity be qualified as *mere* appearance, or *merely* an "appearance"? It may be dim or clear, but if it is actual no one has a right to arbitrarily disqualify its actuality by smearing it with the slur of "mere" or "only." The whole debate has been enmired in confusion, but would have been redeemed to rationality and intelligibility if idealists had simply been content to regard phenomena as the appearance of real essences. The entire complexion of the argument would have been changed in the direction of sense and sanity by the omission of "mere" and "only." These two words insinuated the false premises into the syllogism and distorted the comprehensive view of the whole question. Beyond all cavil, the appearance of existential essence is the appearance of real things. If ground for argument remains, it can only be over the question of some alleged falsity in the appearance. But if falsity is alleged and substantiated, it carries implicitly the human verdict that God did not bring his creative ideas out clearly in his cosmic epiphany. Perhaps we can never appreciate adequately the service Aristotle rendered our human culture in his consecrated effort to correct Plato in this crucial item of his "divine philosophy."

Though the scope of our study can not include a survey of the basic principles of a systematic philosophy, it is difficult to elaborate any phase of philosophical truth without a sufficiently synthetic view to fit the particular aspect presented for emphasis into the *Gestalt* of the picture as a whole. Indeed it is next to impossible to treat luminously of any segment of philosophical truth in severance from the whole context. And certainly our theme of the psychic relation of the soul of man to the world of nature is integrally interwoven with the overall dialectic of God's purposes in thus committing the seed units of his own psychic being to an involvement in "nature."

To glean some rational understanding of his creative procedure, then, it is necessary to grasp as clearly as may be humanly possible the divine motive back of creation. This of course is almost the basic, the ultimate problem of all philosophy, but much will be gained for enlightenment if the most authoritative envisionment of this segment of philosophy is presented.

Universally the mind of mortals has been haunted and to a degree taunted by the question why God created his universe at all. Religion has continually affirmed that divine Omnipotence was able at all times to dispense for himself the felicity of contemplating the excellence and glory of his own being in his omniscient consciousness. Why, then, did he disturb his static immersion in the peace and bliss of perfect beatitude and exert himself in the prodigious task of populating the area of space with the uncountable hosts of creation? Before this awesome interrogation, the little mind of man stands agape and aghast. In the terms under which we must think of it, he could have chosen to remain in the blessed state of unconditioned being interminably. Yet he chose to end his repose, put bounds to his freedom, and set himself to toil at a task of unthinkable immensity under self-imposed conditions of the most extreme rigidity. This involved not only the exertion of his own tremendous resources of mind and energy, but plunged the hosts of his self-created progeny into the task along with him. It was in fact through them as his brain cells and his active limbs that he could exert his workmanship in the project. Of infinite and unlimited power and knowledge, he yet put the agencies of his being under limitation. He put himself, so to say, into the harness of physical instrumentalities to bring to pass the marvel of his creative genius. Mutely the mind of man asks--why?

The reflective sagacity of the greatest minds of the race has finally settled upon a determination which is after all a conclusion reached by the simplest and most naive of reasoning processes. If it seems to anthropomorphize omniscient being as a limitlessly magnified personality, and thus to reduce the Almighty to merely expanded human status, it is inevitable if conceptuality is to be expressed in terms meaningful to the human. A truth of the highest revelatory character is embodied in the scriptural statement that God made man in his own image and likeness. It carries the implication that man may, and indeed must, use the principle of analogy with the principles and realities of his own nature as his only available means of adumbrating truth to his understanding. The attempt to utilize principia totally alien to himself would leave him groping in unrelieved darkness. Kant was right in asserting that deep within man's own interior being and existing *a priori* reside the norms by which human consciousness can gauge the form and meaning of its experience.

Well then, since the ascription of all power and knowledge to the being of God forbids the mind's depriving him of total freedom from any external force or compulsion, the ineluctable conclusion is that God engaged in his work of creation through the exercise of his own free will and pleasure. However anthropomorphic it may sound, man's attempt to analogize the inscrutable motive of the Creator can conceive of no other motive. If man is to adjudge the universal activity by the axiom of like father like son, he must reckon with the traits and characteristics of his own nature to comprehend the nature and behavior of his Father. What does he see in his own life as the pole star of motivation of his every thought and action? He finds his life at every step actuated by a force which overrides all other causes of self-exertion, instinctive and irrational, automatically compelling, and that force he calls *pleasure*. It is the drive back of all impulsions. When he is most child-like and natural, he will without thought do what he best likes to do. Only when sophistication, due to the hard exigencies of experience, twists his mind to weird tactics of expediency, does he act in contravention of the seductive lure of pleasure. This is his family heritage from his Father, who in doing what delighted him best, bequeathed that same trait to his son.

We have to go back to remoter times to find a people who were sufficiently aware of this principle to have given it a distinctive name. That name was *Lila*, and it was given by the Hindus. It has been defined as the delight, the pleasure, the recreation, the sport and play of God. Considered in its most exalted state from a religious or spiritual point of view, it is India's idea of the supreme ecstasy of being--bliss, *ananda*. Throughout the long and at times painful progress of souls from nescience to glory, it is often submerged, lost, diminished in intensity, or deliberately minimized in value at a given moment with a view to its intensification later on. One renounces a present minor pleasure in the hope of a keener one in prospect. Or one in ignorance or folly violates the terms requisite for its generation and suffers pain instead of pleasure. Nevertheless, through and behind all vicissitude glows the *ignis fatuus*, the unquenchable fire of the pleasure instinct. It is the electric magic that points the compass of human motive toward the lodestar of that climactic glory that lures man on to his destined home among the gods.

Like man, God, once he had awakened out of his cycle of sleep at the dawn of a new day of conscious activity, refreshed and thrilling with the joy of the morning, yearned for the vivid exertion of his physical energies. In the rhythmic swing from passivity and dreaming to conscious alertness, he felt the urge and the need for bodily action. He desired the delight in the flexing of his muscles against inertia and opposition. There was work to be done and joy in the anticipation of it. He rejoiced as a strong man to run a race and win a wreath of victory and honor. Life with its challenge and its promise of high rewards lay before him. The thrill of adventure pulsated through his organism; it was the renewal of his youth, the divine compulsion to press forward to life more abundant. His mind teeming with ideas for the building of the cosmos, he was eager to bring his plans to fruition, to throw himself into the work and watch the miracle of his production take shape in finished beauty. And our venerated sacred scriptures do say that after six days of labor he could stand on his hill, survey the work of his hands, and pronounce it good.

The recondite clues that, if apprehended, can lead the mind of man to the basic archai, or principles of understanding by which he can, to the limit of his intellectual capability, rationalize the creation procedure of his cosmic parent, are occultly hidden in the context of the universally operative principle known to physics as *polarity*. All explanation of phenomena in the creative work must be formulated basically on a knowledge of this principle.

In the night period, or sleeping arc of the cycle of alternating activity and rest, God could not be creative. No man creates (except in the phantasmagoria of dreams) when he is asleep. And no man can create until, in waking state, he can bring the resources of hand on the one side and brain on the other, to cooperate in work. When God is in the sleep state that the Hindus call *pralaya*, he can not create because these two necessary agencies for work are both in abeyance, because they are then merged back into their primal unity and identity. For purposes of creative exertion, they must be dissociated out of this relationship and set over against each other in a tension of force that makes every activity the result of mutual interaction between them. This tension and opposition is known as polarity. It is the force that brings the universe into manifestation and holds it together. If it was relaxed for an instant, the universe would collapse and disappear. We see minor manifestations of it in gravitation, magnetism, electricity, and the universal evidence of it is seen in the play of the forces of attraction and repulsion. When the two opposing nodes of this tension are in full force, it is seen that one pole is a positively charged energy, the other negatively charged. And when two positively charged objects, or two negatively charged objects, are brought together, they repel each other, while two oppositely charged objects attract each other. When Empedocles, an early Greek philosopher, said that in the world the two forces of Love and Hate contended with each other, he was stating the scientific truth in terms of animism. And when Heraclitus about the same time said that "war is the father of all things," he was not referring to military combat but to this same polar opposition between the positive and negative nodes of the cosmic energy. For it is precisely at the point of engagement between the two potencies that all things are engendered. This great truth is highly revelatory from every angle. It splits the primal unity of being into the operational dichotomy and arrays the two powers against each other in every area of manifestation. For purposes of creation, it is seen to be as necessary as that if a man is to walk he must have two legs instead of but one. God in his unity is condemned to inactivity; if he desires to enjoy the élan of creation, he must bisect his unity so as to bring conscious purposiveness, on the one side, in position to deal with matter on the other. Only when and where the two potencies are locked in "warfare" of their tensional opposition is something new born into existence. Since their union of forces produces new birth, they take title severally to the parenthood of life, the positive dynamic of the polarity being constituted as father, and the negative as mother. Consciousness, mind, spirit on the male side is the active, aggressive, the generating principle; inertia, matter on the female side is passive, receptive and conservative. By itself consciousness has the business of conceiving, planning and directing the work it designs to accomplish, but it can do nothing to consummate its designs in the world of concrete existence unless it be given necessary tools and materials. Since his own being manifests the dichotomy, both conscious purpose and physical instrumentality are available within the scope of his own constitution. The directing power resides in his mind, his intelligence, his will; the executive agency to accomplish the work is found in his body, the hands primarily. All scriptures speak of the "hand of God" as carrying out the edicts of his creative mind; his hands perform what his mind and will have decreed. His hands have wrought what his mind has thought. By the work of his hands has he formed the world and created the heavens.

This mind and hand become the terms of the polarity in this view. And if mind is always of the positive character, masculine, then hand must be on the negative side and feminine. And such has ancient occult perspicacity invariably rendered it. For it is a surprising fact that in most languages, in spite of the word's ending in masculine terminations (as man*us* in Latin, man*o* in Spanish, cheir in Greek), the word for hand is invariably of the feminine gender. But it is in the semantic representations of the basic archai of truth as found in the literature of ancient Egypt that we have the most startling characterization of the hand in the role and function of the feminine node of the creative dichotomy. The cosmocrator god, personalized in one narrative as Tum or Atum, in another as Kepher, is declared to have created his two children, who became the parents of mankind, from the drops of his blood--meaning his seminal essence--which fell upon the earth from his act of self-creation effectuated by rolling his phallus around in his *hand*. This symbolism earned for him the title of the "masturbating god." We can spare our squeamishness at the baldness of the conception when we reflect that it presents a perfect and most illuminating allegory of the forces of the first stages of creation emanating directly from the body of deity before polarity was established clear out to the periphery of manifested things when, so to say, polarity was interior and not fully externalized. Yet polarity was already in play to the extent that the hand could fill the role of mother principle, negative to active purpose, and by friction with the bodily symbol of generative source, draw forth the productive seed of future life. The two children of Kepher-Atum thus generated to become the parents of humanity were in one version Hu and Sa, but generally Shu and Tefnut, brother and sister. It is quite exciting, incidentally, to know that the *Genesis* account of the creation of mankind through its first parentage in Adam and Eve bears the marks of derivation from the primary Egyptian symbolic depiction. As in the Kepher-Atum legend, man was compounded of the blood of the gods and the clay of earth. It is most significant to know that this term *Adam* initially meant "red earth." Poetry and philosophy have delighted to stigmatize the human body as "mortal clay," and religion has unctuously proclaimed the redemption of man to immortality through the injection into his mortal part of the blood of the Son of God. Egyptian symbolism is vindicated.

It is gratuitous to say that the principle of polarity permeates living existence ubiquitously. More simply it can be said that life can not exist on any other terms. Every living entity can boast of having a north and south magnetic pole, the forces playing between them furnishing the dynamo of its being. This pledges the human mind to the idea that all existence is the product of the conjunction of a unit of conscious force with a material body, the latter being the organism in which the union is localized. If this dialectic is in line with truth, it must be concluded that every living creature must be accredited with sentiency and a soul, however tiny, however feeble.

As Lowell vividly expresses it in *The Vision of Sir Launfal*--
Every clod feels a stir of might,
An instinct within that reaches and towers,
And groping blindly above it for light,
Climbs to a soul in grass and flowers.

Faithful to this conception, the arcane ancient philosophy did not hesitate to categorize the stars of the firmament as living entities, the bodies of the greater and the lesser deities, asserting that humans in the long course of their evolution would become the logoi of solar systems. Every atom is an atom in potency, a future god in potentiality. In organization the atom is a miniature solar system, an epitome of the universe, the microcosmic replica of the macrocosm. And everywhere existence rests upon, springs from and is sustained by the principle of polarity. Life endures only so long as the tension between consciousness and its material embodiment can be maintained.

All this being postulated for purposes of reflection and discourse--and both should enhance the probability of its truth--there is one particular manifestation of the universal principle of polarity on which the present discussion is to be focused. That is the polarization subsisting between the mind and consciousness of man and his objective environment, the world of *nature*. The dissertation will aim to demonstrate that in the terms and in the potentialities of this phase of the universal law the basic archai, Plato's archetypal ideas of the cosmic mind, are clearly to be discerned by competent intellectual acuteness, and that such competent study of nature will bring to light the ultimate canons of knowledge. If the human mind and nature constitute the two poles of the duality underlying man's life, then ultimate truth must be expected to be found at the mid-point of contact where the two are equilibrated.

CHAPTER FOUR

THEISM - DEISM - PANTHEISM

My heart leaps up when I behold
A rainbow in the sky.
So was it when my life began,
So let it be when I grow old,
Or let me die!
The child is father of the man;
And I could wish my days to be
Bound each to each in natural piety.

It seemed felicitous to introduce this pregnant discussion with Wordsworth's lyric to an aspect of nature's charm if only because it gives us the phrase "natural piety." Few have worshipped at nature's shrine so fervently as did Wordsworth. Her revelation to his mind must have constituted for him the heart and soul of his religion. If there was piety in his attitude toward life, it was inspired and conditioned by the influence of his "contemplation of natural objects."

The effort of man to formulate the principles of his religious experience in systems of theology have given us such codes as those of theism, deism, pantheism, naturalism and humanism, prefaced largely by primitive forms of animism. Atheism might be included. Ideas wavered between polytheism and monotheism. It will be instructive to consider the comparative claims of theism, deism, and pantheism, as they reflect man's thought at its highest competence.

In briefest form of definition, theism affirms that God created the universe over patterns of his cosmic thought and supervises its operation from his point of transcendence somewhere at the summit of creation, either that he wound up the universal mechanism and let it run by the power he injected into it by his initial thrust, or keeps his hand constantly on the levers of control. Deism holds that he deployed his mental and physical energies in the construction of the universe and poured them into the organic structure as the soul of man pours its energies into his body, his mentality and dynamism permeating every portion of the organism at all times. Pantheism stands on much the same ground, but has been accused of claiming that the physical structure of the universe embraces the whole of God's being, that God is no greater than his universe. Theism repudiates it because it seems to limit God to his physical manifestation in this one act of creation. As man is conceived to be a power above and beyond his body, so theism avers that God is a power above and beyond the universe, if that is considered to be his body. Deism asserts that God is present in the totality of worlds and therefore the question of his transcendence is irrelevant. Confined more particularly to the life of man than to that of the world, humanism postulates that whatever deific power is in evidence in man's life is comprehended in and exercised by man himself. He is not a puppet to be manipulated by a *deus ex cathedra*. He contains within himself the potential, if not the immediate power, to advance his own life to its highest possibility. This puts it in sharp antithesis to theism. Theism tends to cut man's life out of the order of physical nature, in fact in its Christian expression, directly aims to effectuate this severance as the means of man's final apotheosization. Deism and pantheism would hold any such transformation of his being as the culmination merely of the course of the natural evolution of which man is an integral portion and a product.

The origin of divergence of opinion and the confusion in which the entire debate has been thus involved are chiefly due to the misinterpretation and misconceptions introduced by Christian theology into the purview. It was due to an unbalanced application of the relation of the two constitutive elements of our nature, the natural element on our bodily side and the spiritual element on the side of soul. When Christian mentality lost sight of the principle of polarity, it mistook the functional beneficence of the warfare of opposites for an overt hostility of the negative pole to the positive and heaped upon matter and the flesh the stigma of enmity to the god, whether in man or in transcendence.

A study of Christian history discloses the portentous fact that the concept of the "malignancy of matter," coming into the movement from Hinduism through Zoroastrianism, became an influence overwhelmingly dominating the theology and the ethic. It bred the monstrous cult of asceticism, whose driving motivation was the idea that the instincts of the flesh must be crushed down in the interests of the spirit. Instead of holding the body in salutary relation to the soul, as nature's means of giving the dual parental function of the two their chance to bring to birth the true Christ child in the physical body as its womb and cradle, Christianity tore the two natures violently apart and set the bodily pole in enmity against its positive twin. The opposition of function, all beneficent, was mistaken for the opposition of evil against good, or God.

The tragic consequence of this staggering default of insight are incalculable, but in all conscience overwhelming to any intelligence that discerns it. It lay the Christian mind open to the obsession of a psychological influence that has been nothing less than devastating to sanity, inflicting upon the psyche a trauma that has produced morbidity and crushed to a degree the natural instinct for human happiness. John Dewey has pronounced this supposititious enmity between man natural and man spiritual, rather between man total and his God, as the most deadly dichotomy in the mental life of mankind. George Santayana has re-echoed the accusation in forceful language. Nietzsche cursed it in the most vitriolic terms he could find. Surely the most naive intuition of reason should have averted the debacle from the simplest intimation that God would not thrust his children out of heaven and lodge them in fleshly bodies which would at the same time become the instruments of their ruin. Yet this fatuous misconception is almost fundamental in Christian systematism. By confronting the soul with the necessity of deploying its divine potential through the effort to maintain its balance with the inertia of matter, God did house these child-souls of his own being in mortal bodies. They could not become gods in their own right unless they became masters of the physical forces over which, as gods, they would have to rule. Mastery could be achieved only by a long struggle--Jacob wrestling all night with the angel--with the polar opposition of matter, which should never have been mistaken for an evil element, when it was in fact the spirit's own twin.

One of the most lamentable consequences of this debacle has been that the dominance of the Christian influence has tended to inhibit the spontaneous interest of mind in nature and has therefore delayed for centuries the exercise of mind in its instinctive bent to divine the secrets and the message which nature might have imparted to Western intelligence so much earlier. Obsessed religiously with the persuasion that nature was an evil influence, inevitably there was never that intense motive to fathom her depths of meaning that natural piety would have inspired. The theological contempt for nature discouraged the consecration and enthusiasm that are the requirements for felicitous adventure in such an enterprise. The advance of Occidental culture has been immeasurably retarded in consequence.

Never in the corpus of our revered scriptural tradition bequeathed to us from a sagacious antiquity has there been wanting the forthright averment that the life and mind of the creator pervades and animates his fabricated universe to its remotest range and its inmost heart. In no part or particle of its extent or its essence is it bereft of God's life-giving presence. "The earth is full of the glory of the Lord," sings the psalmist of old. "The world is full of gods," echoes Thales of early Greece. "God is present in all his parts, in every moss and cobweb," chants the American Emerson. What Wordsworth meant by his "natural piety" was just the worshipful recognition of this ubiquitous pervasion of the body and life of nature by the energy and mind of God. And if this unction of divinity could be felt as present and at work in the outer world of nature, far more assuredly was it to be recognized as the leaven of divinely exalted spirit fermenting in the consciousness of man. "There is no part of me that is without god," solemnly asserts the character representing the divine element in our human nature in the Egyptian pantheon. Likewise the sacred writings of the Hindus repeat the declaration of the sovereign Lord that, although he remains total and undiminished in the core of his being above and beyond the range of his physical embodiment in the world, nevertheless he constantly impregnates the universe with a portion of his omnipotence. The creation is steeped in the essence of being, is saturated with the life of God.

Since this conviction was so general an acceptance of philosophical thought, it was bound to give rise to the question whether there could be a parallel between the order of nature and the processes and character of human thought. Gerald Massey, an English Egyptologist of the late nineteenth century, in his penetrating analyses of the Egyptian religious conceptions, wisely observes that there is a near identity of connotation in the words *think* and *thing*. For things in the objective world, if they and their world was to have meaning at all, must have been the product of a thinking process somehow under or behind it. It seemed obviously logical to assume that, as before stated, the mind of God must first have thought what his hands later wrought. Things must have been designed and must bear the impress of their primal thought patterns.

There thus emerged upon the open field of philosophical reflection the basic question: Does the universe express the operation of mind? Is it the product of intelligence and also an intelligence working purposively? Again two schools of thought arose to take issue over this problem, as was the case over the question whether reality was purely noumenal or purely material. Those who predicated the presence of providential design in the structure and order of the universe pointed to a thousand striking, even astonishing, evidences that mind had ordered the processes of nature for obvious and beneficent ends. But the mechanists countered with the contention that the appearance of purposiveness in the natural order was a fabrication of the mind of the observer and was imposed gratuitously upon nature, an importation from outside the physical order, not a revelation from it itself. It is simply, they said, the insistence of our minds in reading design into the course of natural phenomena. Is the world itself a logical structure and process? Or do we, as Kant so strongly asserted, comprehend it according to the patterns of our formal logic? Was it God in the beginning or is it we now who infused logic into the system of nature? It is a momentous question, and its issues are serious for the world of human understanding. Religionists, idealists, moralists, fervently cling to the positive asseveration of the presence and operation of providential design in the life of the world; materialists as obstinately refuse to read purpose and direction into the order.

Preponderantly, however, philosophers have inclined to explain the world as the product of a universal mind-intelligence, directed to benign purpose. Naive mentality when not corrupted by sophistication has been generally impressed, almost subconsciously, by the evidence of omnipresent intelligent direction and set purpose. Erudite philosophers labored at the task of arraying the evidence for design in terms more scientifically substantiated.

The negative position does not lack a formidable body of supporting data on its side. Instead of finding nature a universally kindly and tender mother of all species, carefully shielding all her teeming hordes of living creatures for their happiness and their comfort, close study of her methods reveals the most shocking and terrifying disregard for her multitudinous progeny. Like God slaughtering the enemies of his children Israel in the Old Testament by the thousands, she ruthlessly slays her families in prodigious slaughter. She permits one species to live by consuming another as food, only to be consumed as food in turn by a more powerful ravager. She is inconceivably prodigal of seed production for renewal of life, but enormously and pitilessly wasteful of it. Millions of seeds perish that perchance one may find rootage and survive. Materialists cite these and other facts in refutation of the claims of beneficent design.

But in spite of such considerations, theorists in the main incline to hold to the predication of purpose in the scheme of things. The ruthlessness of nature is itself cited as evidence of a methodology in the process that is designed to promote the advance of life more rapidly. And there is an inclination also to mitigate for our sensitivity of feeling the repulsiveness of the internecine slaughter among the lower species by the reflection that nature herself has means of anesthetizing the pain of death for the orders preyed upon by the stronger. A whale at one gulp consumes a thousand smaller sea creatures, and it is not likely that her dinner comes at the tab of a thousand agonies. That nature sacrifices lower orders for the advantage of higher ones does not rule out beneficent design, especially when investigation views the whole process of evolving life in a longer perspective.

Then again it has to be asked whether we can legitimately expect nature to demonstrate her aims exactly in accordance with tests we would impose as definite evidence of design. After all, are we capable of passing judgment upon her work and her ways? She is demonstrably far wiser than we, her children. Our scriptures pointedly remind us that for us the ways of God are past finding out. "High as the heavens are above the earth, so high are my thoughts above your thoughts," the deity admonishes us. So philosophy has proceeded with great caution toward a positive conclusion as to the teleological intent of nature.

Yet it seems permissible that we may go at least as far as the assumption that she is bent on doing what, by close observation, we see that she obviously *is doing*. We would certainly seem forbidden to judge that she has made the millions of vast and tiny adaptations that spell advantage to all creatures without having intended to win that advantage for them. Our little minds are staggered by the special little inventions, stratagems, provisions, arrangements, even distinct organs, which we find operative in the lives of virtually every one of millions of both her mammoth and minuscule living hordes. The study of natural history confronts us with such sensational evidence of planned schemes, even to the extent of one creature setting a bait outside or inside a trap to catch another creature for its food--the pitcher plant, the Venus fly-trap, the spider, the doodle-bug, numberless similar devices--that we are forced to concede that there truly seems to be no nook or corner in the whole natural realm where intelligence is not visibly at work. A thousand instances are observed, in which, when a species was subjected to some change in the condition of its environment, it met the crisis by a new stratagem, much the same as we humans are now countering the threat of atomic missile with an anti-missile. So multitudinous are these instances of at least rudimentary intelligence throughout the entire realm of living nature, that it is difficult to imagine how the old materialist theory which grounded itself on the chance jumbling of the atomic billiard-ball particles as the origin of world phenomena ever could be held by thinking men. It has been discarded generally, yet incredibly it has some supporters still.

Several considerations would seem to refute it finally and absolutely. It set itself adamantly against the concession of intelligence in the order and processes in nature. Even Darwin's formulas, natural selection and the survival of the fittest, seemed to make evolution intelligible without postulating the presence and operation of mind. The atomic billiard balls or marbles simply were opportunists and seized upon every chance circumstance that appeared to be favorable to betterment or offered advantage. But this one word, *advantage*, along with *favorable* and *betterment*, or similar terms, would seem in itself alone to strike the death-knell of the materialist hypothesis. For such terms are meaningless in relation to something that lacks consciousness and some modicum of intelligence. Conditions around a stone, we must insist, can mean nothing in the way of advantage or disadvantage to it. A billiard ball would not know what would constitute "betterment" for it. How could one situation be more "favorable" to it than another? Without conscious sensitivity, it could take no advantage of things and conditions that chance presented. Thus the materialist thesis was guilty of postulating, as a basic premise of its reasoning, the fact of purposiveness as evidently present in the present outcome of natural processes, while denying it in the operation. That is, if things worked out, as obviously they have done, to the advantage of life in virtually every quarter of its developed status, so that it is possible to speak of a gain, a better status, a higher development at all in a later stage of the process over an earlier stage, how is it logically permissible to introduce the concept of advantage as displayed in the present or the end product when it was categorically excluded from the process at the beginning? The materialist position thus surreptitiously introduces such considerations as advantage, favorableness, improvement, at some undetermined point along the way, in spite of having excluded them rigidly from the start. How could an order of activity that lacked any capability to determine advantage from disadvantage gain the power to do so at any time? That is the fatal flaw in the old materialistic contention. The controversy must end with the realization that purposiveness could never arise out of purposelessness. How could mindlessness develop the patent and multitudinous evidences of mind action? There must have been intelligence present in all natural operation from the start and throughout the course, or there could be none present now. Blank and blind unconsciousness could appreciate no advantage. If "chance" movements in the flux of things presented situations that could be turned to advantage, there had to be intelligence present to recognize and appreciate the good fortune. Thus we can go with the ancient sages who declared that the universe was pervaded and animated and ordered by mind. Without the capability to respond to the challenge of conditions, there could be no such thing as evolution or even growth; and without mind, there could not even be a response. If matter was not initially permeated by potential mind, it could generate it at no later stage. Modern refinements of the evolution theory have established the principle that no process is capable of unfolding anything as end product that was not germinally in it from the beginning. If matter was not rudimentarily pregnant with mind from the start, it could never have developed it.

Then in larger view, it is convincingly evidenced that the course of evolution reveals certain patterns which bespeak the play of intelligence and design. As hinted a moment ago, are we not permitted to assume that what we clearly see life is doing in nature is what it aimed to do? A person may build better than he knows or intended, but hardly nature. Can we not give nature credit with knowing what she is doing? It is beyond all reason to think that the ever-astonishing marvel of adaptability, order and beauty in the external world could have been the chance occurrence of mindlessness. The materialist thesis asks us to believe that if you knock billiard balls around long enough, they will get mad and begin to think. If materialism is to be accepted, it must be on such idiotic terms.

In dealing with the atomistic theory in his special form of monadology, the German philosopher Leibnitz saw the irrationality involved in the thing in its baldest state and was led to endow the single units of existence with an intelligence potential. His theory pointed more or less directly to the concept now being entertained that the monads carrying the life force are themselves units of an energy that may be itself the energy of mind, and not matter--in the old conception--at all. The monads, he said, looked out through a window in its structure, and seeing what was going on about it, used its inherent intelligence to determine how it should act in the jumble of things. By thus acting in response to conditions around it, it developed potential awareness into conscious faculty, first through sheer feeling, sensation, then through the faint flicker of thought in response. Thus out of primeval chaos came cosmos. Life, mind, purpose could never have emerged from *prima materia* to which was denied the conscious potential. If life and mind are born of matter, it could not have been from "dead" matter, but from living matter. Well did the scriptures admonish us to go to the ant, consider her ways and be wise. For as we watch the economy of life in a nest of ants or a community of bees, we see these tiny creatures demonstrating a perfectly amazing schematic program and pattern of behavior. How can we avoid concluding that there is cosmos in the total world when we see that there is rudimentary intelligence in every constituent element of it?

With the presence of mind in the universe accepted as a necessity conclusion of reason, reflection inevitably spurs philosophical thought to pose the question whether there is a kinship, parallelism or identity between the order and harmony of mind action in nature and the order and harmony of thought in the mind of man. The task of dealing with this question takes us into the heart of our theme.

CHAPTER FIVE

KINSHIP OF MIND WITH NATURE

Deeply involved in the thought effort of philosophy generally, the relation of the mind of man to the mind power clearly evidenced in the phenomenal course of nature has absorbed the interest of thinkers at all times. Are the two akin and how closely? If the operations of both seem to show identity, are they the products of the same source? Do they work on the same principles? And how was a harmony of this sort established in the first place? If the harmony is ascertained to be quite close and complete, would it not go far to indicate that man and the natural world were alike products of the same generic power?

It was again the German Leibnitz who ventured to solve the matter by asserting that such a harmony had been established by God, the creator of both man and nature, in the beginning. He declared that such a harmony was pre-established, a natural result of the creational fiat, whose work included nature and then man in the same organic production. It seemed reasonable to suppose that man, presumably the highest branch on the tree of natural life, would have brought to its highest state of development and brilliance that same consciousness which had functioned but dimly in the first stages of biological evolution. If this was the proper view, the mind powers in man at his present stage would in effect be the same as those that function in the world of nature now, with only the difference that they have by now unfolded their incipient potential to vastly greater perfection.

On this thesis it would be legitimate to say that the relation of the two minds, that of nature and that of man, is even closer than that of a parallelism or a harmony, being essentially that of identity, with the difference being only that of degree of unfoldment of primal capability. Greek philosophy cherished this view of the relationship, because Greek thought held man to be indigenous to the natural order. But when Christianity carried the revolt against paganism to extreme limits, it tore man out of his context in the life of nature, and opened out a vast theological gulf between the two minds, making mutual exchange impossible and obliterating traces of the kinship. In fact it set the Christian mind apart in bitterest hostility to the mind of nature. The dire effects have been historically observed, though never adequately estimated.

But the instinctive affinity between man and nature is so deeply grounded in reality that the ostracism of the concept from the domain of religion could by no means inhibit the spontaneous play of the genius of man in sensitive response to its intimations. If not discerned consciously at the intellectual level, it was sensed, now vaguely, now distinctly, through the channels of philosophical reflection, artistic and esthetic sensitivity and above all by poetic fancy and imagination. It is hardly too strong an assertion to say that it has been the deepest soul of poetry. It has been a veritable fount of inspiration for the loftiest exaltations of the poetic genius, the motif of the highest soarings of the human spirit into realms of man's realization of his kinship with the whole of life and mind. It might be said with truth that throughout the history of poetry, it was the minds that had sunk their roots deepest into the world of nature that rose to the greatest heights of vision and intuition. It was as if a mirage reflecting the earth and its scenic phenomena could now and again be discerned in the skies of abstract contemplation. It seldom ceased to haunt, to captivate, to elevate the truth-seeking mind. It seemed to generate almost a mental clairvoyance of metaphysical verities.

It took minds aloft to visions of truth in moments of psychic illumination. Hardly less brilliantly has it worked in the domain of philosophical reflection than in the field of poetry. It has stimulated the contemplative mind to the most luminous discernments of truth and insights into reality that have ever lighted up the area of our human intelligence, as glimpses of this unity of the mind and nature have fleshed into view.

Vision at such high altitude seldom failed to engender the assurance that the truth sensed by thought and truth mirrored in nature were one and the same; that there was no one code of verity for the world and another, disparate and heterogeneous, for the human mind. If the two were the products of the same generic system, their affinity could hardly be doubted. The same tree could not bear two different kinds of fruit. But the fruit might be observed at different stages of its growth, as bud, as blossom, as green core, as luscious ripe perfection. And the sapience of arcane ancient philosophy had averred that it had subsisted in the womb of time and being first as sheer consciousness, as archetypal idea, then was thrust out into existential manifestation in the external world. And the outcome of this predication could be nothing less than the momentous revelation that, if the germinal noumenal form and the one extruded out into the world were two stages or aspects of the same thing, then there could be no question of their "harmony," since in ultimate essence they were one and the same thing.

But, sadly enough, this recognition has not been taken beyond the stage of haunting, enticing, momentarily illuminating envisioning in the mirror of mystical sensibility. It has never been grasped with keen intellectual discernment, never apprehended in the vast sweep of its significance, never recognized as the one ineluctable ground-base of all truth, the one final canon of veritude. It has never been brought down bodily out of the skies of poetic afflation to be organized into a full-fledged authentic science, dually and impregnably buttressed by the most invincible logic of mind on the one side, and the unassailable evidence of living nature on the other. The sporadic glimpses and flashes of the relation never could gather substantiality enough to furnish the material for that complete polarization of the two sides in a consummative synthesis. Never had the vision of the unity, integrity and continuity of the accord between the objective and subjective sides of the equation been steadily enough held in the philosophic purview to solidify the sense of its overwhelming and indisputable certitude. Some thinkers have come close to the achievement, possibly including Aristotle, Plotinus, Schelling and Hegel, the Egyptologist Gerald Massey, Swedenborg, Emerson and perhaps many obscure "philosophers of homespun wisdom." The poetic genius has always been edging toward it. Intimations of its force, even when not intellectually recognized, suffused the idyllic imagination of poets and mystics with shadowy gleams of its presence. Where else could lively fancy go, if it would strikingly portray the loftiest sensings of mind and soul and give expression to the elations of the spirit over the beauty and the glory of the world, if not to the beauty and the wonder of the miracle that God had put on display in the world without? Many minds had felt the reality of the relationship and had stated it as a basic principle of truth again and again. But never has it been formally organized, its fundamental principles systematically formulated and applied, and their overall authority and universal validity established, to be enthroned in the world of mind as the sovereign monarch of truth. It has been left a more or less scintillating mirage of philosophy and poetry, never organically constituted as the science of final understanding, the seal of all intuition and revelation, the vindication of faith and the sanction of all spiritual religion. It so brightens the lens of vision that the picture of truth and reality, dim and indistinct before, leaps at once from obscurity into clarity.

A survey of the place and influence of this concept in world philosophy can hardly fail to be a profitable and engaging undertaking. The testimony bearing on it from noted thinkers is too vast to be marshaled in more than token quantity. The deeper reflection has gone into the investigation, the clearer and more cogent has become the conviction that the human mental processes started from nature, began with and departed from the external physical world and proceeded thence toward the realm of pure ideation and abstraction. Kant made a heroic effort to open up a world of transcendence, in which thought could unfold its own principia completely detached from and uninfluenced by concrete objectivity. He called it the world of the *reine Vernunft*, "pure" reason. The mind, he affirmed, formulated the rules by which the phenomena of the world could be rated, judged and made meaningful. It, so to say, threw a harness upon the objective scenario of things so that they could be drawn into the realm of understanding. But while the form and scheme of understanding was to be provided by these "categories" of our mind, the substance of the understanding was always provided by nature. *How* things were to be understood was the function of the faculty provided by the God-given genius of man; *what* was to be understood was offered by nature. The resultant interaction of the two elements involved the question whether the harness must be constructed to fit the shape of things in the outer world, or the external things so ordered as to settle commodiously into the harness. The history of philosophy reveals the valiant efforts of one vigorous mind after another to construct the harness that would completely and snugly give the mind the power to draw the perfect truth out of the things of the world. Objectivity proved to be a stubborn reality, recalcitrant to theory; and by and large it has been found that the subjective harness has to conform to the shape of outer things often in defiance of the rules of logic.

It is a fact of great significance, though not accorded its due recognition even in Indian thought, that the basic literature of one of the profoundest religio-philosophical systems in the world--the Hindu--stands grounded in nature. The great Vedas of India consist largely of mantrams and formulas that hold religious cultism in immediate relation to nature. Clearly the motif of this epic document sought to express its message of an integral affinity subsisting between the human mind and the outer world. If cult rites and ceremonial forms, as here obviously, were designed to associate man in a closeness of kinship with the external reality, the cult practice must have been inspired by a deep insight into this fundamental interdependence. It was as if man must still be nursed in the lap of the great mother who gave him birth and blessed him with her ministrations. It is questionable whether the best acumen of the Hindu mind has at any later time grasped the key significance of the nature lore of the Vedas. For the later development of the systematism founded on them has soared to so high a pitch of detachment and abstraction from the interests of earth and body that it has severed all direct linkage with its natural ground and has lost itself in transcendental sublimations of consciousness. The central drive of Hindu thought affected to disdain earth altogether, seeking release from mundane duress in the heavens of contentless and unconditioned being.

There is happily increasing evidence, however, that the greatest of modern Hindu thinkers, notably Sri Aurobindo and Radhakrishnan, have sought to amend this bent of India's philosophy and restore its pristine connection with nature. Both have insisted that Indian speculation never really sundered its connection with its rootage in the earth. The primary teaching was that the universe is impregnated with divine mind and that man's association with nature is the salutary source of his well-being and his felicitous advance to the ultimate bliss of nirvana.

If we turn to ancient Egypt, we learn, most authoritatively through the luminous revelations of Gerald Massey's scholarship, that the religious consciousness of early Egyptian civilization was saturated by the aura and influence of nature. The Egyptian people, says James H. Breasted in his history of the Nile country, lived in close and intimate association with nature. The religious literature of the land abounds in nature symbolism. Spiritual conceptualism was profusely adumbrated by natural phenomena. The very gods were figuratively charactered by animal symbols, the figure of Horus, the Christ, having the head of a hawk, indicative of a heavenly keenness of sight that sees all earthly things clearly. With prodigious virtuosity, Massey traces the endless symbol-structures of religious truth to their archaic source in some natural fact or phenomenon. All spiritual conceptuality, he sensed, stalked through the mental world as if it were the shade or ghost of some natural object. The wraiths of divine ideas moved about in the shadowy robes of earthly things. One must read Massey's colossal elucidations to catch the full cogency of this apprehension. Alleging that "metaphysical explanations" have misconceived and distorted the true sense of mythology, he says that "all interpretation is finally futile that is not founded on the primary physical phenomena." He remarks that it is fortunate that we still have left the aboriginal symbols, and we can abstract from them some measure of their semantic message and purport, as best we may. He thinks that early civilization lived through a stage in which it dwelt in closer contact with nature and had developed a deeper sense of nature's "meaning," and that later tendency weakened this rapport, so that we still cling to the symbol only blindly and uncomprehendingly.

He asserts that the great ancient Mystery brotherhoods grounded their rituals on symbols from nature, and that the whole structure of ancient esotericism and occult wisdom, such as the systems of Gnosis, Hermeticism, the Kabalah and the religious arcana everywhere, rested on natural foundations. In fact he sees it underlying the religious and humanistic literature of all the world. Symbols at any rate preserved the tenebrous shadows of truth, which thus haunted the consciousness of mankind as memories preserved in the unconscious. Symbolism constitutes a language extending beyond the written or spoken idioms. It was when ignorance and grossly material misconception distorted the transparent imagery of symbols into caricature and falsity that the interior import of mythology and archetypal concepts faded out and left intelligence holding the husks and empty shells of truth. As the outward and visible form of an idea, a symbol is still the magic wand to awaken intelligence. Outwardly foreshadowing an inner abstraction, it is the most helpful of servants; obscurely or mistakenly envisioned, it becomes the most deceptive and tyrannous of masters. But it remains the one inerrant language of truth.

One of the originators of medical science, the physicist and philosopher Galen, speaks of the Mystery cults as grounding their system of medical morality upon the natural mystery. The rituals were a sacred drama, portraying the principles of moral and spiritual truth by representations drawn from nature. "Nature is the great teacher of man; for it is the revelation of God. It presents its symbols to us and adds nothing by way of explanation. To employ nature's universal symbolism instead of technicalities of language... discloses its secret to every one in proportion to his power to comprehend it."

Massey's view that mankind passed through an early stage in which nature symbolism was a universal idiom in religious literature is well buttressed by all the intimations and root motivations underlying that prodigious creation of the early genius of mankind whose efforts produced the literary wonder of mythology. It is doubtful if modernity has yet grasped the import of ancient mythology as a whole, much less interpreted truly and lucidly the individual myths. The word "myth" itself still carries to our minds the suggestion of primitive ignorance and childish belief. We are not quite sure to what extent the ancients did really "believe" their myths. We are somewhat still in doubt as to whether they deliberately created the myths as obvious fiction, or thought they described realities. We would be sharply surprised if told that these constructions were the consciously designed productions of the most astute and subtle dramatic genius perhaps ever to have gleamed from the human mind and with the keenest philosophical acumen employed to pictorialize the deepest truths. It may well be that we, who in self-conscious pride of modern intelligence superciliously speak in patronizing fashion of the primitive child-mindedness that created the myths as products of puerile fancy, are ourselves still lacking in the perspicacity requisite to comprehend the recondite interior purport of these idyllic fabrications of ancient semantic sapiency. Egyptian, Greek, even Hebrew biblical mythology is still largely a sealed tome. We yet await the coming of the sage who will luminously interpret the myths of old time, those creations of the human mind when it was still alive to the intuitive impression of truth caught by the common consciousness in its reflection from living nature. As Wordsworth has so lyrically revealed to us, the consciousness of childhood absorbs the impress and the spirit of nature with a vividness that is lost in maturity. "Heaven lies about us in our infancy," and the human mind in the freshness of its first impressionism was alight with the roseate coloring of the skies of the morning of human mentality. When we recover the mystical sensibility requisite to read the myths aright, there will dawn a new era of enlightenment, a new opening of the eyes of the mind. All mythology stands in close kinship with nature. Mind and nature worked harmoniously together to produce those fictions that most wondrously speak truth's clearest language.

Massey speaks of ancient wisdom literature as expressing a universal *mythos*. Another writer, Jeremiah Curtin, in his work, *Myths and Folklore of Ireland*, correlates with *mythos* another term of kindred significance--*logos*. *Logos* and *mythos*--the two Greek terms jointly connote the mental constitution of the universe, as this is to be conceived by man. The *logos* is indeed the mind power that created the universe, as even the creeds of Christianity expressly affirm; the *mythos* is the product of mind power in man that discerns the pattern created in the cosmos by the *logos* and endeavors to interpret it at the level of his own intelligence. The *mythos* is the intellectual effort of man the microcosm to discern and interpret to his consciousness the *logos* of the macrocosm. The *logos* is God's thought as embodied in his creation; the *mythos* is man's thought awakened in response to the impact of the creation upon his mind, man's effort to read God's thought after him from observation of the patterns stamped upon the concrete manifestation.

The myth was overt fiction, but covert truth. It was never a true account of things that happened as history, but, as one writer, Eliade (*Patterns in Comparative Religion*, p. 430) puts it, it is "exemplar history," the gist and meaning of all concrete history, compressed, dramatized and illuminated in and by a construction of the ideal imagination. It is not "true," yet tells the profoundest truth. Modern awakening to the true character of the myths has at last discarded the stupid misjudgment of them as errant fancies of naive simplicity stabbing blindly at truth, which has so long blocked all possibility of reaping the rich legacy of occult wisdom so artfully concealed under outward fiction. Myths became untrue only when they are asked to speak for veridical history, which is not their function. Eliade suggests most pertinently that in the ideal system of Platonism, the myth represents a sort of nostalgia of the soul for its lost heavenly awareness of pre-mundane ideality and bliss. He expands this idea to say that a symbol, and in a larger scope, a myth, is a *hierophany*, the imaged appearance of a reality of divine mind. The myth is a more elaborately designed image of a transcendental verity, what modern, especially Jungian, psychology, describes as an archetype in the universal unconscious.

If nature symbolism is a marked characteristic of the literary culture of mid-eastern countries from quite early times, it seems to be accounted for as the dissemination of Egypt's venerable *sagesse* from an unknown antiquity. From this hoary past sprang the clearest exploitation of the meaning-soul of nature. It is to be read with impressive lucidity particularly in a fragment attributed to that legendary figure and mouthpiece of arcane wisdom whom the Greeks called Hermes Trismegistus, "Thrice-Greatest." Regrettable it is that we know so little of the personage to whom this revered title was attached, if indeed he was a person of the human order at all. In our lack of authentic data about him it seems necessary for us to say, as it has jocosely been said of the Greek Homer, that if he was not the individual named Hermes, he was another man with the same name. Hermes is the Greek name of the God Mercury, and the god's name may have been attributed, in a sort of eponymous fashion, to him in recognition of his possession of a near-divine wisdom, suggesting Mercury's "mercurial" nimbleness of intellectual power. Whether demigod in human flesh, or a divinely illuminated human, and whether or not he was the author, as reputed, of that general body of Egyptian religious literature, this person had bequeathed to us a legacy of such wisdom and knowledge as would entitle him to be rated as one of those "holy men of old" to whom, in Biblical tradition, it is declared that God dictated the sacred scriptures. Indeed his identity seems to be merged into that of the god Thoth, or Taht, who in the Egyptian mythology equates the Mercury-Hermes figure in the Graeco-Roman pantheon, and Thoth was the "scribe of the Gods," the recorder of the decrees of fate pronounced on humans as the verdict in the trail of the soul in the hall of Osiris. So his revered name may be but that of the god of mercurial mind, transmitting the codes of universal truth to early humanity. Reputed author of the *Book of the Dead, The Book of Thoth, Book of the Gates,* perhaps the *Pyramid Texts* and other collections that lay buried for two thousand five hundred years in unreadable hieroglyphics, he has left us one golden treasure in the so-named Smaragdine fragment, the *Emerald Tablet of Hermes*. And it is on this greenstone slab that we have the categorical pronouncement of the fundamental truth of human knowledge, the revelation that the two worlds known to man, the ideal and the physical, are identical aspects of one and the same reality. Here are the glowing words that enunciate the oracular delivery:

True, without falsehood, certain and most true, that which is above is as that which is below, and that which is below is as that which is above, for the performance of the miracle of the One Thing.

The "above," or spiritual, was mirrored in the "below," the material. Heaven was reflected in earth below. Matter was the *tabula rasa* on which spirit wrote its message, stamped its archetypal thought images. Projected from the cosmic mind, the ideagrams congealed in matter and stood in concretion before the eye of man. If, then, the material world is the divine thought made visible in solid matter, man has all truth at all times within the range of his vision, and it must be that nature is the cinematograph of truth run on the screen of matter. Nature is the epiphany of the thoughts of the creator. Nature not only represents, but actually *is* the noumenal world transfixed in concrete phenomena.

It is readily understandable, then, that the last of eleven cardinal pronouncements found on the tablet seem to stand as the climactic summary of truth for man's behoof, in the inspiring declaration that "the kingdom of spirit is embodied in my flesh." If spirit has injected its animating and formative power into matter, then, of a surety, is the very body of man the temple of the soul. And most instructive, too, is the statement that challenges, if it does not directly contradict, all philosophies exalting spirit to the disparagement of matter. For in exact reversal of the universal bent of religious aspiration to spurn earth in reaching up for heavenly benefactions, the final maxim on the tablet declares that the power of spirit "is integrating *if it be turned into earth.*" What stunning rebuke is here administered to all conventional religious cultism that scorns earth and its values under the presumption that they are inimical to the interests of the spirit! What a stigma of error it casts on all systems of idealist philosophy, even for that of Plato, in so far as they tear the relevance of the spiritual life wholly away from the actual world and seek to segregate it completely in the ideal realm! What stern rebuff it hurls at those who revel in the mystical delights of dreaming, but who never actualize their dreams in physical accomplishment! Here, we can be taught, is the axial truth that philosophy has needed at all time: that reality and their own growth are not achieved by souls until they have, so to say, brought the power of spirit down to earth and embodied it in concrete performance. There is momentous truth here for all intelligence, truth which stands as an indispensable principle for psychiatry as well as for philosophy and morality, the realization that wholeness, the harmonious integration of the springs of life, is not to be the happy victory of souls that will not resolutely crown their hopes and dreams with outward self-creation here in the body.

The statement on the Emerald Tablet is reinforced by another to the same effect found on one of the Coffin Texts (330) which the author of a recent (1960) study entitled *Myth and Symbol in Ancient Egypt* declares to be the most direct *identification of the soul with nature* that the ancient wisdom has given us. It will bear quotation:

"*Whether I live or die, I am Osiris,*

I enter in and reappear through you,

I decay in you; I grow in you;

I fall down in you; I fall upon my side.
The gods are living in me, for I live and grow in the corn
That sustains the Honored Ones.
I cover the earth,
whether I live or die I am Barley,
I am not destroyed.
I have entered the Order,
I rely upon the Order,
I become Master of the Order,
I emerge in the Order,
I make my form distinct,
I am the Lord of the Chennet (Granary of Memphis),
I have entered into the Order,
I have reached its limits. . . ."

Here is the unqualified declaration of the god that his divine power has been turned into the earth for the sake of the integration of spirit and matter. Had that integration been achievable in heaven, the human mind can conceive of no justification for God's sending souls down to earth to undergo the stress and strain of polarity. Here is sublime truth for lack of which religion has been groping in darkness and distraction over dolorous centuries. What a *volte face* it means for religion if, instead of thinking that souls find their salvation through escape from earth and recapture of heaven, it is known that they win redemption and victory through mastery, as Osiris says, of the order of nature in the earth that religion has so unctuously despised!

And what a light of understanding shines out for us from a brief statement in the *Book of the Dead*, where it is said that the souls of Osiris and Re are twins! It is stated that when Osiris visits the so-called "Underworld," which is our earth and not, as has been mistakenly assumed, some limbo of Hades character even below the earth (another correction which would clarify a host of misconceptions about ancient religion), he meets there the soul of Re, and the two gods "embrace each other and so God exists in two forms." The brilliant illumination that this bit of mythicism can give our minds has been kept dark because modern mentality lacks the genius to identify those gods of ancient Egypt and Greece. How dull and slow we have been to realize that those ancient deities were the personifications of both natural and spiritual forces! Instead of being fictitious entities, they were the living potencies of universal life.

What powers, then, were Osiris and Re, these twins who embraced and so made God dual? From every intimation given in the texts of this marvelous Egyptian literature, Osiris is that unit of God's own spiritual soul-power that descends into the lower ranges of material creation to be the god of this underworld, there to lie in inertness, bound in a coma, asleep and helpless, until his son Horus comes to arouse him out of his dormancy and raise him from the "dead" to newness of life. Precisely like Jesus, he descends into the underworld, goes to his "death" on the cross of matter and is resurrected by the divine power. Renan in his famous *Le Vie de Jesus*, came close to revealing, and later Gerald Massey did reveal, a secret which could jolt and jar Christianity into a recognition of its true origins in this majestic ancient wisdom of Egypt: the irrefutable etymological fact that the name Lazarus in John's Gospel is but a Judeo-Latinized expansion of the original Egyptian name of Osiris, which was *Asar*. As the Egyptians generally referred to him as Lord Osiris, the Hebrews prefixed their short *El* form of "God," making it El-Asar, and the Romans completed the transformation by suffixing the "us" termination of most Roman masculine names, making it El-asar-us. The initial "E" "wore off," as the scholars say, the "s" shifted to its brother "z," and we have Lazarus. Horus, the Son of God, raised his "dead" father at a town called Annu (Anu). Jesus, the Son of God, raised Lazarus from the "dead" at Bethany. This Anu likewise suffered a sea-change at Hebrew hands, as they prefixed to it their word for "house," which is *beth*, making it *Beth-Anu*. As the "u" of ancient Greek words transforms into "y" in English, the outcome in Hebrew hands was "Bethany!" So the miracle of Jesus raising Lazarus is definitely the rescript of Horus' raising Osiris. And this presumably removes the incident from the domain of history over into that of spiritual allegory.

But what does it mean for the identity of the soul with nature? Everything pertinent and revelatory. Osiris is the divine soul of God that, like the seed in the soil, is emanated by the Father to impregnate and animate his material body. Then who or what is Re? Evidently the Egyptians, inheriting a supernal wisdom from some mysterious source, knew something of the nature and power of this deity, for they represented him by the symbol of the sun. Now after possibly three millennia, modern man has suddenly become acquainted with the god Re on terms that may make consorting with his personality analogically perilous and smiting as the rays of his celestial symbol are blinding to the eye. If this god is the power at the heart of the sun, he is also the power that modern science has at last learned the secret of the releasing in the infinitude of tiny suns that we call atoms. Modern man indeed knows much of the god Re, and he now realizes that perhaps he has been as blindly and suicidally curious in his fell desire to split the atom as is the moth that flies again and again into the candle flame and dooms itself to destruction. Yes, Re is the gigantic magic locked up in the atom, the constituent of matter.

As such, then, he is one of the two parts into which total godhood has segmented itself for purpose of creation, the other part being spirit-consciousness, which Egypt called Osiris. The descent of Osiris into the underworld brings him into the relation of polarized "opposition"--which is really the potentiality of love--with the terrible might of Re, in polarity these two embrace each other, and the mainspring and dynamo of creative activity of the two-part God are set in motion. Every time a soul from the heaven world enters into incarnation in earthly body, the drama of the meeting and embracing of Osiris and Re is reenacted. And most propitious is this glint of knowledge from ancient Egypt for the validation of our basis thesis, since, if Re is the animating soul of the atom which is the underlying essence of nature, and Osiris is the unit of divine spirit thus involved in polar association with it, then all debate as to the kinship of mind with nature is at an end. For the law of twinship is similitude.

CHAPTER SIX

THE NATURAL REVELATION

It seems certain that St. Paul had been deeply indoctrinated with the Greek legacy of wisdom from a hoary past. He was educated at the impressionable age of one of the three most important centers of Hellenic philosophy, Tarsus. We should not be surprised to hear the great Apostle echoing the Hermetic maxim in the clearest terms. We find such a succinct declaration of it in his *Epistle to the Romans* (1:20): "That which may be known of God is manifest. For the invisible things of him from the foundation of the world are clearly seen, being understood from those things which are made." Having, in the aura of Plato's idealist emphasis, told us that the realities of the unseen world are far greater than those of the visible world, he admonishes the Roman brethren that "so they are without excuse" if they fail to discern the nature of God in his mundane revelation. Whereas philosophy has droned for centuries that the unseen things are the reality behind the visible phenomena, Paul says that the seen things are the reality of the unseen; in Hermetic idiom, the below is the substance of the above. As Hermes had amplified his formula on the Emerald Tablet, the sun is the father of all life and truth for man; the moon is its mother, and the wind carries it in its sweep over the earth.

But we find the acme of clear and ringing proclamation of the great truth in a concise statement in the Talmud of the Jews, which could have come out of the Hermetic spring through Philo, the Jewish philosopher. The ancient Hebrew esoteric Kabalism was in close touch and affinity with Egypt's esoteric profundity. It states the axiom with the utmost directness and simplicity and therefore with the greatest cogency: *"If thou wilt know the invisible, open wide thine eyes on the visible."* Perhaps this is the acme of all philosophical instruction given to the human race. It hits us with the inescapable logic of obvious fact: the visible universe is the work of the creator; he puts his mind into his work; study that work and you will know the mind that created it. Aristotle had arrived at that consummative conclusion, which had long before been proclaimed by both Egypt and India, that the divine thought and the objects of that thought in the world are the same.

The great Greek philosopher's dialectic was based on his predication that the material mode of being was pure potentiality, which could not be converted into reality until infused and enlivened by the energy of spirit, by which transaction it achieved its only title to entification and meaning. It received its gift of reality from an act of mind upon it. Hence neither matter nor spirit could claim the status of real being until matter and mind-form had effected a union in a concrete structure, matter being the passive instrument, mind the active agent. The formless material embodiment thus came to be the concrete substantialization of the ideogram of mind. The act of spirit on matter established an identity between the lower physical and the upper noumenal. The philosopher spoke of the product as a "mixture" of the two modes. He harped constantly on the theme that in the world of inanimate things, and there only, do we find the ideal shapes of the real essences that Plato wished to grasp in their ethereality, those archetypal images of transcendent reality. All bodies are composed of sheer potentiality of matter and actual forms of thought and exist only through this conjunction.

One of the most voluble expressions of the identity between the two poles of being is found in the *Zohar*, the voluminous text embodying the system of esoteric teaching of the early theosophical Hebrews, the Kabalists. Constantly reiterated is the Hermetic principle: the spiritual above is imaged in the material world below. That which is unmanifest in the immateriality of divine consciousness comes to manifestation in this underworld. It speaks of the undisclosed spiritual reality, which, however, is disclosed here on earth. That which is hidden on high is revealed down here. And the conclusion that necessarily arises out of this knowledge is that for the interests of the soul's orderly progression in the flesh, the two segments of the human duality must be unified in a synthetic of consciousness and its objects. And, it is worthy of emphasis that the Kabalist thought laid insistent stress upon the law of life that in the tensional relation between spirit above and body below, with the active potency resting with the spirit, the latter remained incapable of the exertion necessary to deploy its aggressive energies in the interest of the passive lower or bodily part, until it was aroused and its powers awakened by the call of the entity below. The higher nature was unable to act for the benefit of the lower until the latter provided the incentive, as well as the conditions, for the exertion of its latent capabilities. All realistic occult science envisaged the soul as bound in dormancy under the coarser sluggish vibrations of the body--poetized as its prison-house and tomb--so that it had to await the higher perfection of the organism for the implementation of its higher purposes. The relevance of this basic insight for all religion and philosophy is tremendous, since it establishes for spiritual cultism the truth that the initiative for spiritual growth must originate with man at his human level. He dare not sit still and expect the gods to descend and raise him up. The god in us stands ever ready to dispense his largesse of blessing and beatitude, but he must wait for man to invite and facilitate the influx. Hence we find the sacred scriptures exhorting us to seek, to knock, to beseech fervently for the beneficence desired. Man below must at least clear the path for deity to reach him, through the jungle of bodily passions and sensualities.

The *Zohar* quotes R. Judah as commenting: "That which God has made on earth corresponds to that which he has made in heaven, and all things below are symbols of that which is made above." This plain statement virtually summarizes the message of our study. It is Plato extended and actualized by Aristotle. But Plato swings strongly to the Stagirite's view when he says in the *Phaedrus* that there is only one way to take care of things beneficently, and that is to give to each the food and motions natural to it, so that in adapting itself to the harmonies and beauties of the natural life it shares here, each soul becomes attuned unto the noumenal thought aboriginal in the universe. He dilates on the beauty which the soul has enjoyed in heaven and longs to regain here. In the *Phaedrus* he says:

> *I repeat again that we saw her there shining in company with the celestial forms; and coming to earth we find her here, too, shining in clearness through the most transparent apertures of sense.*

Despised, dishonored, vituperated as the senses have been by religion as the instruments of Satan himself, Plato reminds us that it is through their ministry that man is to regain his felicitous rapport with God. Plato agrees with the *Zohar* that, however distorted, shadowy and blurred is our recognition of the ideal forms now embodied in nature, still it is our even unsensing contact with them, our friction with them, that awakens the recollection of that divine enchantment they held for us in the empyrean. It is this encounter of the soul with the existential reproduction of the divine ideas that gives the soul the felicity of its divine reminiscence. The consciousness is one in the subject and the object, and it is the brushing of the one against the other that lights the spark latent in the unconscious. The soul is bound to recover her lost memory of divine things. What seems not to have been sufficiently clarified in this situation is that, instead of a *recovery* of memory of a more perfectly cognized knowledge of sublime truth experienced in the superconscious felicity of heaven before descent, it must be for the individual ego the *first,* the pristine, awakening to knowledge that was never as yet roused out of latency and germinal potentiality to self-conscious functioning. Plato's theory of the soul's felicitous acquaintance with and enjoyment of the divine ideas in its antecedent life in celestial regions subsumes as a premise for his idealist system a presupposition that seems never to have been subjected to challenge, yet which would appear to be summarily overthrown by very simple and direct logical dialectic. It has ever been a predilection of religious thought to include everything in any way connected with "heaven" in the category of "perfection." Imperfection may be the state of things on earth; but in heaven, all is complete. No consciousness is less than the fullness of perfect beatitude and bliss. No condition of being is in default in any way. Looked at with closer scrutiny, however, the theory, as basic in Plato's theorization, seems to be almost childishly naive and unsupportable. And to see it so, one has only to hold it up beside the theses which underlie the generally accepted views which rationalize soul's incarnation and earthly life for souls at all. These acceptances are virtually unanimous to the effect that souls are sent to earth, as Christianity assumes that Jesus was sent to earth to suffer and "die," for training, for experience conducive to growth, for education in the work of cooperating with the Father in his creative activity. But how can a soul that is bathed in the blessedness of heavenly felicity and the transfiguring power of divine ideation be in need of education through coarse experience? If a soul is reveling in the light and beauty of supernal glories unknown to man, from what status of the situation springs the necessity of its being torn away from that beatific life and thrust down into an underworld of darkness, ignorance and the actual dangers of being lost in sensuality and blind waywardness? Why the deprivation of its benign happiness above and its loss of these memories of felicity?

Then what principle of divine logic or divine necessity becomes the ground for the rationalization of the procedure which drags a soul away from its achieved felicity and puts it under the necessity of recovering it? And if it had won beatitude, lost it and won it back, what assurance is there that it may not lose it again? In fact on the basis of the doctrine of reincarnation of souls in many successive bodies on earth, a more or less universal obsession of the religious consciousness of antiquity, the soul would merely repeat the ordeal of losing and making the lifelong effort to recover its heavenly memories each time it descended into body. Unless it is an integral predication in this theory that the soul returns to the empyrean after each life below positively enriched, advanced in evolution, exalted in capacity for larger and more exuberant life, with expanded consciousness, the endless repetition of loss and recovery of blissfulness of the seraphic sort intimated by Plato would be definitely an irrational futility, the subjection of the soul to a treadmill routine of the most stressful sort that would never advance the soul's interests the least degree.

The confusion and the wreckage of rationality here has been occasioned largely by the attribution of a wrong connotation to this word "perfect," "perfection." By direct etymological root it means "finished," completed, aim achieved and process ended, final stage reached. In applying this meaning to the embryo souls, the progeny of God's mind, as they are projected from the mind of the Father in the noumenal realms above, one sees at once how impermissible it is to connect the term "perfect" with these fledglings of divine mind. How can perfection be imputed to them when they have not even begun their climb up the ladder of evolution? They are the "Innocents" of the Christian legend (the fabled victims of Herod's fear), the "younglings in the egg" of the Egyptian allegory, the Kumaras, or young "virgin" males, "celibate young men" of Hindu myth--young divine souls not yet "married", by incarnation, to their female counterparts, the fleshly human bodies. If the word "perfect" be insisted upon, it could be applied to them in the narrow sense that they are perfect in themselves at their stage; that is, that, even though only in their infancy as spirits, they are "perfect" as such. This argument would rest on the assertion that, as between grown oak and tiny acorn, even the acorn can be perfect--as an acorn, not, of course, as an oak.

And perhaps this side-light on the question enables us to see how the confusion has invaded this area of religious conception. The common and uncritical religious mind has always held this vague conception that associates "perfection" and finality with heaven. But heaven is also the place of beginnings, and how can we attribute perfection to beginnings? This failure to distinguish between the mere perfection of condition (at any stage of process) and perfection as completion of cycle, has thrown the religious mind quite off balance in this regard. Lacking any certain knowledge, or at least rational theory, such as that of reincarnation, as to how conscious life achieves continuity, without which a philosophy of life is impossible (since that which ends and disappears can have no history), the massive idea in the general mind is that one earthly span of existence ends the soul's brief spasm of mortal agony and opens its eternal career to some sort of "spiritual" existence. From many points of view this naive persuasion is insupportable dialectically. Until we have more certain knowledge of the basic terms of the relation between known physical existence and predicated spiritual existence, with such an entity as a soul passing, either once or many times, from one state to the other, we have the premises for neither a criterion of "perfection" nor of reality. Is the experience of souls "real" when they are in embodied residence on earth or in disembodied state in heaven? If it is so in one state and not in the other, by what standard is "reality" judged? If God's thoughts turn into earthly things, and soul's heavenly dreams are realized, in whole or part, on earth, how can reality in the one case and unreality in the other be asserted? If the soul has experience in both states, how can reality be imputed to the one experience and denied to the other? Until we have, as said, trustworthy factual data answering these questions, we are philosophizing from practically blind premises. Plato told us much about the soul as a migrant through the regions of being and of history, but he seems to have failed to maintain the equilibrium between the two worlds of existence for the soul entity, inclining to glorify its disembodied existence and experience in the noumenal world to the disparagement of the reality and value of its embodied sojourn or sojourns on earth. His successor Aristotle sought to adjust the balance more equitably. His system seems the more rational.

It therefore seems necessary to subject Plato's charming theory of reminiscence of lost paradisaical felicity to the stricture that earthly gains in spiritual intuition and vision of divine things are not strictly a recovery of lost genius but more likely the soul's initial achievement of higher vision. For this is the divine purpose or motive of the Father in pushing his Sons out of heaven's Eden into the limbo of earth. It is for their education, their chance to convert Edenic potentiality into concrete conscious actuality, as Hermes distinctly says, here on earth. Our chief concern with this phase of the dialectic is the role that nature plays in this process of the soul's spiritual education through the stresses and the logic of living experience.

If Plato did concede, in the *Phaedrus,* that "all the great arts require discussion and high speculation about the truths of nature; hence come loftiness of thought and completion of execution," it remained for another poet of lofty thoughts, the English William Wordsworth, about twenty-three hundred years later, to chant in lyric verse perhaps the most exalted panegyric ever sung in tribute to nature's elevating power. Our work could not well omit his lines from the "Tintern Abbey" poem. Prefacing with the statement that he has felt in nature the presence of a spirit that inspires in him the most elevated thoughts and "rolls through all things," he says that he is therefore

> *. . . well pleased to recognize*
> *In nature and the language of the sense,*
> *The anchor of my purest thoughts, the nurse,*
> *The guide, the guardian of my heart, and soul*
> *Of all my moral being.*

He expatiates on the theme at greater length, saying that nature can so inform the mind, so impress it with lofty thoughts, that not all the dreary intercourse of daily life can destroy the deep assurance "that all which we behold is full of blessings." Nature, he says, can generate in his consciousness a blessed mood of exalted feeling, so powerful that he is lifted into a veritable trance of ecstasy, in which he is "laid asleep in body" and becomes a living soul, and "sees into the life of things."

Of ancient thinkers following Plato, none has surpassed the Neoplatonist Plotinus in his insight into the relation between soul and sense. An insight into the profound dialectic of his analysis of the mission of the soul in descending from the realms of pure intellectual being into the world where truth, beauty and blessedness are seen only in transient partial glimpses, would be most enlightening. This great visionary of the truths of the soul centers his main thought effort upon the "philosophy" of the soul's descent into the mundane sphere. Firstly, it was God's maneuver aimed at effecting the conversion of chaos into a cosmos, by projecting the units of his spiritual mind into the physical universe so that they might leaven the material mass with the interior dynamic of self-conscious intelligence. In this he agrees with Hermes, that the procedure was directed to "the performance of the miracle of the One Thing." Even though suffering the temporary dismantling of its spiritual integrity in scattering its divine bread upon the waters, the soul sent from God bears in its tiny unit an inextinguishable spark of the divine creative fire, and if it does for an initial period permit that spark to be almost snuffed out by the "moist nature" of the sensual instincts, it will become a living center of radiation for the force of the God-mind itself in its quarter of the creation. It bears its portion of the divine formative fire into the heart of matter, there to work its transforming power on matter. God's second object in sending the souls of his Sons into the world, the philosopher analyses, was the necessity of their education through the experience of wrestling with the opposition of matter under the terms of polarity. If they were, as designed, to become the coadjutors with the Father in his creative enterprise, they had to be placed in relation to matter that would develop masterly control of its atomic energies. They were sent here, as Plotinus says, "for the purpose of developing their own powers and faculties." Most significantly he says: "It is not enough for souls merely to exist; they must show what they are capable of begetting." They are to impregnate the universe with intelligent directive power. The dual divine motive for plunging souls into incarnation is, then, the schooling of their own intelligence toward mastery of their own divine intelligence, and then the use of its mastership in the developing economy of the total creative design.

Plotinus announces in this connection a truth that could be of inestimable value to religious understanding if well digested. In declarations that flout openly the ideas that the soul besmirches its spiritual purity by contamination from earthly bodily sensuality, this philosopher stands almost alone in asserting that the soul "need not regret knowing the nature of evil and vice" in her contact with body and its sensualities. It is this very contact with "evil" that is going to be the stimulus and goad to her education. It needs this adverse condition "for the purpose of developing its own faculties and powers," which would without it lie fallow and stagnant. Soul would not know the nature and extent of her own potential if she did not wrestle with the inertia of matter. To encompass eventual divine poise and tranquility, she must "begin by considering the images stationed at the outer precincts." Remote as these external objects seem to be from their source in divine mind, they still bear the impress of their original thought formation and can thus be a reminder of the eternal truth and beauty.

This universe," he declares, *"is a living organized effective complex, all comprehensive, displaying an unfathomable wisdom. How, then, can any one say that it is not a clear image, beautifully formed, of the intellectual verities? No one seeing the loveliness lavished in the world of sense. . . could be so dull-witted as not to be carried by all this to recollection and gripped by reverent awe . . . Such a one could have neither fathomed this world nor have had any vision of that other. We must recognize that even in the world of sense and part, there are things of a loveliness comparable to that of the celestials, which fill us with veneration for their Creator and convince us of their origin in the divine forms, which show how ineffable is the beauty of the Supreme.*

Here surely is the ringing asseveration of Thales some seven hundred years before Plotinus, that "the earth is full of gods." So realistically was this sense of the divine animation of the earth that in the imagination of the Greek a deity of some rank, be it Naiad, oread, dryad, mermaid, nymph, faun, gnome or other spirit, lurked in every dell, stream, or grove. It may be conceded that a gross crystallization of the spiritistic concept traduced the idea into a form so crude as to rebuff intelligence and to condition the pagan consciousness for acceptance of the Christian shibboleth "Great Pan is dead" when it reverberated from the lips of the fanatical pietists of the Jesus cult about the first A.D. century. But it must be asked at the same time what chilling winds, blowing over the general consciousness deadened the quick and mercurial sense of the actual presence of deific mind in the natural world. However grotesquely personalized the conception could have become in bucolic mentality, it is from any angle distressing and fatalistic that the pagan spell of a warmer and more directly intimate kinship between man and nature effervesced out of the ancient consciousness. If Christianity may have brought its devotees to a closer awareness of the pervading influence of God in the spiritual area of our life, it did so at the cost of the loss of that enlivening sense of the nearness of the divine presence on the physical side. This loss must be accounted the greater one, since in the balance between the inner spirit and the outer world which a truly beneficent philosophy must inculcate, paganism idealized the deific constitution of nature without derogating, much less nullifying, the function and power of the spiritual forces, whereas on its part Christianity gave all glory and paid all worship to the spiritual element and completely shattered the equilibrium by negativing utterly the physical weight in the dichotomy. The Christian murder of Great Pan cut the currents of a lively and sustaining sympathy between man and nature, so that from that day there set in over the Western world an obtuseness and insensibility toward the natural world, which, ever hardening over the centuries, has led to a ruthless wantonness in the human attitude toward the soil and its vegetation, with widespread devastation of its bounties and its beauties. As between a civilization deeply softened by a profound reverence for the assumed presence of deity in the earth, and one dulled to any such sensitivity, one must give the rating to the pagan over the Christian.

Heraclitus, doubtless in the same tenor of philosophical thought as Thales, declared that "Wisdom is to see true things and to act according to nature, listening to its voice." (Fragment 112). In consequence true religion must spring from the merging of one's thought with the divine thought, which is a living fire pervading and animating the universe. He states that the Logos is both the divine thought that percolates through all nature and also the human thought in so far as it participates in that single cosmic and eternal movement. This profound sense of the identity of the truly balanced human thought with the living spirit of the universe was the primary and basic foundation of the Greek philosophical system. The perfect harmony of man's thought with the mind of the Logos, Heraclitus saw, would fulfill all the demands of the moral and spiritual laws of life.

Passing over the abundant witness of medieval philosophy to the kinship of mind and nature, and especially the resurgence of concern with nature that came with the great Italian Renaissance of the fourteenth century--a veritable back-to-nature sweep in all essential elements--a cursory view can be taken of modern testimony bearing on the theme.

It can hardly be denied that one of the most telling blows that cut the chain of ecclesiasticism and dogmatism that had bound the European mind in fetters for fifteen centuries was John Locke's declaration that there could be nothing in the mind that had not entered through the gateway of the senses. While, to be sure, this startling pronouncement did not commit philosophy to a gross sensualism, it did enforce attention to the relation of idealism to the outer nature.

Spinoza recognized the parallelism between thought and outward things in his notable summarization of the concept: The history and connection of ideas is the same as the history and connection of things. He insists that all things in nature must involve and express the idea of God as their primary *raison d'etre*. We come to greater knowledge of God in proportion as we understand natural things more clearly. The mind itself becomes one with the eternal Logos to the extent that it seizes upon the primal archai of truth as they are illustrated by natural objects.

The prodigious elaboration of philosophical speculation that was carried on by Medieval scholasticism must not be overlooked in the survey. Its most profound elucidation was the work of the great Aquinas, denominated tersely as "Thomism." What place was given to nature in it?

The ultimate Thomistic position is a reasonable compromise between the Lockian sensualism and the Platonic idealism, between the world and the mind. It can be succinctly stated in the form: knowledge begins in the senses and is perfected in the intellect. This formula allows for the play of both sides of human nature, and permits both to contribute their influence to the final summation of experience.

Aquinas bridges a wide gap in the dialectic between the unknowable thing-in-itself and pure consciousness, by the device of postulating an intermediate agency inherent in the divine endowment of man, the active power of the imagination. If in abstract dialectic he conceded to Kant that consciousness, as being immaterial, can not become identical with a material object, and therefore can not know it in reality, nevertheless this active agent, the imagination, is able to "desensualize" or psychically disintegrate the physical object, so as to transform it from unknowable object into a mental image or ghost of its reality, clear enough to bring it into man's conceptual world as an object of knowledge. So if they are to be truly understood, objects must be illumined by the mind.

The great Kant, though not preoccupied with the theme as central in his schematism, gives nature due place in his critique of our mental mechanics. Nature as necessary foundation for true conceptuality is implicit in his famous maxim: "Thoughts which lack content are empty; precepts which lack concepts are blind." Without the power of sense we should be aware of no object; without the power of intellect we could think of no object. From these predications there springs by irrefutable dialectic the necessity that all sound human ratiocination must be the conjunct interfusion of thought and thing. Contending that we could not *know* the world as thing, yet he could not deny to it its indefeasible factuality, and its substantiality for thought. Nature furnished the raw material for our psychic reinterpretation. It presented something that mind needed to introspect and interpret. Cognition without objects is void, he said, and would be meaningless. There would be nothing for the faculty of thought to work on.

The Prussian thinker speaks volubly of the metaphysics of nature. By this he refers to the superworld of laws, principles, intuitionally conceived structures of logic and meaning which exist *a priori* in the transcendental area of the human consciousness, to which he has given the name of "categories." Nature yielded its meaning to us when we discerned its phenomena and gauged their significance by the rule of these categories. He fully acknowledged the dependence of our ideation upon "our sensual contact with the objective world, however imperfectly we could know it":

But the existence of external things is absolutely requisite for this purpose; so that it follows that internal experience is itself possible only mediately and through external experience.

It is surely to be wondered if the Konigsburg philosopher ever followed the dialectic of this determination to the limit of its implications. If, as he avers, it be true that our highest intellectual or intuitional cognitions of truth are dependent upon and mediated by our experience of outward things, then it must be concluded that the content, the form and the structure of our conceptions are determined primarily by the shape of these external objects and phenomena. Would this not have instructed him that he might better look outside to find the forms and norms that give shape to our truth concepts rather than search for them in the vacuous upper region of transcendental idealities? Might it not have occurred to him that, inasmuch as those outward things had already been structuralized by divine thought, presumably the same source from which the transcendental *a priori* forms and molds had emanated, there could be expected to be an identity between the two? Some deep intimation of this identity of inner and outer it was that swept Fichte, then Schelling, and then Hegel on to grandiose conceptions of such a harmony between the two modes of being, spiritual and material, in the universe. It had of course been a recondite perception of the Hindus long before. We do hear him saying:

All phenomena exist in one nature, and must so exist, inasmuch as without this a priori unity, no unity of experience, and consequently no determination of objects in experience is possible.

If all things exist in one nature, there can be little debate over the question whether reality for man lies in the subjective realm of idealism or the objective realm of nature. Each wing of the bird of life and mind can carry the body of true existence only if it is balanced by the other. And the unity of experience Kant speaks of is the result of this balance.

Whatever accord with truth our philosophy may claim at present owes an immense debt to the German savant for his revelation of the hollowness of the claims of those who expound a philosophy of extreme and uncompromising transcendental idealism, such as the supra-intellectual absolutistic nihilism in some Hindu systems and in mysticism. That reality is to be achieved by transcending all sense and even thought in a void above them, while consciousness is stilled in a repose that annihilates all sentience, Kant denounces as the abject folly of unreason. Of such thinkers he speaks contemptuously, saying that "they beat their wings in vain against the eternal walls." The air of that region of the void is too thin to buoy up the wings of consciousness.

CHAPTER SEVEN

MIND'S SOURCE IN NATURE

It is perhaps true to say that the concept of the unity of world soul and nature was carried to its highest point of accentuation in the splendid surge of idealist realism in the great romantic movement that swept German thought to its finest flowering following the Kantian stimulus. If Kant had contended that we can not know external things as they are in themselves, reaction to this determination was certainly not in the direction away from nature. It did not indict nature as valueless in the search for knowledge or aid as an incitement to spiritual intuition. In fact Kant's work spurred a recoil of thought back upon nature, enhancing its function and significance to the highest degree. If nature could not declare its own order of being to us, might it not be able to reveal to us something of that Logoic thought that created it? Could it perhaps be the voice of the Logos, the spokesman for God? Was it not the self-revelation of the creative mind and purpose?

This at any rate was the thrilling concept that gripped the German philosophic mind and carried it to its highest elevation perhaps in the brain of Schelling. It would be an enchanting revel to quote liberally from the flights of this exuberant spirit into the airy region of this alluring philosophy. In his *The Philosophy of Nature,* he expands the theme of the world as the epiphany of the creative Logos. His axial thesis may be condensed and consummated in one brief citation: "The system of nature is at the same time the system of our mind. Nature is God's mind made visible, and mind is nature made invisible." This is as forthright a manifesto of the doctrine as could be made. In the creation we see the marvel of the God-mind expressing itself. "Nature," he felicitously says, "is the cosmic process in the bud stage." The poetic mind sees nature, as the stage antecedent and preparatory to the emergence of spirit, standing to spirit as bud to rose.

Another German thinker of eminence was Schiller. His view of nature may be graphically summarized in a sentence from his *Philosophical Letters*: "The universe is a thought of deity. This ideal thought form overflowed into actuality, and the world born thereof has realized the plan of its Creator."

While Hegel only confirms and further applies Schelling's theorization, his contribution to its authentic claim to veracity is too great to be omitted from the survey. The historical and the rational natures are in substance one, he asserts. And--a most profound discernment--it is only because life has in the beginning--as Heraclitus argued--split itself into two opposing forces, that it can and must reintegrate itself in the finale. The necessity for the division--the inevitable query of naive logic--is seen in the law of polarity, positive against negative, since without the balance of conscious mind against unconscious matter nothing could be created; and without the expression of his will and purpose in fresh creation God himself would stagnate in non-being. Creation could not take place as long as God remained asleep in his unity. Creation requires a thinking planning creator and matter with which to create; and these two are arrayed in tension against each other only when polarized as opposite forces. Hegel's elucidation of the dialectical necessity for the dichotomy of spirit and matter is perhaps the most inexpugnable since the day of Plotinus, and it is a contribution vital for all philosophical exposition henceforth.

Hegel in his early writing asserted that the Greeks were masters of their own inner and outer life, and so had no need of theological systems or ecclesiastical institutions. The moral law was instinctive in their consciousness in an natural undisturbed harmony with reason, as *their whole life was in complete harmony with nature*. (This logic can with equal truth be applied to the ancient Egyptians.) Hegel saw that truth and beauty, and goodness with them, are intellectually represented to man in and by nature. Nature faces us with its undeniable spell of beauty; it must be true; and, except in much Hindu thought, must be good. Spiritual life, he says, objectifies itself to itself, and thus turns back upon itself and swings full circle for the purpose of self-enrichment. Inner life is revealed by a symbolic extrusion of itself in the outer world, and the reflex from the outer transforms it into a vital inner experience. In this experience, soul completes a synthesis of itself with its own objectivity. The active intellectual nature of soul, through the ordeal of separation and reunion of its subjective and objective phases, achieves its perfect self-recognition. In short it could not come to know itself until it has precipitated an objectification of itself outward in matter and can thus observe and study itself. Intellect, he affirms, is not an element or faculty separated from and opposed to spirit, as so much mystical propensity has insisted, but it is a phase or moment of spirit itself. Therefore its determinations, if logically unimpeachable, can not impugn the nature and purposes of the total spiritual being. This is a most important principle, since intellect has been derogated with the charge that through its analytic processes it dissolves the primal unity of life and thought into multiplicity and so distracts and confuses the soul's pristine "vision of wholes." The rebuttal of this unbalanced judgment is seen in the primary fact that life itself has initially broken away from unity, dispersing its outward movement into infinite plurality, and it thus becomes the business of intellect to analyze the endless diversity in such a way as to discern the jig-saw interrelation of the parts, and so to turn the analysis into the ultimate synthesis. Putting it a little differently, Hegel says that what the intellect separates--rather what life has separated--and objectifies, spirit reunites and resubjectivizes. Human thinking accomplishes this by the logic of reason and its highest expression is intuition, which, like intellect, is an integral element in the unity of total consciousness. This logic, he says, is a logic not only of knowledge, of thought, of the living self, but also of basic being, existence and reality. In this reach of insight into the nature of *Geist,* or spirit, one commentator well observes, Hegel has achieved the inseparable connection between mind and spirit, between the human and the divine, and it must be rated as a great philosophical feat.

In a notable passage, the German thinker develops as clear a dialectical elucidation of the necessity for the incarnation of souls in mortal bodies as modern speculation has at any time advanced. Plotinus had enunciated this dialectic in masterly fashion in the third century. "To actualize itself," Hegel writes, "to work out the basic identity of ideal and real, mind has to wander through the spheres of Nature, as its great opponent, its own nothing,' and it has to find its own essence in its opposite," as the latter reflects back to it its own basic forms. Nature reflects the soul's own divine forms back to it. In heaven it may, as Plato predicates, bathe its consciousness in the eternal verities. But, just as the acorn can not comprehend its oakness, nor the human child its blissful immersion in pure ideality, soul-mind must leave paradise in order to make unconscious ideality consciously real to its slowly-evolving self-awareness, as that is born and matures through battling with the external forms. "The mind," he expounds, "must return from its apostasy as victor over itself,'". Paradoxically to be sure, the soul must leave its home in heaven in its youth and immaturity in order to meet itself returning in its maturity. As the eye can not turn to inspect itself, the soul must see itself pictured in the forms which its parent has projected in nature, which forms are the likeness of itself. In the static inertness of unified being, consciousness can not become aware of itself, can not objectify itself to itself. It must brace itself ideally against itself materially to become self-conscious. Spirit becomes acquainted with its own selfhood by looking its material opposite in the face. Spirit plunges to its own "death" as spirit when it goes forth to parade in the world of substance, and then stands off and watches itself as it stalks through the worlds. Thus it endures "death" on the cross of matter, but in the reflex it recovers its true selfhood and arises anew from the "dead." "There is neither being nor life without this antagonism, this self-negation, this death."

Making a daring leap ahead in the field of modern speculation toward the conclusion that matter and mind are essentially one, or that matter is stamped with the impress of mind, that the two exist as a dually conditioned monism, Hegel boldly proclaims that, "since the Absolute is intrinsically Thought, the doctrine of thinking must be the doctrine of being." The world would then indeed be the crystallization of the divine Thought. Vigorously expressed is his assertion of the falsity of the position of those, predominantly Oriental philosophies, which seek to eliminate the conflict between the soul and the world by dismantling the apparatus of the sensual, the emotional and even the mental human equipment. In place of this blind effort to kill the influence of the world and man's modes of experience with it, his preachment is to apply the intellectual faculty to the task of rationalizing the conflict. Conflict is not to be dissolved, but to be understood, and so seen as beneficent, not a miscarriage of divine intent. For its issues are the body of experience which constitute the soul's education. To destroy the conflict untimely would be to take the child out of school.

In full accord with Hegel's view, the author of a work, *Philosophy and Ideological Conflict,* Charles S. Seely, writes that everything in the universe has an opposite, and nothing can exist without its counterpart; one explains anything in terms of its opposite. If one is destroyed, the other disappears with it. Many writers speak in similar vein.

In a work, *God in Search of Man,* A. J. Heschel says that the German romantic movement, itself owing much of its impetus to the prior Italian Renaissance, "resurrected nature," and the influence lingers to the present. It placed nature in a position of close to ultimate significance. Enthusiasts sought to cultivate a sentimental sympathy with nature. He ends, however, by saying that this worship for the most part brought not the golden rapports so ideally anticipated, but revealed its inadequacies, clearly pointing to the need of something higher than nature to satisfy a deeper hunger of the spirit. A discussion of this disappointment or failure will come in a later phase of our study.

Hegel's great message in philosophy is, of course, the thesis that the advance of the life movement in the world is the expression of the Absolute Reason. The law according to which all being unfolds is reason, and as divine mind is its dynamo and generator and nature its product, the two, mind and nature, are essentially one and the same power. As Spinoza put it, one is *natura naturane,* life generating its product, the other *natura naturata,* the generated product, the one seed, the other fruit. The divine idea, giving form and meaning to the procedure, is the only genuine reality.

As fine a mind as that of the German poet-philosopher Goethe gives his verdict on the theme under discussion. It may be summarized in one sentence: "Everything that happens is a symbol; and it can perfectly reflect the world." This does not assert that the world itself is the total symbol of the divine thought, but it points to this idea.

And in the same theorization, it can be said that the concept launched into formal philosophy by Berkeley, the *esse est percipi* formula, by transferring the naively sensed outer world into the ego's inward experience, virtually leads to the necessary identity of the two worlds.

Suggested in the context here is the famous couplet of that prolific artificer of sententious aphorisms, Alexander Pope:

All nature is but Art, unknown to thee;
All chance direction which thou canst not see.

The capitalization of Art hints at the creative Artist and his works.

Echoing Schelling and Hegel, Bosanquet says that the content of mind is the content of nature; and everything in mind is, on the Lockian thesis, drawn from nature. As Pope says that nature is seen but not understood, Bosanquet sets forth the view that what we classify as the spiritual world is this nature--understood. That is to hold that the natural world finds its true inner meaning in our spiritual intimations induced from reflection upon its phenomena. He emphasizes the idea that the highest spiritual realizations are not in an upper world, but are cognate with the existent order.

A singularly lucid exposition of man's life in its intermediate position between inner consciousness and outer world is the former Harvard philosopher, George Santayana. At the beginning of his admirable work, *The Life of Reason,* he speaks of the "crushing irrationality of life itself." One face of this irrationality is the basic fact that life is the result of the cosmic procedure that launches souls, or the transcendental principle of conscious selfhood, in earthly bodies, inspires them with passions and subjects them to buffetings from the environing world. This is the prime condition of all observation and inference, and all failure or success must be rated in relation to it. This is to say that this embodiment of souls in mortal flesh is the foundation of life and therefore is the ground of all meaning reference for humans. The first task for both curiosity and intelligence would then seem to be to study and understand this physical environment in which incarnation has consigned the soul entities, this "animated engine" called nature. Clues to the meaning of the soul's immersion in this kind of a world will obviously have to be sought in the phenomena of this natural order. Imagination and reason must work on nature to descry in its operations the principles of its ecology. So mind primitively knows no mystery that is not rooted in phenomena, and "fancy can build no hope that would not be expressible there." Thought would have no fuel to feed its activity unless the reality of the cosmos presented itself to its notice. If in his study man finds nature exhibiting the evidences of rational procedure, he can begin to formulate a philosophy of his relation to the world. If he does not find these revealing indices in his scrutiny of nature, where else may he look for light on his life?

Human attention, he writes, *is riveted on temporal existences, on the fortunes of particular objects, natural or corporeal. There is then a primacy of nature over spirit in social life, and this primacy, in a certain sense, endures to the end, since all spirit must be the spirit of something, and reason could not exist or be conceived at all unless a material organism, personal or social, lay beneath to give thought an occasion and a point of view . . . Things could not be near or far, worse or better, unless a definite life were taken as a standard, a life lodged somewhere in space and time.*

The sanity and indefeasible logic of this simple dialectic could have saved the philosophical effort from the endless dispute that has seethed in the kettle of speculation over the Hindu doctrine of *maya,* the "illusion" of matter and our experience with it. The argument whether the world is real or only an illusory dream has agitated the waters of the philosophical pool at all times. In this, as in so many other matters, the naive conscious reaction to the ego's contact with the outer world need never have been distrusted or questioned. Santayana is saying that even if sophistication of logic may make the point that our immediate experience with our world is a mere ghost of reality, it is still the *actuality* of our life, which no logic can invalidate as real experience. For, in brief, if our contact with earth does not yield us reality, there is no other source from which we can have it. If we renounce this world as unreal, we have access to no other world that is real. Our experience here is our one chance to know reality.

And of course Santayana is in agreement with others who recognize that the objects and phenomena extant in the physical world constitute the idioms of the language which eloquently conveys the essence of truth to human intelligence. He well recognizes that the objective processes stand as symbols of cosmic truth and inner reality.

Nature's works, he elucidates, acquire meaning in the "commentaries" they provoke the mind to make upon them; they seem to bring mind to a kinship with the life expressing itself in them. Mind imputes to nature its own values (as Kant insisted) retroactively or in reflection, but nature plants the first impressions. "The mind spreads and soars in proportion as body feeds on the surrounding world." Consciousness sees nature from the point of view of its own ideal interests and measures the flow of things by its own ideal standards. It translates nature into the categories of its own conception.

The philosopher cites as evidence that nature is the fertile soil out of which springs higher intellection in the fact, previously noted herein, that in Hinduism, "the national religion seems to have been nothing but a poetic naturalism."

Strangely, however, in one place Santayana seems to waver in his general position regarding nature. He says (*The Life of Reason,* p. 207) that "the phenomena of nature, intelligible, rational, but immensely impressive . . . while they compel attention, they do not after a while enlarge the understanding." Husbandman's lore, he says, is singularly stagnant. Since the idea that inspired this work is the thesis that nature is the ultimately true enlightener of the understanding, this statement of the philosopher must be scrutinized.

We do not deny the truth of his remark that in common life people's daily contact with nature does not enlarge the understanding. The aim of this work is in fact to amplify this state of things and to "enlarge our understanding" of its causes, its meaning and its implications. The blindness of people generally to the esoteric message of nature is precisely our theme. It is part of the dreariness of common life that people accept nature as commonplace daily routine, entirely obtuse to her subtle intimations of meaning. This simply attests that the "average" of humanity takes nature as it comes, sinks to a level of familiarity with it, lets custom stale any profounder interest in it, and remains unreflective about it. And, save in rare instances, the husbandman is the last person likely to develop a semantic interest in or understanding of nature. His interest in soil and weather is so grossly utilitarian and practical that poetic sentimentality about them is a remote possibility in his life. Santayana is looking at the wrong people in gauging his view of nature's instructive potential. Our work aims to demonstrate that nature's power to enhance our understanding demands the function of the highest, not the average, refinements of the human intelligence. The thinker himself gives evidence of the correctness of our view, for while he drops this comment on the dullness of the general response of thought to nature, he has on his own part pierced deeply into the inner meaning and revelation of truth suggested to his keener mind by reflection on nature. He says it is to nature that man must look for models and goals, for instruments and materials which thought must have as fundaments for thinking at all. He says that nature can be trusted to be true to its word. If he allows that the external world provides the basic material for all thought, and that this material furnishes the very paradigms of truth, he is strictly in line with what he so often forthrightly asserts as to nature's allegorical and semantic function in our mental life.

We read such sweeping categorical declarations that "Mind grows self-perpetuating only by its expression in matter." Again: "The ideal is a constant emanation from the natural and has no other possibilities,"; we have to accept the "appearance" of things--so much belabored and stigmatized as mere "illusion"--as the best medium of our knowledge of things. Realities become knowable by virtue of their ability to present themselves to us in these appearances. "In no region can the spirit find itself so much at home as among natural causes." The reflective mind can find no ground for doubting that the principles which it sees illustrated by nature are in close harmony with the canons of rational thinking. Nature furnishes thousands of intimations of such a kinship.

The more intense and even poetical becomes a man's sense of his spiritual state, the more clearly will he realize his utter dependence on nature and discern the identity of the animating drive in his life and hers. Nature is a region where mental form, the spirit ideal, breeds an existence to express itself. Mind is the entelechy, the goal aimed at, of an organic body. Nature at its human station is destined to give birth to divine mind. Every theme or motive in the life of reason expresses some instinct rooted in the body, which is a natural instrument. "Reason cries aloud for reunion with the material world." This single sentence should be recognized as one of the most important truths ever uttered. Mystical enthusiasts drop the world in order to grasp reality. This he calls "an exquisite suicide." Nature is like a new mythology; the purely fictitious idea has a certain likeness to nature, finding itself mirrored in her forms and habitudes. Nature helps mind to maintain an equilibrium with reality, its perennial forms serving to dissipate the shadows and fogs of haunting fancies and illusions that besiege consciousness when drawn too far away from actuality. So long as the will or the instinct is in large measure blind, unenlightened by intelligence, the life of reason is still swathed in ignominy, "and the animal barks in the midst of human discourse." The individual will is lost for the most part in frivolous pleasures and less worthy spurs to action. Nature banishes illusions and provides an exit out of psychic distortions and aberrancies; illusions dissolve in the presence of nature's obvious insistence on the real. So wisdom basically consists in recasting natural impulses in the furnace of experience.

And how splendidly he grants to natural life its salutary role when he says that . . .

Were it not for what we know in the outer world and of our place in it, we should be incapable of attaching any meaning to subjectivity. The flux of things would then go on in their own medium, not in our minds, and no suspicion of illusion or of qualification by mind would attach to any event in nature . . . It is our reliance on the world's material coherence that marks our awakening, and that constitutes our discovery that we exist as minds. Mind is an expression, weighted with emotion, of natural relations among bodies . . . There is nothing stable or interesting to contemplate except objects relevant to action, the natural world and the mind's ideals.

And Santayana, in a side glance at Greek thought, pays a notable tribute to the benignant influence of nature when he remarks that "if no single phenomenon had been explained correctly by any philosopher from Thales to Lucretius, yet by their frank and studious contemplation of nature they would have liberated the human soul." This liberation would have come from the realization that but two things existed in the world, nature and mind, the latter the power of consciousness, the former something to be conscious of. And it is possible that our Harvard savant, with perhaps as keen faculty to picture the forms of abstract thought as any philosopher has ever displayed, has caught the truth of a relation between these two constituents of life that none other has so clearly delineated. For he has taken a most radical position on this relation. He has in fact gone clear to the extreme view that, so far from spirit's being the absolute antithesis of matter, a thing alien and without dependence on matter, it is in truth as much a product of matter's creativity as any material object. It is simply the ripe fruit on nature's tree. In short, spirit, consciousness, mind are in and belong as much to the world of nature as does a tree itself. The automative springs of unreflective action, which we call instinct, we have agreed to think of as located in and a product of our animal nature. But mind, thought, intuition, spirit we have segregated off from the domain of nature and claim that they come down to us from some supernatural order of essence even existent prior to nature. No, declares Santayana; these essences that we like to think of as "higher" than instinct are just as truly the production of nature and its forces as is instinct. Spiritual intuition is only instinct evolved into sharper perception, more sensitive appreciations, more luminous and numinous insights. The entire range of life is not a process that proceeds under the banner of nature, then at some point switches to the banner of spirit, but is an unbroken continuity of the same order. And if the early stages of the movement involve the preview and anticipation of the later and higher stages, how can it be denied that the process and the motivation are spiritual throughout? If, as in the case of the acorn, the spiritual end product is implicit in the beginning, then again the whole order must be considered spiritual. It is all one process, but the human mind in its limited view, contrasting initial and rudimentary status with developed manifestation, insists on a division and difference between the two moments. It names the seed stage as one order of being and the fruit stage as another.

Santayana would subsume both stages under the one category. He asserts that the entire life of reason was generated and controlled by the animal life of man in the bosom of nature. Blind impulse of instinct, leading to now happy, now unhappy outcomes, stirred thought alive and so unfolded the powers of cognition, reason, moral and spiritual consciousness. If it turns actually spiritual in the end, it must have been similarly so in the beginning. So, the philosopher insists, it matters little whether you extend the concept of the natural right on to the spiritual consummation, or pull back the spiritual to cover the primary grades. Santayana will be charged here with an illegitimate redefinition of the term natural that extends its meaning to make it include the spiritual, and even by inference makes the spiritual side include the natural. By so doing he may be accused also of making both deism and pantheism the true religion. He says intuition is pathetically animal.

He confesses that he does not know what matter is--in itself. But, in a rigorous critique of the vaunting claims of "metaphysical idealists" as to the primacy and sole reality of spirit, he finds that, if spirit is the reality behind all appearances, then this spirit is precisely what he calls matter, since it is the living energies inherent in matter that drive the life movement forward. And he adds that he finds this concept of the world process much more interesting and beautiful than the mystical rhapsodies of the idealists, and much more likely to be true. Further he says that our loftiest intuitions of mystical rapport with the being of God depend on nature and matter for their foundation and generation. By its grand sweeping harmonies, it is nature itself that gives wings to the soul. This view, he says, is supported by the popular definition of "spiritual," because intuition, when it thoroughly introspects animal experience, transmutes it into pure flame of conscious illumination and renders it religious or poetical, which is as competent an estimate of the meaning of "spiritual" as the popular mind can ever reach. He declares that most metaphysics are simply imagined experiences, flouting the possibility that true experience of real essences could go on in a void, without any material foundations. This position put him at sharp variance from most Hindu spiritual systems, which he does characterize as baseless vaporings of feeling and chimerical infatuations. Love itself, he says, is a brilliant illustration of a principle universally discernible: that the human reason lives by its power to turn the friction of material forces into the light of ideal verities. The intuitions which we take to be the afflations of spirit flow out from the experience of the ego with the crude forces of the world and take form under the felt pressure of nature, but definitely require the existence of nature to generate them.

Incarnation, the presence of souls in physical embodiment on a planet, is by no means an anomaly. The spirit is no intruder on earth, but is here by proper assignment in the order of cosmos. It is not a fall, not a miscarriage of divine ordinance. Then the philosopher dares to give utterance to a statement that throws the imputation of the grossest possible error in the face of orthodox Christian theology, when he says that it is a fatuous and unfounded prejudice to suppose that spirit is contaminated by its contact with the body of flesh. The very opposite of this doctrinal axiom is true; the immersion of soul in the flesh is intrinsically beneficent from every point of view, as it is only through the device that spirit-soul is itself generated. Every brush of the latent essence of spirit against the objective confrontation of the outer world produces its bit of friction which warms potential soul quality into life. Every impulse of man or beast fans the flame of spirit one degree higher. Ideas that have no deep roots in the world are unrealizable and cause psychic indigestion. His climactic indictment of spiritual mysticism as wild libertinism of the imagination is voiced in his statement that if you cut your lines of attachment with the animal bases of your life, you run mad. When the soul cuts her umbilical cord with her Mother Nature, she risks detachment from the sources of her well-being.

CHAPTER EIGHT

THE WISDOM OF AUROBINDO

Devastating as Santayana's strictures would seem to be to the transcendental subjectivism of India's religious philosophies, it is to an Indian thinker that we turn now to find another strong pleader of the case for the truth. No survey of the place and role of matter and the objective world in the life of the spirit dare overlook the contribution to this theme made by the man widely reputed to be India's greatest and most illumined modern philosopher, Sri Aurobindo Ghosh. His splendid two-volume work, *The Life Divine,* and other literary productions, reveal the shining light of a mind capable of objectifying before it the essences of abstract conception and examining them with the most lucid transparency. All the more notable and quotable are his insights into the panorama of truth because his authoritative voice sounds a clarion call for a rectification of falsely oriented trends and goals in centuries of Hindu philosophical systematism. He sends out epochal appeal for Hindu thought to forsake its insistent bent on straining to attain the assumed ecstasies of unconditioned being in nirvanic entrancement above the range of human sentience and to turn back to earth and strive for wisdom and enlightenment from the very ground of earth and nature. The significance of a movement indigenous to India itself, that will turn the Hindu religious aspiration from the detachments of spiritual yoga back to lowly earth, can not be overrated in the world today. But this work is so extensive that even the briefest synopsis of it must run to some length.

A starting point may be found in his exposition that man's life is clearly the impact on his consciousness of two apparent realities, a duad of worlds, one of material objects in a domain external to himself, and another of consciousness or spirit. Aiming to correct so much Hindu thinking that essays to find blessedness in the spiritual area by negating and suppressing sensual experience with the objective world, he strikes ringing blows for the truth of the conception that the beneficent outcome of human endeavor is the consummation of a living experience that reaches fruitage through the union of the elements and forces of the two spheres of being, the spiritual and the physical. Flying directly in the face of that enormous body of Hindu speculation, which not only ignores earth and its values as essential to the glorification of consciousness, but thinks that more enriched and exalted being for man is to be achieved by suppressing, nay, killing, out agencies by which human life is attached to the world, the senses, the emotions and the mind itself. Aurobindo declares in the most positive terms that the higher divinity latent in us can never realize its potential until it makes a complete union with the actualities of earthly sensual experience, and not in remote areas of the void "above" all existential consciousness in utter abstraction and entrancement, but right here in the world of sense and objectivity. This radical revision of time-honored Hindu persuasion by India's leading modern thinker constitutes a virtual revolution in ancient Aryavarta's mystical religionism that is destined to lift its people at last out of their passivistic lethargy and awaken them to face the realities of objective existence with other peoples in a world of this kind. He describes both the spiritual and the materialistic views of existence and concludes that both disfigure the truth. To regard all physical experience as an illusion and a dream; or on the other hand, to hold our sensual contact with the world as the only reality, and all ideal recognitions as even a far thinner dream, is a mistake either way, a falsification of the true position. For spirit to deny the reality of matter and its reaction to it, or for material consciousness to negate the spiritual factuality, is equally an imbalance. Each view simply bespeaks the inability of the one cast of mind to recognize the validity of its opposing view.

But, asserts this wonderfully astute and clear-sighted philosopher, we can see the truth which both views disfigure. In almost a direct reversal of the predominant religious philosophy of his land, he says that, on the side of the spirit, no mystical experience "is entirely valid until it has possessed itself of our physical consciousness and manifested on the lowest levels in harmony with its manifestations on the higher summits."

It is equally true that form in the spiritual Platonic archetypal sense and matter, each asserting itself as a self-existent reality, is an illusion of ignorance. Form and matter can be valid only as the shape and substance of manifestation for the incorporeal and immaterial. They are in their nature an act of divine consciousness, in their aim the representation of a status of spirit.

This is thrillingly prophetic of a new epoch opening for Hindu reflection. What the philosopher is daringly saying to his countrymen is that in the play of life's polarization between positive spirit and negative matter, neither segment can exist and function apart from its tie-in with the other, and if the tension magnetically holding them together *could* be broken, all manifested existence would dissolve back into primordial non-being. If there is to be conscious existence at all, it must be under the terms of polarization of spirit and matter.

In the most lucid forms of expression, he expounds that if the Absolute, Brahman, wishes to enjoy the delightful exercise of his energies in creative activity, it must engage its forces in the task of working in the area of the relative, the conditioned and the phenomenal. Its own self-awareness can only be awakened by this tension set up between the two opposites in its whole being; its only possibility of finding genuine delight in creative expression lies in this self-exertion and self-revelation of itself to itself. Speaking with the authority of self-evident truth, he oracularly says that in the progressive advance of God's self-manifestation, if we, as participants of this experience, cast aside or belittle the physical life that is our basis and status at the lower level, and then in reaching the mental and spiritual heights we discard and stifle the vital forces that have brought us this far up the line--if in our infatuation with the spiritual we reject the lower energies of the mental and the physical, we limit and stifle the fullness and free movement of God's manifestation of his own being in and through us. However high we climb toward the shining summit, "we climb ill if we forget our base." This is magnificent beyond all acclaim; here is the sanity, the truth, the light that may lift not only Hindu religion, but religion, generally out of murky shadows into the daylight of real knowledge. And majestically he swings into the full orbit of the implications of this bright discernment:

Not to abandon the lower to itself, but to transform it in the light of the higher to which we have attained is the true divinity of nature. Brahman is integral and unifies many states of consciousness at a time; we also, manifesting the nature of Brahman, should become integrated and all-embracing.

What does this imply? Nothing less than for our integration and ultimate perfection we dare not ignore or neglect the physical foundations of our life, since only by maintaining a balance with them can spirit realize its own capabilities. One must ask what it could have meant for the stability and happiness of the world if religious ideologies everywhere had been sanified by the decisive knowledge that, as he says, "we do not need to give up the bodily life to attain to the intellectual and the spiritual," nor do we have to give up the intellectual and the spiritual interests to blot out all lower grades of conscious experience in order to gain the nirvanic release--moksha--into the imagined unconditioned world. The revelation of so brilliant a light of truth by one of India's own spokesmen should open that nation's eyes to a realization of the semi-darkness in which its idea of achieving spiritual bliss by suffocating the life of the body has enwrapped it for doleful centuries.

If there are spiritual powers transcending the levels of world life, they embrace the universe, they are one with it, and are not excluded from any part of it, nor is any part of it excluded from their overall presence. The world of form and conditioned manifestation is permeated by the entire immanence of the timeless, formless and unconditioned real being of Brahman. The harmony of the two segments is the condition of all life that aims to be basically divine.

One must wonder if the religious mind of our day is able to grasp the staggering truth of Aurobindo's sledge-hammer logic when he says that if those aspiring spirits who, by persistent zeal may attain the state of liberation, may pass beyond the world of the senses and the mind into nirvanic repose in an upper void, thus by their very illumination abandon their obligation to human society and so remove themselves from the human scene, "the world would be condemned to remain eternally the scene of unredeemed darkness, death and suffering. And such a world can only be a ruthless ordeal or a mechanical illusion." The thought here is that if for their own selfish grasping at the alleged bliss of liberation these higher and more advanced souls take themselves out of human society, instead of remaining in touch with it and thus contributing their uplifting influence to their lesser developed fellows, the world would never rise above the status of the mediocre, the blind and the ignorant. If the alumni do not continue to help the undergraduates, how can the latter advance?

We glean a new understanding of our own nature when he says: "In the conscious individual Prakriti matter turns back to perceive Purusha spirit; the world seeks after the Self; God, having entirely become Nature, Nature seeks to become progressively God." And can orthodox Christian theology escape the stigma of ignorance and error when reading Aurobindo's flat declaration that the confusion and darkness into which the soul falls in consequence of its plunge into initial nescience for the sake of incarnation "are not the punishment of a fall, but the condition of a progress." The status of existence the soul takes on here "are the elements of the work he has to fulfill; the price he has to pay for the crown he hopes to win; the narrow way by which nature escapes out of matter into consciousness; they are at once her ransom and her stock." How far more benignantly could Christianity bless its devotees if it did not first strike down the innate will to good and the inherent sense of the dignity of the soul by the doctrine of man's primal affliction and corruption through the sin of his first progenitor!

Invidious as it may be to emphasize it, the rebuke his forthright utterances of inerrant wisdom administers to idealists, spiritualists and mystics, or those who preach the gospel of the soul's need to tramp nature and its elemental energies ruthlessly underfoot, decrying the alleged evil of the soul's subservience to them, can not be ignored. The overt rebuttal of these fallacies comes clear with the philosopher's interpretation of the ever-baffling problem of the good and evil of life. Against India's insistent claim that by sheer negation of his sensory and even intellectual contact with life man should seek release from all limitation by dissolving the duality of consciousness and matter, he explodes the devastating bomb of the reminder that, if we could be successful in dismantling the duality and the opposition that we stupidly (according to Buddhism) maintain by our ignorant desire for sentience, we would presumably eliminate the conflict, but along with it we would achieve also the unforeseen consequence of eliminating our own existence in the cosmic movement! We hold our existence here only by virtue of the tension between positive and negative force in polarity.

It would seem that there at long last is the end to the whole doleful chant of religious and philosophical derogation of the bane of humanity's physical sensual life on earth. It would seem to be the decisive refutation of India's lament over the duress of bodily life and the claimed necessity of escaping its oppressions.

The apotheosization of man is not to be delayed until all sense life is abolished and soul floats ecstatically on wings of bliss above the world consciousness. We exist on earth by what is in the mind and the body. If to attain to the glories of the One Existence-Consciousness-Bliss (the triadic unity of being), we must abolish the operations of body, life and mind, then a divine life here is impossible. The world is the playground of pure ideation, expressing itself through the agencies of the body's equipment. The process is not a maya, an unreal play of deceptive forces, but the real play of conscious being. The spectacle seems to us to lack unified or integrated purpose and harmony; but this is because we see its multiple diffusion into infinite complexity and diversity. But since it is the essential condition of advance for unit soul entities from initial nescience to divine integration that they should achieve their ultimate glory through just this experience in matter, the beneficence of the whole scheme becomes apparent.

It can not be hidden that there is forthright rebuke in Aurobindo's vigorous dialectic to all pious insistence on the illusory character of mortal life, the vanity and evil of the world, on the one side, and on the other, the fatuous idea that by some psychological stratagem we may escape its full incidence and cut a short road to consummate blessedness. The philosopher says that this problem is wholly one of relative values. We are equally in error if we expect quick attainment of perfection through the path of unchecked sensual life, or if we look for a magical flowering of being through a strangling inhibition of sensuous existence. Here rings out the voice of true wisdom on this eternally controverted point in philosophy: "A relative good linked always to its opposite is all that here we can seek." If we govern our thought and conduct of life by this knowledge, we can apply the Vedanta teaching to the fulfillment of the life objectives, without beating down our basic natural forces in the fantastic and futile effort to escape their actuality. Purusha, the infinite spirit of the universe, is the active cause of all movement in the world of Prakriti, the universal matter. The ego in the human person is a limited unit, monad, or spiritual atom, functioning at a certain place and stage in the universal process. The office of this tiny entity is to give the life of God, of which it is a fragment, its chance to impregnate the whole universe with its active power. Its life here implements the creator's desire to revel in Lila, his delight in creation. It is the distribution of the joy of creation from the One out among the many. "I have come that ye may have life more abundantly." In the phraseology of the Greeks, "The gods distribute divinity," and these souls are the seeds of a prospective divine harvest in the autumn of the cycle. Prakriti, the outer matter, mothers them into stem, bud, blossom and fruit. Toward this fruitage of infinite delight the whole creation moves, as St. Paul affirms. "This," says Aurobindo, "is the supreme birth which material nature holds in herself; of these she strives to be delivered." There is nothing to be evolved out of matter which is not already seminally in it.

To correct the blindness of sense, the errors of ignorance and the initial stupor of mind evolution counts on experience to develop the faculty of reason as the means by which man may secure and harmonize his position of balance amidst the forces of his environment. The books of Egyptian wisdom speak of the first god Atum long seeking a place of stability and solid ground on which he might take his stand amidst the primeval chaos. Matter, crystallized into substantial form, provided that platform amid the void. Nature is the ground-base of the universe and the preparatory stage for the later epiphany of spirit. Extension is not a delusion; duration is not an illusion, as is sometimes argued. Through the dissemination of its infinite units of soul force throughout the visible universe, Purusha is moving towards its goal of purpose and its delight in the activity of creation. Aurobindo again positively refutes much negative Hindu philosophy in declaring that the movement toward becoming is the only Being. (Certain systems assert that all becoming is illusory, unreal.) The world advance is the ecstatic dance of Shiva; its sole motive is the absolute joy of the god in the dance. If the infinite mind, being able to become active or remain quiescent, to throw itself into forms or retain the forms within itself; if it indulges itself in the delight of exertion for recreation, it can be for only one reason--for Lila, the divine joy in creation.

The world, then, is the free play of the cosmic mind, self-impelled to cast itself into the infinite forms, and avid of conscious experience. Aurobindo speaks of this Lila as the spontaneous child's play, the poet's pure joy in beautiful expression, the actor's joy in reproducing living moments, the inventor's thrill of discovery, the builder's happiness in construction, the eternal exuberance of the soul of things, everlastingly young, irrepressibly romantic, perpetually shaping and reshaping things for the sheer bliss of self-expression. The God himself is the play, the player and the playground. These three elements in the world process, Maya, Prakriti and Lila, contradictory as they may outwardly seem to superficial view, are yet complementary and necessary to a total integral view of life. If we can see this underlying interrelation of harmony of the three, we are able to discount the apparent jangling of their interlacing movements.

The world is conscious divine idea throwing itself into mutable forms of its own plastic substance. The world expresses a premeditated truth and obeys a predetermined will; it is an initial emergence, in conscious self-knowledge, of that which lay in unconscious inactivity. The outer forms have been created, not outside, but in and as a part of the working of the divine Idea. And it is a caustic stricture on great Plato's asseveration, and that of a thousand philosophers, when Aurobindo says that

there is neither reason to suppose that there can not be any real play of the higher divine consciousness in a world of forms, nor that forms and their immediate supports, mental consciousness, knowledge of vital force and formal substance, must necessarily distort that which they represent. It is possible, even probable, that mind, body and life are to be found in their pure forms in the divine truth itself, are there in fact as subordinate activities of this consciousness and part of the complete instrumentation by which the Supreme Force always works. Mind, life and body must then be capable of divinity.

Might not, then, the denunciation, the evil stigmatization by theology and philosophy down the centuries have been a most disastrous perversion of sane understanding in the run of human life?

Amid all the seeming random jumbling of the multiple individual expressions and embodiments of the pure spirit in the world, it is sensible to presume that all the separate units, each seeking its fitting place and office in the melange of energic forces, is carrying out the supreme will of the unitary Being.

The purely formal abstraction of thought that asserts our inability to know things in themselves has virtually no practical value since, whether they are things in themselves or mere appearances of more real things, our minds are obliged to deal with them as ostensibly real things, at any rate, real enough for us. The natural order, as it is a production of the Supreme Mind, must be viewed as generating not perversions and falsehoods, but the varied objectifications of universal truth.

Aurobindo directly affirms the daring theorization of the most advanced scientific minds that, "as we have already discovered that matter is only substance-form of Force, so we shall discover that material Force is only energy-form of Mind." And it is an epochal revelation he makes in putting forth the theory that "Material Force is in fact a sub-conscious operation of the Will."

We may say, therefore, that it is a sub-conscious Mind or Intelligence, which, manifesting Force as its driving power, is executive Nature, its Prakriti, has created this material world.

What, then, is Life, the philosopher asks, and what relation does it bear to Supermind? By what necessity of truth or illusion does it come into being? Ringing down the ages is the cry of religionists that life is an evil, a delusion, a delirium, from which we must flee into the repose of eternal Being. But how is it conceivable that the Eternal has wantonly inflicted this evil, this drunken stupor or insanity upon--himself, since we are units of his being and he thus partakes of our experience? Clearly it must be rationalized as some impulse of the being of God to try out his powers by engaging his energies in the recreational exercise of his strength that would otherwise, in the static condition of non-polarized being, languish in inanition and stagnation. As sharing the nature of the whole unity, the individual entity, the soul, finds itself subject to two principles: the necessity or the will of the separated ego to act and survive in its identity; and the pressures imposed on it by nature, by which it must seek its way of advance along with the other units of being.

Purusha and Prakriti, being one in supramental harmony, are here a two-aspected single truth or being: "There can be no disequilibrium or predominance of the one over the other. The one Consciousness-Force, having dispersed itself into its millions of forms, and each having the right to fulfill itself, the world becomes the scene of a multitudinous activity, with the key to the jigsaw puzzle of the proper harmonious relations lacking, due to *avidya,* or primary ignorance. But what to the minds still steeped in *avidya* seem to be contraries, negations and evil eventualities are to the Overmind complementaries and balances, checks, safeguards, securities and compensations, what the Hindus call karma. All untoward fortunes of the separate egos, all errors, blunders, miscarriages, are all necessary and ultimately, if not immediately, salutary as leading to self-discovery. For the soul to expect the achievement of pure unconditioned beatitude and imperishable existence here is by itself a contradiction of truth and reason. The vicissitudes and contrarieties of life, which the reason refuses to ascribe to an arbitrary fiat of the Creator, find their rationalization as inevitable phenomena of a higher consciousness, emerging, like a moth from the cocoon, with struggle and difficulty, out of its binding encasement in the physical.

Aurobindo is in accord with Heraclitus in affirming that the whole drama of the alternate cyclical action of life in throwing itself out of equilibrium and then restoring the balance is the basis of all phenomena and the principle of all understanding. The outer is no negation of the inner, the below of the above. The lower and external is one term, one formula of the above and eternal existence. If the two are locked in absolute harmony in the unity, life is imprisoned in quiescence; it remains static and inert. To achieve movement toward her goals, she must throw herself out of equilibrium. When one of her endless cycles comes to its end, she returns to an interval of rest. The two phases are not alien to each other, he insists. An apparent duality is created in order that there may be a free action of nature working itself out with the support of the spirit, and also a free and masterful action of the spirit controlling and working out nature. In her hegemony of the process, spirit maintains its liberty to advance deeper into the heart of nature to construct her living forms, or to withdraw and dissolve the forms when they become too binding and unwieldy. Purusha and Prakriti go always together, and the status of nature at any time discloses the action and aims of the spirit. In each step of the progressive gradations of nature spirit takes a poise of its own proper to the stage: in mind-nature it becomes mental being; in life-nature it becomes vital being; in matter-nature, it becomes physical being; in supermind, it becomes the being of knowledge; and in the supreme spiritual state, it becomes being of pure existence and bliss. Nature as it is known to us is a limited expression of that Super-Nature. What nature does is really done by spirit, acting through it. If spirit draws back from its working in nature, the whole operation relapses into quiescence, and its silence we also cease to be. If we are to share its adventure and its advance, we must enter into the tension and the conflict by which it throws itself into action. So all the "evils" that ensue upon the fission of unitary life into duality have their beneficent function in the order. Perhaps this is the most crucial and necessary axiom of truth that philosophy has to learn. The things called evil can be no mere mistake of the divine spirit-force and without relevant meaning. It must be justified as purposeful even if it remains to us an insoluble mystery.

Taking issue with Plato, Aurobindo holds that, although to us world objects remain shadowy symbols of the reality they adumbrate, nevertheless they represent reality itself, not illusion. This statement rings the theme-note of our essay. Our aim is to vindicate nature against the obloquy of reporting truth falsely, or even dimly or in distortion. The imperfection is in our feeble powers of reading, not in nature's reporting. Clear, legible, articulate, she prints her manuscripts for us in all her forms. Without the objects she presents for our minds to work on, our conceptions would remain as formless as the void it would wander in. Mind can only discover what nature has presented to view, can grasp only the truth that nature pictures. If God's version of truth as he has portrayed it in nature can not be received explicitly, from what other source may we expect to gain a vision of it? The real maya or illusion is not in the natural forms, but in the mind's propensity to conceive or project forms created by its own inventiveness, but which do not agree with the truth extant or potential in nature. So much of mystical afflation thus becomes a real illusion, a sad and wasteful quixotic tilting at windmills of phantasy. Aurobindo draws out this thought to its ultimate status, that the untrue and unreal can give no true vision of reality.

And the philosopher registers a subtle and most significant discernment that stands in sharp refutation of the maya doctrine, in his logical perception of the self-contradiction implicit in the Buddhist philosophy which maintains that ignorant desire for sentient existence is the woeful cause of the soul's involvement in mortal body. For if ignorance is the cause of our existence, then the knowledge that would be considered the supreme value would extinguish our existence. We have here a strange answer to the Hamlet soliloquy, in the self-negating proposition that the highest value for existent being is its extinction. The only good thing about a toothache is its cessation, we may think. But to regard the extinction of sentient experience as its sole blessedness is to have placed life in the category of the toothache. Aurobindo is here subjecting to a sharp critique the doctrines of Buddhism, Jainism and some other Hindu systems that classify life as an evil that is to be avoided at all costs.

But how a non-existent being can have a preference or make a choice of values, or conceive of any values at all, does not appear. Yet much Hindu thought before Aurobindo rests predominantly upon this very presumption. Aurobindo quotes the Upanishads as stating that Brahm exerts his energies in both the light and the dark sides of his being, for the promotion of life's progress to immortality. To attempt to escape the really beneficent pressures due to the ignorance, and to live in the superconscious cessation of the experience of *samsara* is to shut oneself up in a featureless consciousness of unity and in ignorance of the manifested Brahman and "is itself a blind darkness." The final outcome of reasoning here is the realization that the divine consciousness is not shut up in either compartment of its dual nature, "but holds the immutable One and the mutable many in one eternal, all-relating, all-uniting self-knowledge."

He rebukes the so-general depreciation of the mental faculty as being obstructive of the divine in us, with the rebuttal that the function of reason in distinguishing the multiple aspects of truth, and thus appearing to break up the unity of life, is for the very purpose of coordinating and integrating the manifold in its unity. The point of consummate value here is the knowledge that the highest mystical apprehension of the unity of all being possible to man is as nothing for light and knowledge when compared with the perception of the same unity as the cohesive, coordinated, organic unity of the total when this is seen as the marvel of the fitness of all the parts to each other and to the grandeur of the whole. The one sees unity without distinctive parts, but the other sees it through the vision of the organic structural unity of all the constituent parts. It would seem that the view of the many blending in a marvelous harmony of interrelations, as a sheer intellectual achievement, is a far more moving and mystically thrilling experience than any view of unity that extinguished all diversity in blank homogeneity. A view that dissolves all differences leaves the mind trying to make something out of a meaningless emptiness, which can in no way bestir the soul to the exaltation of wonder, love and praise. It deprives mind of all *points d'appui* on which to take meaningful hold of the world. Aurobindo's demonstration that the mind can gain no leverage by which to exercise its directive rulership in life in a vacuity and indeterminateness is revolutionary, not only for the philosophies of his own land, but for the entire field of philosophical speculation, or of that segment of it which argues the desirability of inhibiting the world of conditioned being to reify the consciousness of unconditioned being--if such a consciousness were possible.

In concluding the survey of this outstanding thinker's contribution, it could not be missed that he makes nature the very foundation of his schematic philosophy. Nature, he shows, is the epiphany of the mind of the creator. To seek for knowledge of truth and reality without consulting the record of it inscribed by Brahman himself on the face of nature is one of the most disastrous forms of the *avidya*.

CHAPTER NINE

THE INSIGHTS OF CARL JUNG

To present the testimony of another great figure of modern literary distinction as to the message of truth in nature, we are taken from the province of philosophy into that of psychology. It might at first sight be regarded as unlikely that psychology would find itself as closely related to the meaning of nature as philosophy or religion. In the investigations of the eminent Swiss psychologist, Dr. Carl G. Jung, however, the relation between psychology and nature constitutes a revelation of the deepest import. This should not be surprising, since the influence of nature must reach man through the channels of the sensibilities and the mind, as directly in the life of the psyche as in the intellect specifically. A sketch of Jung's findings and discernments must lamentably be all too brief.

He strikes the keynote of our theme in the sententious statement that "there is in material things a certain truth not seen by the outward eye, but perceived by the mind alone. Of this the philosophers had experience and found its virtue to be such that it worked miracles."

We may presume that these were miracles of luminous insight and understanding rather than a physical magic.

Saying that Christianity is based on a psychological process which demythologized the Christ-myth of our inherent potential of divinity into the legend of a human personality raised to the supreme spiritual coefficient, he asks: "What is the use of a religion without a mythos, since religion means, if anything at all, precisely that function which links us back to the eternal myth?" And he it is who in our modern day has gone farther than any one else in revealing that the mind's only approach to the inner meaning and power of this eternal myth is through the mediation of the "divine archetypes," and these are all supplied by nature.

Jung's insights into the necessity of dualization of itself in order to become self-conscious are clearly discerning of this great fundamental truth and are set forth with the sharpest distinctness. All in all, they are most enlightening.

The epochal break of soul force out of the initial nescience and automatism of subconscious nature into full self-consciousness he calls the process of individuation. This is the actual creation of the human soul, endowing it with awareness of its animal body and its ideally conscious natures as well as with the sense of freedom to utilize these powers. It is the birthing of souls. Then the psychologist unfolds the same basic discernment which Aurobindo has so solidly affirmed: that if the individuation process, so long antecedently pursuing its course as unconsciously as does the acorn in becoming the oak, or the child an adult, is to metamorphose into self-awareness, it is only to be achieved through the polarization of the potential powers of conscious awareness with the unconscious forms of truth objectified in nature. The higher octaves of human consciousness, to which it is legitimate to assign the term of "divine," are designed to be awakened into cognition of their function by being confronted with the images of truth concretized in natural forms. This situation sets the conditions of the problem of the ultimate reconciliation of the "pairs of opposites," which becomes the problem of, in psychological terms, "integration." Asserting that this task is not made possible by the sheer agency of logic, he says that for its successful resolution the psyche is dependent upon the intuitional spur of symbols, which make the irrational union of opposites possible. These symbols "are produced spontaneously by the unconscious and are amplified by the conscious mind." But, one must ask, whence does the unconscious mind derive "spontaneously" these intelligence-provoking symbols that are the foundation stones of all truth and all reality? Certainly the unconscious can not pick them up from any area outside of, unrelated and alien to its experience. It must therefore entify them out of the context of its experience with the actual world, with nature. Jung may not have stated this conclusion in any formal and explicit proposition, but it is deducible in his system from many forthright statements of the dependence of the mind or psyche on natural objects.

"The parallelism between symbols is astonishing to any one who knows both the psychology of the unconscious and alchemy." This statement could perhaps better have been phrased to point out, not the parallelism between symbols, which are multitudinous and all-various, but that between symbols and the mental concepts and the eternal verities which they adumbrate.

But Jung says that the difference between the "natural" individuation process, which runs its course unconsciously, and the same process continued under the conscious control of the matured ego generated by it, is tremendous. In the first phase consciousness does not intervene; the development proceeds space instinctively. In the second phase, the darkness of unconsciousness becomes illumined by the first gleams of conscious intelligence, which continue to grow ever brighter as advance through experience goes on. The light shines in the darkness, and this time the darkness begins to comprehend what the light reveals. What is of climactic importance is that the human psyche, living amid the ubiquitous crowd of nature's symbols, comes to comprehend the light cryptically concealed behind nature's array of symbols. This esoteric language of the symbols, however, Jung and others assert, is not to be read simply with the physical eye, but can and will be descried by the sharpened vision of the intellect. Using alchemical symbols, he says that the *filius solis et lunae,* that is, the mental product of the union of spiritual truth in embryo, symbolized by the sun, and the forces of the physical body symbolized by the moon, or the individualized soul born of the union of these two ingredients, is in its development the integration of the union of opposites. It is, he concludes, the alpha and the omega of the process.

Since, now, through the psyche we establish the fact that God acts upon us, and we know by now that we are in turn acted upon by the unconscious, must we assume that God and the unconscious are two different entities, or two aspects of the one God force? Empirically, he says, it is established with a high degree of probability that there is in the unconscious an archetype of holiness, which manifests itself "spontaneously" in dreams and other forms of heightened impressionability. It does seem probable, he thinks, that there is an instinctually acting divine archetype in the unconscious. This is manifestly an important conclusion, and if it had to be arrived at by the most involved processes of empirical investigation, it only confirms what naive thought might have presupposed. This would be the idea that if God is the author of our being, his presence and power would be as active in the unconscious as well as in the conscious areas of our experience. It is reassuring, however, to know that methodical scientific procedures give certitude to the simpler and more direct intimations of the naive view. If Jung has on logical or clinical grounds buttressed the religious faith of mankind that the mind and spirit of God are at work in the unconscious background or underground of our life, he becomes to that extent a benefactor of the race. His life work is a study of the most revealing and significant result of unconscious elements in play in the field of psychological causation. It is not without some sense of fear that we come into the knowledge that our lives are mysteriously influenced by forces of intelligence operating outside the range of our own consciousness and control. Can we be sure that these forces are beneficent at all times? If it is logical to assume that evolution is laboring to expand and intensify the powers of consciousness from dim darkness to clear and revealing awareness, how can it be that the forces in play in the lower limbo of unconsciousness appear to have more immediate control over our lives than those of our conscious experience, for which alone we could assume our karmic responsibility? Does this mean that we are puppets on the acting stage of life, being manipulated by strings in the hands of unknown managers off in the wings? Could it be after all that we are not beings of free will, shaping our own destiny according to our wise or unwise direction? Can we count on these unknown forces that haunt us out of an unseen world to deal with us beneficently, justly, to give us at least our due? Can they be influenced in any way by the action of our conscious lives?

Jung's entire production, the content and substance of his comprehensive deliverance of discovery and knowledge, constitutes so far the most rationally valid answer to these questions. As Darwin sought answers to the questions implicit in the evolution theory, so Jung searched over the wide field of psychic manifestation, studied all available phenomena and by methods partly inductive and partly deductive, arrived at a high degree of certitude as to basic principles of a psychic science. By endless study of the symbolic structure and meaning of dreams, by researches into the general science of semantics, by exhaustive reading in the field of ancient mythology, religion, anthropology, and by the cultivation in his own mental equipment of a keen scent for the tracing of analogies between symbolic forms and abstract principles of truth, this exceptional genius has left his world well equipped to answer the challenge of the discovery of the "unconscious."

On the whole his findings and determinations offer reasonably satisfactory evidence that the influences affecting us from the side of the unconscious are of a beneficent character, not discernibly hostile to our well-being in any arbitrary or whimsical fashion. The magician that appears to be watching and guiding us in the shadows of the subconscious seems to be a good fairy and not an impish demon.

It is beyond question that Jung was tremendously impressed by a phenomenon which he became cognizant of as he pursued his investigations over a wide terrain in mythology, religion, and even such an exceptional interest as alchemy. This was his observation, if it was not a fresh discovery, that in all these varied ramifications of the psychological interest, virtually but one code of symbols composed the language by which ideological conceptions and values were embodied or expressed. This was significant enough, but when to this realization he was able to add the further discernment that essentially this same universal code of symbols was also the medium of the representation of thought images which the unconscious mind cast up to the conscious in the dreams of his clinical patients, the psychologist felt that he had established a valid basis for the formulation of a fairly definite science of the psyche. By the accumulation and comparative study of data thus amassed, he was able to develop a certain degree of mastery of a universal language of symbolism. And he was able to use and apply this knowledge with more exactitude and more edifying results than any one before him. His lucid interpretation, in particular, of the symbols employed in medieval alchemy is a quite extraordinary achievement. His exposition of the cosmic significance of the number four is likewise a remarkable feat of introspection.

However dark and mysterious lay this realm of the unconscious in the hidden area of our life, it was a long step toward an insight into whatever intelligence was there at work in our behalf to have so fully decoded the language by which that intelligence conveyed its messages to our conscious area. The more clearly its peculiar language was understood, the more specifically could the nature of that subliminal mind be apprehended. And if indeed it was the mind of God or his Logos speaking to his earthly children from out of the deeps of our unconsciousness, it was a prodigious truth that had at last dawned on our human intelligence. If there was a specific language, or lexicon of symbols, by which God, lurking in our subconscious, communicated his ideas and meanings to us, mastership of this recondite code was at once elevated to the place of highest concern in this life of ours. If, as the sacred scriptures seem to hint, God in early times spoke in some direct fashion to "holy men of old," but did so no longer, we could still catch the burden of his message if we learned how to make articulate this ubiquitous mute vernacular of deity.

If symbols then embodied the substance of the message of the Logos, they were certified beyond doubt as the essence of truth. They were the letters of the divine Word, the alphabet of the language of verity. It must be inferred then that they bore somehow the similitude of the divine ideas themselves. Indeed were they not to be facsimiles of those ideographs of the creative mind? To represent an idea, a noumenal form, the symbol must present some likeness to it, else it would wholly lack suggestive purport.

The link between Jung's great work in semanticism and nature was then the symbol, what he liked to call the archetype. He could not avoid turning to nature, because the whole vocabulary of the symbolic language was drawn from that source. Nature, with her correlative ramification in mathematics, geometry, physics, as well as man's constructive manipulation of these elements in imagination, furnished the entire dictionary of potential meaning representation. Of these elements were constructed by the subtlest human powers of dramatization the material substance of myth, allegory, drama, fable, parable, number graphology and finally astrological pictography, all designed to fabricate constructions dramatizing noumenal forms of truth in one way or another. Covering the whole field of ancient cultural and literary expression, this semantic methodology gave form to every mode of religious representation, whether in books, where allegory was the invariable norm of writing, in architecture of temple, pyramid, image or icon, in ceremonial and ritual, in festival celebration, in social custom, even in governmental structures.

A universal persuasion of this sort could not have arisen had not the mind of antiquity, inclined as it was toward deistic and pantheistic assumptions, been obsessed with the conviction that the forms and phenomena of nature bore the image of the archetypal concepts of deity. Nature spoke mutely the language of God. Therefore to nature every sage and prophet seeking to indite a "sacred" book of religious truth turned for the materials of graphic literary power. Likewise Jung, seeking to interpret literature of this stamp, turned to nature to find the keys and clues to the mysteries veiled in semantic forms. And he says that it is just this apprehension of the presence and meaning of the God-mind in nature, realized for a long time in unformalized intuition, then later discerned in clear intellection, that the human mind must grasp if the world is not to stand bereft of significance. The deep soul of man, of its own divine impulsion, yearns for wholeness, for sustaining knowledge and, above all, understanding, "and therefore lays hold of the images of wholeness offered by the subconscious." From these premises emerges the final determination of the problem in full-orbed clarity: the subconscious has these divine images because it is itself the tablet and depository of the divine thought.

But man, in whom this subconscious finds itself in function, along with the attribute of consciousness, is a product--and the highest--of nature. And since these two divine attributes have flowered out of the germinal potentialities hidden deep in the basic natural order, the inescapable logic of the situation points to the conclusion that the world of nature harbors within it the seminal essence of consciousness and mind.

Jung's work bears more or less directly upon two much debated elements of philosophical speculation, Locke's theory of the mind as at the outset of life a *tabula rasa,* or consciousness unmarked by any impression until sensory experience stamps sensory images upon it; and the theory of "innate ideas," developed by Descartes, Spinoza and Leibnitz, but rejected by Locke. The general concept of consciousness as an unwritten slate at the start is perhaps a loose idea of the truth. But once the ego has been immersed in the conditions of conscious experience and bombarded with impressions from the world without, the once pure slate becomes voluminously stamped with both images of outer things and the flare-back of its own reactions to the outer contacts.

The theory of "innate ideas" stands in immediate relation to that of the *tabula rasa,* as it predicates the idea that at the beginning of the conscious life of the individual, God stamped a whole encyclopedia of divine ideas on the pristine matter of consciousness, which would emerge into active manifestation in the course of evolution. Philosophy rather inclines to the idea that God at the outset generated the potential of consciousness and trusted to the experience of the ego units with their material environments to register upon it the forms of ideation adequate to buoy up the soul units in the stream of life. All mental capability must be germinally innate in the soul in embryo. Experience will bring it out. It could not unfold its conscious inheritance except by undergoing the tension between its spiritual nucleus and opposing matter.

The status of things here, which Jung envisaged and clearly demonstrated, is simple enough to be comprehended in the succinct statement of the principle that soul, with its initial endowment of conscious potential, had remained in static inertia in the empyrean, its slate of consciousness would never have been written upon and would, as Aurobindo, Plotinus and Jung contend, never have developed any ideas at all. The ideas are only given birth, as are all other things, by the union of pristine soul force with material reality. Jung, the psychologist, deals with the situation in terms of the relation of the conscious force to the unconscious. If in the individuation process consciousness is to advance to ever higher powers, it must from the start and throughout win this glorification by wrestling with the inertia of the unconscious, and so find its balance with its opposite--which, be it never forgotten, is only itself objectified to its subjectivity. This requires its plunging into the world of nature, where the contents of the cosmic unconscious are made visibly extant. A theology which had lost its soul and its vision mistakenly interpreted this plunge of embryo gods into matter as the expulsion from Eden and the fall from Paradise, whereas it is the sallying forth of souls in the bright morning of their existence to take the road to Paradise.

Jung indulges in a number of enlightening ruminations upon the differences in the psychologies of East and West. He says that while the West is seeking the aggrandizement of life by looking outward and upward, the East seeks it by sinking thought ever more deeply into the interior of consciousness. It presents a sharp contrast, broadly speaking, between the materialistic and the psychic views of reality. Jung admonishes both parties that the true view is that which brings the two movements together in the understanding of the conflict of the two trends in the basic polarity. The West may in a deeper view of existence agree with the Orient that eventually souls must disengage themselves from their entanglement in the meshes of matter. But it also would remind Eastern mentality that the epochal achievement is to be consummated not by the obliteration of physical experience, but by fulfilling its demands.

In a notable passage Jung shows how the human psyche, if it is not integrated by the sanifying power of acquaintance with the divine archetypes, is subject to wayward tendencies and suffers many forms of psychic dissociation. As a cure for this dismantling of the soul's integrity, he advocates the return of thought to nature, where the salutary influence of the archetypes of wholeness are to be, even if unconsciously, encountered. He says that nature's semantic cinema "reflects something that lies hidden in the subject himself, in his own transsubjective reality." The mythology of the divine life speaks of the dismemberment of the God-nature as it fragments itself to provide and distribute the eucharistic spiritual bread to all beings. This is the treasure of infinite worth that is not to be hid in the napkin, but to be sown as the good seed that will take root, germinate and produce fruit for a hundredfold harvest. In Jung's philosophy it is this engagement of the units of potential consciousness with the archetypes lodged in the unconscious of nature that will restore the individual souls to their integrity and harmony with the cosmic consciousness. He closely matches the Platonic ideas in saying that the soul suffers psychic dismemberment in its immersion in the distractions of sense and must reintegrate its wholeness by the acquisition of intelligence and wisdom through the exigencies and pressures of its experience with nature. He says that if there was a general clear understanding of this dissociation of the ego into its own limited measure of open consciousness, on the one side, and the vast encompassing area of the unconscious on the other side, "we would know where to attack." The distressing reality of the situation, he believes, is that the deciding factor in our life lies with the individual man, "who knows no answer to his dualism." This is indeed the nub of the human problem, as it commits an enormous volume of human effort to a futile pitching at fantasies and fantastic unrealities fabricated by quixotic theological aberrancies and unsound philosophies.

Jung's magnificent achievement is an immense contribution to an enlightenment of this darksome condition. His theory of the archetypal base of our potential knowledge, along with his own lucid interpretation of many of the symbolic images of truth will tend to focus research and interest upon the true sources of understanding and thus help to keep the human psyche in harmonious relation with the archetypes of verity embodied in nature.

CHAPTER TEN

THE HEART OF NATURE

Any survey of the history of naturalistic theory pretending to be comprehensive would be immensely voluminous. Our relation to nature is so close and crucial that no philosopher can formulate a system rationalizing our life without including it organically in the purview. Nature enters into the heart and soul of poetry and provides at least the setting of all romantic literature. Anthropology must deal intimately with it.

But a limited survey of its treatment on an eclectic basis is eminently sanctioned, as the insights and theorizations of the profoundest thinkers on the theme will prove to be highly stimulating and will help in the formulation of the theses and the rationale of the philosophy of nature at which this work aims. It is an educative enterprise of the highest cultural value to gain a panorama of the views of our deepest thinkers on this basic element in human life. While much repetition will be unavoidable, selection of material will be guided by the effort to present diversity of approach and viewpoint.

In *A History of Philosophical Systems*, Vergilius Ferm, the editor, it is well stated that a summary definition of naturalism would be: Nature is the sum and substance of all that is, and to know nature is to come to terms with it in the most productive or effective way, by study and reflection. Not to take it as the sure ground of truth, or true reality, is to assume that life is to be explained by something beyond it that excludes it from the context of real being. One of the writers states that nature is the ultimate inspiration of all poetry.

A variant view of naturalism is expounded in another work, likewise a symposium of essays by a group of authors: R. B. Perry, S. Butler, J. E. Boodin and others, which speaks of a synthetic naturalism. One of its presuppositions is that matter and spirit are not to be considered as opposites, but a composition of complementary forces, effecting a synthesis. S. Alexander is quoted as proposing that the universe is evolving toward deity in mankind; and he thinks that religion needs to explore the mine of inspiring truth that nature may conceal in her depths of meaning. He asserts that matter and energy are inert or grossly coarse. Neither are they morally evil; there is no sin involving matter. One ought to disenchant one's mind of traditional views, which, in ignorance of the real essence of either spirit or matter, followed superficial notions that they were opposite and mutually hostile. This is well discerned and brings these thinkers to the grand visions of the early hierophants of the sage wisdom of the past.

Dr. George P. Conger, eminent savant in Minnesota University, has given expression to a sharp point of logical deduction, in asserting that it is only in a world in which God is not fully and adequately revealed that a special extraneous revelation assumed to emanate from the delivered oracles of God can have any valid importance. A world of God's creation that would not present the full epiphany of his nature and being, but that would need his publication of a separate manual or commentary, or gloss in literary form, would seem a bizarre idea. If God is assumed to have thrust his children into a world where the terms and significances of that existence would not, as it were, automatically educate his progeny in at least the basic import and the practical management of the situation, his action would belie our concept of his omniscience and omnipotence alike, and convict him of failure to match his performance with his ideal program. On the ground of our hypostatization of the God character, this view of the human situation is dialectically unpredictable. His revelation of himself in his creation, then, must be accepted as adequate, if not complete. (It is supposable, however, that it may not be finished.) This reasoning at once becomes a formidable challenge to all "revealed" authority in religion.

In fact it seems patently illogical that we should think it necessary to look outside the order of the physical world structure to detect the principles that must be inherent in the structure to constitute it what it is. It is closely in line with this train of thought that Bernard Shaw, in characteristic fashion, has expressed that, "although the life-force supplies us with its purpose, it has no other brains to work with than those it has painfully and imperfectly evolved in our heads." The inference here would be that nature, in evolving as her top product creatures with competent brains, intends to make her own revelation of her secret purposes through those brains.

Dr. Conger gives expression to another keen insight in classifying the analogies that can be drawn between natural things and the concepts and principles of truth as "cosmological categories." That is to say, that the world known to us would not have developed without a ground-source of its form and nature subsisting in the original creative concept. Protesting that our problem surely is one of living rightly *in* the world of matter rather than trying to escape it, he concludes that in spite of many fond hopes of mystics to win release from conditioned being, "escape from the world of matter, at least during our present condition of life, is impossible." He quotes Emerson to the effect that without movement through matter's domain toward something more perfect, there would be stagnation and death. Evolution is not blind change or chance; it is advance of life to grander status. Its aim is revealed in every step forward, if there is discernment in the witnesses.

The progress of science and culture achieved through the increasing effort at reflection certifies that the principles of harmony that human reason exhibits are the same as those embodied in the life of nature itself, is the conclusion of another writer, Joseph A. Leighton (*The Field of Philosophy*).

Carlyle proclaims that nature, standing as symbol of a reality in the noumenal world, is the outspoken revelation of the Infinite in the finite.

James Royce harmonizes nature and mind on the ground that evolution tends to bridge the gulf between the two forms of being, matter and consciousness. There is no break anywhere in the continuity of process. William James agreed with Heraclitus and Aristotle that "the perpetual flux in the authentic stuff." In the flowing stream of the movement of life was to be found the manifestation of the divine ideal and real being.

Rabindranath Tagore, Hindu poet, analogizes the progress from ignorance and imperfection to intelligence and self-mastery, from nature to mind, with the transition from bud to rose. We for convenience separate the two stages, but they are phases of the one existence.

In his *Novum Organum*, the great Francis Bacon states categorically that merely mental ideas and notions, formed apart from reference to the physical reality of the world, should be disallowed, and all understanding based anew upon the actualities of experience, "since there is no other entrance open to the kingdom of nature than the one to the kingdom to heaven, in which no one may enter except in the form of a little child." The passports giving entry to the one realm are the same as those admitting to the other. Crisp and clear is his assertion that "reality only presents itself to us when we look out upon the world of the senses. The senses alone provide us with realities, the realities of empirical knowledge." This is a ringing echo of the Egyptian Hermes.

The modern John Dewey articulates this same recognition in stating that actual life transcends intellect. It does so at least in the sense that it grounds all intellectual activity. He takes issue with Kant's affirmation and mystical claims that a higher or supra-intellectual faculty is needed to consummate a consummative synthesis of the data of experience, asserting that experience itself demonstrates and teaches the principles of righteousness.

"The organization intrinsic to life renders unnecessary a supernatural and super-empirical synthesis. It affords the basis and material for a positive evolution of intelligence as an organizing faculty within life."

Nature herself, both as the external support of life and its expression through man's own growth, will provide the guiding principles of understanding and action.

Many writers voice the idea that the life of the inorganic world is just as wonderful, and just as significant, as that of the organic.

Dr. Guy P. Rohrbaugh, in *A Natural Approach to Philosophy*, argues that if evolution establishes that higher forms have emerged from lower and the organic has evolved from the inorganic level, it follows that the inorganic world had carried in its original womb the seed potentialities of the later higher development. Even now nature must be harboring the unknown shapes of future life. He finds a law of continuity to pertain to all types and reaches from the lowest to the highest forms of existence. No one can locate a sharp line of demarcation between living and non-living matter.

J. S. Haldane expresses the conception that the material world, which has been so long regarded as a world of blind mechanism, is in reality the spiritual world, seen only partially and imperfectly, the only real world there is. This was of course the thesis of Henry Drummond in his formerly quite influential work, *The Natural Law in the Spiritual World*. John Locke virtually made the natural and the moral law identical.

Then there is Sir Oliver Lodge, one of our first nuclear physicists, who declares that the universe has never been other than rational. Its operations reveal a harmony with the human mind when that is sufficiently illumined to perceive the grandeur of nature's revelation of truth.

The eminent modern Physicist-philosopher, Eddington, maintains that our knowledge of the physical world is symbolic of the ideation that gave it existence and form.

A modern writer of keen insight is Etienne Gilson. Since the universe is born of a final cause, i.e., created for a purpose, it is saturated with finality, so that we can never dissociate the explanation of things from their primal-ultimate *raison d'etre*. If, as the modern bent in science tends so completely to do, we look in nature only for the how of explanations, we must not be surprised if we miss the why of it. There is no true finality to understanding unless we posit intelligence at the source and at the heart of things and conceive creation as an act of intelligence.

This scholar quotes Duns Scotus, medieval schoolman, as saying that intelligence is identical with its essence, implying the identity of mind and matter, so that the universe is conceivably mind materialized.

Nature, he elucidates, has depths which exceed its external expression; they involve metaphysical realities and prepare the way for the mystic. But since causality flows from actuality, it must be seen that nature outwardly presents a face which is the reverse side of itself, so that what we tend to read on the one side in terms of force, energy and law can be translated on the other side in terms of divine ideations, or seen as the analogies of these. For one who can make this translation the physical world takes on the character of a sacred world and religious values take strong hold on the mind.

As one reflecting and justifying the Church's philosophy, he still sees fit to condemn the ecclesiastical contempt for the natural life and attempt to suppress its sensual proclivities which instituted the harsh rigors of asceticism and mortification of the "fleshly lusts which war against the Soul." The Fathers of the Desert, he says, driven mad by an insensate hatred of nature, embarked on a life which is a radical negation of all wholesome human values. He says they mistook desert solitude for peace. The negative and defamatory Christian view of nature, he enlarges, can not be upheld. On the authority of St. Thomas, illumination consists in the gift made by God to man in his creation, which is the very thing it was the essence of Augustinianism to deny. Thomism, Gilson claims, closed the era of the theological blight on the natural potential for illumination, and let the light of God's revelation of himself in nature henceforth shine out for the edification of doctrinism. Aquinas' philosophy made possible the function of empirical contact with nature as a force designed to generate the concepts of truth in man's mind, since nature is herself the expression of truth. *Coeli enarrant gloriam Dei.* If the heavens declare God's glory, it is because they, and earth, too, bear his image. The great medieval doctor, Gilson says, penetrated into the heart of nature and touched there the very roots of causality. The work of the Almighty can not be inert and meaningless, for thus it would give no testimony to the divine craftmanship. So to attempt to exalt God by vilifying his handiwork is both a glaring logical fallacy and an insult to the deity it would aim to glorify. The things God has created partake of his perfection in such a way that any detraction of his performance detracts also from his glory and his power.

The eminent early Orientalist, Max Mueller, has commented on Christianity's contempt for nature as a danger to Christianity itself.

Another discerning writer, F. W. Dillistone, in his *Christianity and Symbolism,* holds for man the possibility of aligning himself harmoniously with the eternal time sense and the rhythm of nature, if he will withdraw his consciousness sufficiently from the superficialities and distractions of his life in time. He may then find himself becoming sensible of his even movement with the groundswell of the pulse of the universe. And only in that orientation of consciousness can he find his ultimate satisfactions and his peace. But Dillistone more positively, if less poetically, relates man to his world in saying that the pattern of existence and exalted consciousness predicted for the future is analogous to the existential mode in this world. He avers that if man is to survive, he must rediscover the meaning of organic wholeness in his relation with nature. Man's chief need and task of today is to harmonize his life dynamically through symbols. He must find in them the principles that will integrate his life happily with his environment. The eminent Harvard theologian, Paul Tillich bemoans the Church's loss of the moving power of its own symbols as stifling the spiritual life. Father Gerald Vann, in his *Water and Fire,* agrees with this view, saying that our age has lost the power to register cathartic regeneration from the efficacy of symbolism.

The British physicist and philosopher, Sir Bertrand Russell, forthrightly declares that "it is only in marriage with the world that an idea can bear fruit; divorced from it, ideas remain barren." He amplifies this by saying that to read the book of nature with the conviction that it is an illusion is just to miss the possibility of understanding.

Bacon and Goethe alike insist that we must find the bond of kinship between nature and the subject reflecting upon it. We are continually bent on making nature conform to the schematism of our ideologies. On the contrary, it is inevitable that we must bend our ideas into conformity with the paradigms which nature holds up to us.

It is the pronouncement of W. E. Hocking, former head of the Philosophy Department of Harvard University, that "to lodge meanings somewhere in nature seems to guarantee their genuineness, as if all meanings must be made to touch base in a region of indifference before they may spin their alliance with feeling and action." This says simply that nature is that realm of which we can predicate certitude of real existence, all others resting upon suspicion of fantasy. In its unchallengeable objectivity it is the one thing that we can trust for reality.

In her *Logic and Nature,* Marie C. Suabey writes that since no individual genius is competent to account for the infinitude of natural processes, it seems necessary to abandon the perceptual view of existence and assume instead that nature's criteria of truth are to be tested by logical rather than by sensual evidences. Nature--as shall be brought out later in this study--will not yield up her meanings merely to the eye; her redaction into significance demands the intellect and one with a keen edge. A logical order must be assumed to be the ground of the temporal.

Even the mystic realizes that to override and neglect or negate the natural, the personal, the human aspects of life in the reach for higher being--to push the natural out that the divine may enter--is to unhinge and unbalance the salutary order of existence. If to give existence to God in personality one has to depersonalize the human and sever it from its sources of health and power in nature, then personality itself is thrust out into meaninglessness.

That keen analyst of philosophical concepts, T. V. Smith, is forthright enough in his view of the relation of thoughts to things to assert that beyond doubt the outcome of thought "grown prideful of its emancipation from things, is lunacy." This would point the finger of a psychological dementia at most Hindu religious systemology. He fortifies this judgment with the logical principle that for the Eternal to produce something less perfect than himself is shocking to human reason and is contradictory as well. Those who besmirch God's physical creation with the moral stigma of imperfection and evil cast the stigma of incompetence and error upon the Almighty. This is to set man psychologically at odds with his mind and thus at odds with his universe.

In addition to the leading psychologists, many savants in philosophy dilate on the function of symbols in conceptual science and deplore the obvious unreceptivity of the mind of our age to their nuances of significance. It is declared that the domain of once living symbols has become a morgue of mummies. The fires of esoteric meaning in these archetypes has all gone out. This unfortunate situation conduces to blindness of the mind and paralysis of the spirit. The inevitable result is bound to be psychic debacle. The symbol is ultimately the only means by which a law, a principle, a truth or abstraction of any sort can be represented and purveyed to intelligence. Our regulative ideas take form and exert living influence through their representation to consciousness by symbols.

Dillistone finds much of the difference between Greek and Hindu systematism traceable to their divergent attitudes toward nature. The Greek view, he dissertates, lays prime emphasis upon the operation of mind in nature, whereas in the main the Indian approach reflects an indifference to the form, the rhythm, and orderliness of the world. The Hindu thought saw nature's luxuriant profusion of images as mere surface movements upon the ocean of a single cosmic life. But the Greek mind, as the Egyptian before it, could not rest content with such a conception; it was convinced that nature revealed the rule of a principle of world-order underneath the surface manifestations which could be discovered or at least comprehended by the human mind. The Greek concept did not look upon nature with the idea of controlling it for his own grandiose aims, but to understand it, to interpret its message. Instead of attempting to conform nature to his own patterns of thought, he sought to bring his thought into line with nature's patterns. In so far as the Egypto-Greek conception attempted to plot the form of any future existence for man, it moulded the view of the future over the pattern found in this world. In this conception, the assumed presence of mind in nature made a true science of nature possible, if there was developed a power of introspection capable of discerning it. Prof. R. G. Collingwood elaborates this same analysis in his work, *The Idea of Nature*.

That mind is dependent upon nature for all concepts that would give it an insight into truth is the conclusion of the Indian philosopher Das Gupta. In the interplay between mind and object, if for the object its title to being rests on its being perceived, so mind's claim to reality is based on its power to perceive. It is impossible for us to think of a mind perceiving or being active in any other way than through its perception of objects. Without objects confronting it demanding explanation and understanding, mind would but stare into a void. It would be in the same predicament as a man floating in the air, unable to move in any direction for lack of something resistant to push against. There can be no apprehension without something to be apprehended. Therefore mind had to be confronted with objects.

The modern humanitarian-theologian Albert Schweitzer has given expression to a direct assault upon the traditional theological attitude of negation and condemnation of nature. The world is now free and ripe for a higher religion in which the ego in man will be able to utilize the influences of nature as aids to its spiritual aggrandizement, instead of having, as the old theology dictated, to alienate itself from it, push it aside and trample it underfoot. The new attitude will be to penetrate to the heart of its secrets, where the discovery will be made that the laws and principles of its own spiritual life are surprisingly exemplified in every operation.

The deeply piercing mind of the German Hegel rejects the philosophies that posit the development of some kind of transcendental faculty of consciousness as a necessary instrument for apprehension of the highest truth. He finds the eternal truths adumbrated in the present order of things. He does not find it necessary for the human mind to abandon the lower road of its purely human capabilities in an effort to find a higher road on which travel is somehow magically easier. The pathway to absolute knowledge is also the pathway of the natural consciousness. He says that the experience of the soul in conscious existence becomes the history of consciousness itself, and by the process it transforms itself into self-consciousness. For the fulfillment of this prodigious evolutionary transformation, the polarized opposition of conscious units to an external natural world of objectivity is indispensable. The German thinker would probably have agreed with Santayana, who went farther than any one else in the way of disqualifying the much-exalted faculty of "intuition" as allegedly superior to intellect, in saying that intuition is itself pathetically animal.

CHAPTER ELEVEN

GOD AND NATURE

The material of the preceding chapter is a brief and sketchy survey of what might be denominated the effort of the human logos, through its best minds, to delineate the structure of the Logos of God. It portrays the fruits of the human attempt to glean the noumenal import of the universe from observation and reflection on its phenomena. If it has not been registered on the minds of the readers, it is to be pointed out as a fact of notable significance that, as evidenced by the collation of the testimony presented, there is seen to be agreement, if not virtual unanimity, of the world's best philosophical opinion on the basic thesis--the idea that the natural world is an epiphany of the creative thought of the mind of God. It stands before us as the divine theophany. God has revealed his nature and his thought and purpose in his creation. Likewise it is seen that there is agreement also upon the idea that the message inscribed by deity on the open face of nature is legible by the mind of man, if that instrument is sharpened to a certain adeptship in interpretative adroitness. It is obvious from the opinions advanced that many great minds had caught a vision of the possibility of a stupendous achievement of the human mind itself: of finding in nature *the ultimate canons of knowledge*. Back of and instigating this feeling must have been the conscious or unconscious haunting of the thought that these ultimate principia of truth, if they were to be discovered anywhere, would be found inwoven into the texture of the living universe. Many a mind must have put to itself the question: If they are not to be found there, where else, in all conscience, could they be looked for?

And these observations enable us to analyze the thought situation respecting this fundamental question of philosophy in its elementary simplicity. If not localized in the external world, there was but one other place to search for them: in the human mind. and so the philosophical quest for them advanced along two paths, the one external and objective, the other the path of introversion and subjectivity. It may be said that in so far as reflection suggested and pursued the possibility that both paths might be found or made to converge, that both at any rate led to the same destination, and that there was harmony, if not identity, between them, philosophical effort made substantial progress toward discovery. The nub of the ideological conflict was just this question: Was man only the detached spectator of the truth and reality of things; or was he himself the arbiter, if not quasi-creator, of the universe? The ancients seemed to possess authoritative understanding of the matter. But their sagacity was forgotten for the middle centuries, and it was Locke, Hume, Berkeley, and finally Kant who brought the issue out in sharp outline. The Greek philosophers had urged man to find the archai of truth within himself--"Man, know thyself, and thou wilt know all things." But the Greek philosophers realized that in knowing himself, he would find himself a being poised between two worlds, an outer objective and an inner subjective one, and that, through the operation of that majestic axiom laid down by thrice-greatest Hermes, he could in the main only know himself as his experience with that outer world revealed himself to himself. Religion, obsessed with the idea of the supremacy and hegemony of the spirit, lost sight of this balancing qualification to the science of self-knowledge and attempted to find the more stable realities in disdain of and detachment from the outer realm, to a large extent carrying the straining effort out into an ideal vacuum and warping devotional life into eccentricities and abnormalities.

Alexander Pope, reaching back to those Greek Mystery teachings, reminded the modern world that "the proper study of mankind is man." This gave the cue to Kant, who turned thought in upon itself and studied the structure of the human mind as no one in the West had done before him. He recognized the fact that man found himself immersed in an environment that vitally affected his existence and laid down some axioms that went in a corollary fashion with his determinations. So it was left for Fichte, then Schelling and Hegel, to attempt romantically to seek for final answers in the harmony and asserted identity of the order of man's mind with that of nature. An essential ingredient of man's knowledge of himself is that he is on his physical side a generic product of the natural order. Whatever he may be as a spiritual entity, a unit of the God-mind, he is one-half animal, as Plato told us. Theological infatuations swept religion into the persuasion that the animal portion of his nature was a horrible mire clinging to his feet, which he must stamp off at all costs. The romanticists, on the other hand, realizing that he was the child of Mother Nature, contended that the rationale of his nature was to be found in a deep study of the *modus vivendi* of that Mother's organic life. Whatever codex and modus of being the total system of the living world revealed, it must deliver to man also the fundamenta of his existence and constitution. His life, as religion so fervently contended it was, could not be so drastically alien to his natural parenthood. Religion had long asked man to renounce his parentage, to revile his natural Mother. It even threw her out of the primordial Trinity. The romanticists were swept into high afflation of philosophical intuitions in contemplating the vision of the widely supported thesis that deep within the heart of nature would be found the cardinal principia governing man's life. Their enthusiasm and the exhilaration of the enterprise carried them some distance toward the supreme vision of the unity of our minds with the logos of nature, but not far enough to have established the relation on an authentic platform of scientific demonstration, and the grandiose movement faded out.

It is now our task to inquire into the causes of this failure and that of many previous movements toward the consummative goal to which they should have led. This quest will take us into one of the most challenging mysteries in the field of religio-philosophical history. We face an anomalous fact of that history itself in this situation. Here was a principle of the best human thought that was endorsed in principle by all leading thinkers; yet in every case, in every age, it failed of substantial or general verification and has not achieved that status even yet. In spite of its having been accorded the accolade of approbation and endorsement by the greatest intellectuals in history, it is yet regarded with suspicion and distrust in the philosophical world, and considered largely as a poetic sentimentality and pretty theoretical fantasy.

Few realize how generally and almost unanimously endorsed by the consensus of opinion formerly and recurrently ever since. It was a maxim of the cryptic methodology of the Kabalists, the esoteric party among the early Jews. It was understood by Josephus, who attests to the fact--the significance of which has been disdained and ignored by the orthodox Hebrew religionists--that even Moses, the eponymous hero of Jewry, wrote the Pentateuch in a vein of figurism, rather than historically. In fact he says in the Preface to his great history that, now having completed his devoted task of recounting the history of the Jews in its external aspect and objective reality, it will be his purpose, if God gives him the strength and the time, to rewrite the substance of the Mosaic scriptures in their sub-historical and esoteric sense. Had the Jewish historian been privileged to produce this work, it is conceivable that the entire history of Western man could have altered in the direction of a humanistic uplift and the relapse of Medieval European mentality into servitude to ecclesiastical dogmatism been obviated. But while Josephus failed to bring his lofty purpose to accomplishment, effort of a quite similar kind was made by a perhaps even more perceptive contemporary, the philosopher Philo Judaeus. He developed the cult of semanticism to a fairly high degree of lucidity in his writings, as the basis of his undertaking to effect a synthesis of the Mosaic Hebraism of the

Torah with the Platonism of Greece. His work was the inspiration of Ammonias Saccas, the founder of Neoplatonism, as well as that of Pantaenus, Clement and Origen, which found expression through these leading theologians of the great school of Christian exegesis at Alexandria, with their influence reaching on to Augustine, the prime formulator of the doctrinism of the Church.

But our claim will be challenged on the ground that this flourish of semanticism was in the domain of theology and had no connection with nature symbolism. The reply to that is that when theology is expounded allegorically and esoterically, it becomes an enterprise in semanticism, all processes reverting back to the archetypes furnished ultimately by nature. Incarnation of soul in body is seen as the death of the seed planted in the soil and resurrection its germination; or, under changed figure, the setting of the sun at eve or in the autumn into night or winter, or again as the fiery essence of soul going down into water--the human body being about seventy percent water--and thus in danger of drowning in the red sea water of the human body blood. The semantic genius of ancient sages grasped at a thousand aspects of nature's life and employed them as analogues of spiritual truth. It has not been recognized that this was the predominant motif in most ancient scriptural composition. It may be said to constitute in essence the lost key to the interpretation of the sacred scripts of old. Clement and Origen made a valiant attempt to formulate Christian theology by this methodology, with a limited degree of real achievement. But again it was not virile enough to carry conviction. Sporadic movements followed through the Medieval period, but were mostly summarily suppressed by the jealous power of the Church, committed as it was to the literal-historical exegesis of the Scriptural legacy.

It has to be true that humanity in its historical evolution passes through crucial situations of the most momentous character, with future weal or woe contingent upon the issues, but never fully aware of the critical nature of the turn of events. That is, we can seldom be fully cognizant of what we have by the tiniest margin of luck happily achieved, or by the trickiest quirk of fate just missed. It is the humble opinion in this literary corner that the human family suffered one of the most catastrophic misses of this kind in all its mundane career when in the early centuries of our era the cult of esotericism in religion, with its foundations in semantic modes of literary expression, faded out and was replaced by gross literalism which kills the spirit by the deadness of the letter.

He who will succinctly expound the causes of this calamitous failure of intelligence at a most critical juncture in human affairs will render his fellow man a service of the first magnitude. It dimmed and almost totally extinguished a light that had previously gleamed in the minds of men of undoubted title to the status of Initiates, Hierophants, Illuminati, minds of near-Buddhic enlightenment. It marked the turn from intelligence to mental darkness, by which the ancient light of occult truth that had been kindled by perhaps the greatest luminary of all, thrice-greatest Hermes, suffered diminution and eventual obscuration. It produced that precipitation of the fogs that carried spiritual opacity into the night of Medieval Dark Ages.

Mystery it is and will long remain, but indications seem clear enough to warrant the explanation that the efforts of Philo and Origen simply did not achieve that degree of clarity and cogency, that brilliant luminosity in semantic imagery, requisite to establish the authenticity and authority of the method upon the mentality of the time. It was at any rate not adequate to bridge the enormous gap that always subsists between the power of genius to visualize clearly the concepts of abstract intellection and the stolid crassness of the dullard. The infinite tragedy in the case is that the down-draught of gross exoteric misconception that literalized the Scriptures overwhelmed and smothered out the candles of inner illumination, and took charge of two thousand years of history. That this debacle plunged these years into a darkness profound and disastrous is the accepted verdict of history.

In view of the recurrent efforts of sages and cult movements from time to time to resuscitate the allegorical-symbolic mode of interpretation and their invariable failure, it seems necessary to conclude that at no time has the consummate artistry, the subtle technique and the overall proficiency requisite to establish the methodology as incontrovertibly sound and valid been demonstrated to promote it to acceptance. That many minds of deep reflective apperception have been assured of its adequacy as the most competent tool for the apprehension of truth, but no one has ever apparently succeeded in formulating the principles that would make it operable as an applied science. As said, it has been left floating in the upper region of poetic fantasy, mystical rhapsodizing and rare flashes of vision that could never be marshaled into the semblance of organic systematism. And lacking such character of structuralism, there was nothing to restrict it to legitimate compass, to prevent wayward and whimsical fancy from running wild with it and in the end discrediting it with irrational excesses--much the same as Freud's adventurous efforts to interpret dreams symbolically have run out into ludicrous extravaganza. It seems necessary to assert that no one has ever formulated the organic principles under a system of rationalization that would have given the method title to the character and name of a scientific technique. It remained in the status of loose visionary ideality.

A vast and formidable deterrent to its more authoritative vogue emanated from the side of dogmatic religion in the introduction into Christian theology of a tenet that came into the Church as a product of Hindu negativism--the doctrine of the so-called "malignancy of matter." Matter, the "opponent" of spirit, was loaded with contempt and stamped as the evil principle. Acceptance of this dogma inevitably inspired a hostile mental attitude toward nature, the material world. If nature reeked of poison to the soul, surely one should not look to it for any salutary message for the spiritual life. It is not to be denied that this noxious misconception inflicted a centuries-long blight upon the natural tendency of the mind of Europe to learn what nature could have taught it. The break-out into humanism and naturalism in the fourteenth century with the surge of Renaissance romanticism, and the secret and semi-occult and the first adventures of Roger Bacon, Paracelsus, Philalethes, Raymond Lully, Cardano and others in empirical science marked the first emergence of a drive back to nature. An Isaac Newton could find in the esoteric lucubrations of the mystic Boehme intimations which led to his formulation of the laws of motion. Sensing peril from the challenge of nature, entrenched pietism fought the interest in nature with a blind bitterness that, when the chilling annals are read, leaves one wondering whether faith and religion are not the most devilish of all human persuasions. When the obsession of a hypnotic power that might be called "sanctitude" can so warp the human mind that a purely physical phenomenon, the rotundity of the earth and its circulation round a central body, can drive fanatical zealots to the point of inhuman savagery against the humble individual who announced the discovery, there is ground for speculation whether religion is not all in all more demonical than angelic.

From the beginning of the resurgence of interest in nature, it required three or four centuries for dawning modernity to emancipate itself from the suppression of ecclesiasticism and proceed triumphantly on its course of ever deeper penetration into the interior wonderland of nature. Now the search has gone deep enough to have given us contact with a magic so mercurial that we can surpass the legendary feats of alchemy, convert a waterfall into light, waft a sonata across a continent and watch a baseball game three thousand miles away.

But this is all on the physical side. The dynamism we have extracted from matter can give us light for the eye; still we linger in the murky dimness-- also largely produced by the shadow of the same religious obscurantism--that prevents us from extracting from nature its consummate blessing, *light for the mind*. Still our blessed and truly holy Mother is thwarted in her benign purpose of bestowing upon her children her most sanctified gift of all--knowledge of eternal truth.

Our quest over years for an explanation of the failure of all attempts since the day of Hermes Trismegistus to recover the ancient arcane science of nature-wisdom was happily rewarded by the discovery of one terse and sententious sentence found in one of the Upanishads of India's religious lore. This sentence will provide the golden text for most of what will follow in this work. It is truly a priceless treasure for understanding, a formula for knowledge. The reference pointing to the central creative mind-soul of the universe, the statement stands: *"By sharp and subtle intellect is he beheld."* These words well deserve to be inscribed in imperishable characters, as Carlyle says, "on all walls,"--most appropriately those of churches, seminaries and universities. Here is the vindication at last of the religiously defamed *intellect*. Not besmirched with the calumny of its supposed baneful opposition to spirit; not belittled as the dissipator of integral unity of knowledge; not vilified and scorned as the block to intuition; but placed in its true and beneficent role as discerner of truth, at last intellect presides in our kingdom of intelligence. As far as nature is concerned, it is, in Wordsworth's felicitous phrasing, "the master light of all our seeing."

The key, then, to understanding all previous failure to demonstrate the ineluctable legitimacy and cogency of the nature-mind kinship as source-spring of the highest intelligence, must be the fact that neither the Hermeticists, Plato, Philo, Origen or others who essayed to establish it as basic canon of knowledge, possessed or exercised the requisite sharpness and intellectual subtlety to certify its validity and command its acceptance. Their probing into nature was not done with sufficient acuity of mind or keenness of discernment to have lightened the darkness of the dullest minds and put the principle beyond denial. When they had done their best, the message of truth did not ring out with the enchanting clarity that would have made its music impossible to miss its effect on even the common level of mentality. All honor goes to them for their heroic championship of nature's mighty Cause. It is still the unfortunate truth that their effort was not brilliant enough to carry their mission to ultimate victory.

And now the world of religion and philosophy is challenged to muster that "sharp and subtle intellect" by which finally the meaning of God written upon the creation of *his* intellect is to be grasped by his earthly children.

William Wordsworth, one of nature's most fervent worshippers, has made us aware of three stages in the evolution of our adoration of nature in an individual's lifetime. We begin, naturally, with sheer sensual delight in her forms and wonders. The beauty she flaunts before us in bush and tree, grass, sky, field, mountain and stream, sunshine, moonlight, spring and autumn, simply bend our spirits in thrall to her majesty and splendor. This is felt in our youth. Ruskin speaks with reverent feeling of the enraptured awe which his first sight of a mountain produced upon his mind and emotion in very early childhood. Wordsworth gives us a lively picture of this enthrallment of his senses,

"when like a roe

I bounded o'er the mountains, by the sides

Of the deep rivers and the lonely streams.

Wherever nature led; more like a man

Flying from something that he dreads than one

Who sought the thing he loved. For nature then
(The coarser pleasures of my boyish days,
And their glad animal movements all gone by)
To me was all in all. - I cannot paint
What then I was. The sounding cataract
Haunted me like a passion; the tall rock,
The mountain, and the deep and gloomy wood,
Their colors and their forms, were then to me
An appetite; a feeling and a love,
That had no need of a remoter charm
By thought supplied, not any interest
Unborrowed from the eye."

The keen perceptiveness of our sight and hearing in childhood brought to him the full registry of nature's charm and panoply of marvel. He needed only to roam at random amongst her rich display of beauties to revel in the fabulous wealth of her enchantments. So he says

"That time is past
And all its aching joys are now no more.
And all its dizzy raptures. Not for this
Faint I, nor mourn nor murmur; other gifts
Have followed; for such loss I would believe
Abundant recompense. For I have learned
To look on nature, not as in the hour
Of thoughtless youth, but hearing oftentimes
The still sad music of humanity,
Not harsh nor grating, though of ample power
To chasten and subdue. And I have felt
A presence that disturbs me with the joy
Of elevated thoughts; a sense sublime

Of something far more deeply interfused,
Whose dwelling is the light of setting suns,
And the round ocean and the living air,
And the blue sky, *and in the mind of man;*
A motion and a spirit that impels
All thinking things, all objects of all thought,
And rolls through all things.
Therefore am I still
A lover of the meadows and the woods,
And mountains, and of all that we behold
From this green earth; of all the mighty world
Of eye and ear--both what they half create
And what perceive; well pleased to recognize
In nature and the language of the sense,
The anchor of my purest thoughts, the nurse,
The guide, the guardian of my heart, and soul
Of all my moral being."

This may stand as poetry's most lyric tribute to the enchantment of the earth for God's children, whom he sent into this paradise, this Edenic "garden of delight."

It is in this citation that we find the poet's delineation of the second stage of our response to nature. In it he has made the transition from simple sense delight to the beginnings of *reflection,* which, being mental, gives rise to emotion and sentiment. He begins to see in nature analogues to the life of man; he sees it mirroring aspects of human experience. Spring brings renewal of life, autumn steals it away, and winter seals its death. Morning suggests life in its freshness and novelty; evening shades and night's darkness just as obviously depict for thought the fading out and extinction of everything positive and conscious. The aspects of nature begin to parallel the nuances of reflective meditation.

The clouds that gather round the setting sun
Do take a sober coloring from an eye
That hath kept watch o'er man's mortality.

This poet's motif in virtually every one of the thousand places he molded in verse was the abstraction of some felicitous moral apologue, some touch of similitude caught by fancy, some pertinent and revealing affinity between the natural scene or object that came under his observation, and some moral, intellectual or spiritual intimation of inner truth. For him nature came to be a never-failing panorama, if not an open book, of moral apothegms. If in contemplating a tumbling brook, a butterfly, a single daisy or a host of daffodils in a meadow, he caught the pattern of some idea in the area of human life, his mind seized upon it with avidity and sought to express it in lines of beauty. Nature thus has been the inspiration and soul of most poetry.

This, then, is the second stage. It is an intermediate and transient station between the first and the third. And into this upper story of the house of nature-revelation it must be said that few poets, philosophers, mystics or even intellectuals have lifted their message, and when they have done so, it has been more by a happy inadvertence than by following a known methodology. For into that exalted realm of vision and understanding the passport of admission is this sharp and subtle intellect. And the attainment of this talisman as an open sesame to this crowning hall of enlightenment is not too common.

A number of achievements in this third stage have been registered in poetry, but there is one performance of the kind that both deserves quotation for its own majestic beauty and will serve to illustrate the third type of nature appreciation. It is by our same English bard, Wordsworth. It has often been regarded as the most sublime poem in our English language. In this one piece at least, he soared into the third stage and gave us a masterly exemplification of the type. The poem is -- one would readily guess -- his *Ode on Intimations of Immortality From Recollections of Early Childhood*. Here a higher vision than massive feeling, delicate sentiment or felicitous fancy was in command. In a moment of insight, probably flashing into thought as he was reading something of Plato's philosophy, he became vividly aware of a parallelism between the glow of brilliant color in the early sky of dawn and the brightness and joyousness in the mind of childhood. There it was, a beautiful thing in mind matched with surprising fidelity by a beautiful thing in nature, the one occurring in the morning of the day, the other in the morning of life, a correspondence between mind and nature to make a poet's heart beat high with discovery and wonder! Just as this brilliance in the first--and only the first--brief moments of dawn lights up the sky, then quickly "fades into the light of common day," so in the first years of life there glows a splendor of happiness in the consciousness of childhood, as, lingering,

Heaven lies about us in our infancy,

then it, too, dies out in the commonplace, and

There hath passed away a glory from the earth.

The basic theme of this majestic rhapsody was thus an idea that took shape from the sudden perception of a similitude between a natural phenomenon and a purely conceptual one, of a fact of human experience mentally conceived, and in it we have beyond question a magnificent instance of the play of the "sharp and subtle intellect" demanded by the Upanishads for the envisioning of deific mind in the related worlds of man and nature. It is safe to surmise that in the intellectual exhilaration engendered by this discernment, Wordsworth's mind experienced a sublimation to a "lucid moment" that inspired also the beauteous forms of language which alone would match the beauty of the conception. It stands as one rare and glowing illustration of the cathartic power that nature may exercise to purify the human mind and soul that can stand reverently enough in her presence to "see into the life of things."

CHAPTER TWELVE

FINDING TRUTH WITHOUT SCIENCE

Evidence that these illuminating analogues of truth require this highest acuity of intellect for their apprehension is found in the expressions of many thinkers. Plotinus states that if we are to catch the voices of spiritual truth, we must keep the "soul's perception bright and quick." The wisdom of ancient Egypt admonishes that there is a little sun of divine light within the core of the being of man and that we must keep it bright and shining, star-like." The deep mind of the great Medieval reformulator of Catholic theology on the basis of Aristotle's system, Thomas Aquinas, wrestled with this problem of discovering the divine images from the contemplation of nature. He dilates on the necessity of the mind's utilizing to the utmost the resources of *imagination,* so that it may reify before it the structure of a spiritual concept in such sharp and clear outlines that it is transformed into virtually another physical object itself. Thus held clearly before the inner eye, its likeness to some object in the external world may become apparent and so find still greater clarification. Obviously what is required for keen perspicacity in this high art is a nimbleness and mercurial alacrity of thought, a readiness and aptness to trace analogies between seen things of the world and their noumenal ghosts or shadows--or, as Plato would have it, their true formal realities.

Many authorities inclined to idealism have loudly extolled the legitimacy of the claims put forth for the principle of analogy as ground for truth-finding, or at least as a sound and reliable guide to it. But minds geared closely to the exactitude which scientific investigation demands, have always been inclined to depreciate the value of the analogical method. It has always been repudiated as too diffuse, too loose, too indefinite and in the end, fallacious. It invariably lacks dependability.

The exponent of the validity of analogy, while recognizing the deficiencies thus advanced, contends that its alleged defects do not disqualify it as functional technique for truth discovery, and asserts that they only come in because the scientific mind asks that the method do more than can legitimately be expected of it, or should be required of it. Science rejects it because it fails to produce what is called "proof." But the idealist insists that the production of proof is not its function and is in fact not in its power. But what it is fully qualified to do is to point to similitudes of pattern and principle between the known and the unknown thing, in such a forceful way that a mind of sufficient alertness and acuity will catch an intimation of relationship not otherwise discernible. It is hardly in all cases able to offer verification, but it points the direction of search and renders the mind keen on the scent, as it prods with hints and suggestions. It may not furnish proof, but it can almost unfailingly point to the region where proof may be found. As an illustration of the idea, if science had been awake at any time since at least the seventeenth century to the utility of the analogical principle, it could have divined the degree of certitude that if and when the atom was to be dissected, it would be found to be organized over the more or less general pattern of a solar system. Indeed ancient and Medieval "occult" science had predicated this fact. Analogy would have furnished the general conception; now the marvel of electronic techniques can come up with the "proof." The scientific mind is impatient and skeptical about the serviceability of analogy because he demands that it shall present not merely parallels and correspondences, but precise copies exact to every detail. The similitude can be expected to carry as far as pattern and principle; it should not be asked to reach as far as to minute detail. Nature everywhere is loudly vocal about genera, but always she has introduced variations in the species and goes on to infinite variety and diversity in the individuals.

With so much factual corroboration of the principle now before us, it should be possible, on an accredited basis, to use analogy in all speculative enterprises. What can be said with finality on the matter is that there can be no impugning the method of analogy as a mode of enlightening the mind. As far as our acquaintance with objective things is concerned, the mode of acquiring knowledge is by direct observation, then inferential digestion of the sensual data. Man could not know his world in the first instance if he had not sensory apparatus to contact it. But when it comes to knowledge of things which have a semi-existential reality only in consciousness, as to which not his senses but his mind or imagination gives him a secondary kind of apperception, there is really no other instrument available to his capacity but analogy. Even if it be claimed that some logical faculty--of the kind Kant called *a priori*--operative in the void above the strictly intellectual reach was able to conjure up and imprint images on his secondary or subconscious mind, he still would have no way of giving them classification or meaning save as he could discern a likeness to images already made familiar through sensory experience. This is the confirmation of what Locke meant when he said that there can be nothing in the mind which had not been first in the senses. And if this be true it virtually validates the principle that nature furnishes the fundamenta of all ratiocination that leads to knowledge. And that it is true is a main contention of this essay. It is the summary conclusion underlying and justifying all that either Plato or Jung have in mind in their predication of the divine archetypes. And it is obvious that nature furnishes all of them.

In broad outline, Jung's position has been set forth, but his vast and penetrating researches have brought to light some vital elements of nature symbolism that it will be most profitable to rehearse. In his scintillating interpretation of the symbols of the occult alchemical system of semantic values, he quotes an excerpt from a Medieval document called the *Roasrum Philosophorum*. The "salt" referred to when the Jesus figure, speaking in the Sermon on the Mount, likens the divine spark in the heart of man's life to the "salt of the earth," and reminds that if its savor be lost the body is deprived of its vital force, suggests interesting connotations. The alchemists used it as the light and power of life, considered chemically. They even developed the thesis that in the correspondence between mind and matter, and in the balance of the subtle forces of nature, the particular force implemented by the influence of each sign of the zodiac was congenitally related to a certain chemical salt, so that persons born under each sign would always stand in a close affective affinity with the salt connate with his sign. So the passage quoted by Jung from the document runs:

Who therefore knows the salt and its solution knows the hidden secret of the wise men of old. Therefore turn your mind upon the salt; for in it alone, that is, the mind, is the science concealed and the most excellent and most hidden secret of all the ancient philosophers.

On this Jung gives the comment or exhortation of one of the astute purveyors of Medieval science, Khunrath, as follows:

Therefore direct your feelings, sense, reason and thoughts upon this salt alone. The work must be performed with true and not with fantastic imagination.

Here we find a Medieval alchemist echoing the Upanishad's "sharp and subtle intellect."

Another excerpt cited by Jung from this same source proves amazingly apt for our theme:

The philosopher in the Book of Dialogues said: "I walked around the three heavens, namely, the heaven of composite natures; the heaven of discriminated natures; and the heaven of the soul. But when I wished to walk around the heaven of intelligence, the soul said unto me: This is no way for thee.' Then nature attracted me, and I was attracted."

If the crypticism here veiled for the "initiated" means that insights into the truth of things is sought in realms of fancy above and detached from the ground reality of nature, but is not to be found there, and instead is to be found in nature, it strangely corroborates our thesis. Jung summarizes the theme by saying that as a result of the projection of the salt archetype in the mind, an unconscious rapport is established between the psyche of the alchemist and the arcane transforming substance, the spiritual "salt" impregnating matter.

The assumption underlying this train of thought, says Jung, "is the causative effect of analogy." And he quotes another writer, Dorn, as stating: "From this the attentive reader will conclude that one must pass from the metaphysical to the physical by a philosophic procedure." It would seem that the writer here is attempting the analogical rule in reverse, as the natural direction is from the physical to the metaphysical. However, once the mind has long dealt with the natural archetypes and through them envisaged their noumenal significances, it often finds itself searching in nature for the physical analogues of spiritual conceptions.

"There is in natural things a certain truth which can not be seen with the outward eye, but is perceived by the mind alone (*sola mente*). The philosophers have known it and they have found that this power is so great as to work miracles. In this truth lies the whole art of freeing the spirit (*spiritus*) from its fetters, in the same way that, as we have said, the mind (*mens*) could be freed (that is, morally) from the body. As faith works miracles in man, so this power, the *veritas efficaciae*, brings them about in matter. This truth is the highest power and an impregnable fortress wherein the philosopher's stone lies safeguarded."

The first sentence of this excerpt directly states the thesis of our work: the things of the natural world yield their appearance to the eye, but they only yield their meaning, their cosmic import, to the mind, and a subtle one, adept to trace analogies.

As to the power of such mental perceptiveness to work miracles, it seems obvious that the reference is not to physical miracles but to exaltations of mind. It is intimated here also that the alchemist's aim is to free the soul from the incubus of body. This idea seems to be an objective of religion and philosophy generally, and it has operated to throw the mind into a negative posture toward the body. Ultimate release of soul from its physical vehicle at the end of the cycle is understandable and unobjectionable. But this attitude must ever be held in proper balance by competent understanding of the beneficence and high evolutionary purpose of the soul-in-body relation in the first place, being the prime condition of life's advance, its escape from static inertia toward expanded being. At this point nature offers one of its illuminating analogies of the type under discussion, and its robust cogency is at once evident. The persistent persuasion of so much assumedly "spiritual" philosophy that the soul's immersion in watery body is an evil to be expunged by tearing it loose from its anchorage to "set it free," matches in error and folly the stupidity of the gardener who would think to promote the growth of his plants by (prematurely) tearing them out of the soil. And it is not overstressing the "miraculous" efficacy of the natural archetypes, when intensively lucubrated upon, to declare that the soulful brooding upon these analogical parallels does truly work intrinsic cathartic prodigies. Numberless highly sensitive minds have testified to this transforming power, beside Wordsworth.

Another sentence from this astute Khunrath begs for our consideration:

I pray you, look with the eyes of the mind at the little tree of the grain of wheat, regarding all its circumstances, so that you may bring the tree of the philosophers to grow.

Jung subjoins: "This seems to point to the active imagination as the thing that sets the process really going." This is indeed the core of this heightened use of the *imagination* that is the specific function of the mind essential to the sensing of correspondences. A nimble fancy, not wayward but pursuing true leads, is the spur that goads into activity the intelligence lying latent in the unconscious. Every concrete object and phenomenon in nature thus knocks at the door of mind to open and come forth to behold a truth. The difference that measures the yawning gap between our stolid incomprehension of nature's mute eloquence and a keen sense of her message, is just the failure of the living world and its objects to bestir in us the lively powers of intellection in catching the analogues between things and their meaning.

Reflection suggests the mirror, and this is one of the symbols of Medieval alchemy that challenged Jung for interpretation. He handles it most competently:

The mirror' as an indispensable instrument of navigation' doubtless refers to the intellect, which is able to think and is constantly persuading us to identify ourselves with its perceptions (reflexions'). The mirror is one of Schopenhauer's favorite similes for the intellect. The term instrument of navigation' is an apt expression for it, since it is indeed man's indispensable guide on pathless seas.

It should be noted that, as Jung puts it, this faculty of intellect is constantly prodding us to identify ourselves with its operations. India's supreme philosophy centers about the concept that we are identical with the great Total, Brahm. "Thou art That." Here the psychologist says that the world is at every instant trying to bring us into awareness of our community with it. It is silently pleading with us to open blind eyes and recognize the identity. Until this awakening we are much like Wordsworth's rustic bumpkin, Peter Bell:

A yellow primrose by the river's brink,
A yellow primrose was to him,
And it was nothing more.

Jung's study of the archetypes and their provenance from nature gave him the insight by which he could challenge the position of idealists and mystics who eternally huckster the shibboleth of the superiority and validity of "intuition" over the solid work of the intellect. It flaunts defiance also in the face of India's philosophies of flight into the void above the mind. Referring to an exponent of this transcendental philosophy, he makes this notable statement, which we deem worthy of emphasis:

But when the ground slips from under his feet and he begins to speculate in the void, seduced by soaring flights of intuition, the situation becomes dangerous.

It is inevitable that the free and unstable mind will speculate, both in wayward roving vacancy and in earnest search for truth, in all possible directions. But speculation, says Jung, becomes a peril when it abandons the ground of reality testified to by the objective creation of the cosmic Mind and attempts to fly off into regions where there is nothing to give thought a foothold. The hazard arises from the fatal tendency of minds not too strong to mistake in time the chimeras of its own fanciful origination for the veridical forms of truth. In weak minds these fixations of uncritical thought become veritable Frankensteins dominating the entire consciousness. Man can not fly to heaven without at least the resistance of the earth to give fulcrum to his thrust.

In view of the devastation of human sanity which the wild excesses of irrational religiosity have inflicted upon the human mind, one is impelled to dilate more at large upon this pronouncement of the psychologist. It holds the potential of an epochal reassessment, "an agonizing reappraisal," of cardinal elements in the life of religion; it should dictate a radical reconditioning of religious technique. Intellect must be elevated from a secondary and subservient position to feeling and faith and steady the vagrant impulses of arrant pietism. To whatever extent it may be legitimate for souls to attempt to fly the mystical heavens of some transcendental superconsciousness, the effort must be made with eye steadily fixed on the realities on the ground. For at least the soul must have some place to land and be at home after its dizzy flights. Does this decry and disqualify mysticism? Not at all. Mysticism is ineluctably a station on the upper reaches of the pathway souls must travel on the road to grander being. It can lift us into truly diviner experience of beatitude. But the afflations that loft the soul into those giddier heights pose dangers to the adventurous spirit if they are not kept in close relation to the realities of the earthly experience.

At his peril man attempts to substitute his own wild vagaries of unrestrained fancy, buoyed by extravagant and unwarranted hopes of imagined bliss and liberty, and beauty extant in the living world. His mind is susceptible to realizing a blessed exaltation of sense and thought that arises naturally out of his contact with and reflection upon the order and beauty of the world. Jung elsewhere has endorsed our thesis that a mysticism that is generated out of the real experience of souls with its incarnational realities is safe, sane and salutary; whereas a feeling extravaganza concocted out of the errant and unreasoned fantasies of a misdirected imagination are hazardous. Intellect must stand guard to hold the soul in paths of safety. The Greek myth of Phaeton, son of Apollo, who essayed to drive the chariot of the sun across the heavens, and letting the horses of passion and wild free adventure have their way, with the result that earthly vegetation was consumed, points the moral of this situation. If we attempt to build our castles in Spain and eyries in the sky without solid foundations on earth, they are bound to collapse.

It is a psychological problem, whether our straining to launch ourselves on the wing is based on fantasy or on reality. If "divine love" be the power to thrust us off the ground, it must not be love in the abstract, but love of something real: love of an adored one, love of music, love of nature, love of the delights of reason, to which all philosophers testify as the most exalted of human experiences, love of health, bodily exercise, duty, skill, and happiness that can flow forth only from these achievements in the earthly sphere. When souls can soar into mystical realizations from these grounds, they can fly with safety, because they will maintain a balance with the world of present reality that will hold their chariot in its normal orbit. Whenever man abandons earth for the vacuity of the skies, physical or ideal, he risks losing his footing on the ground and being blown about by wind of fantasy. He can not maintain his balance in midair. It was neither for purposes of punishment nor on a whim of deity that souls were sent from heaven to earth. Part of the divine motive was that they should face the pattern of the Logoic thought stamped upon the physical world. Their education in cosmic creativeness--for they are destined to become co-creators with their Father--could not better be consummated than by confronting them here with the forms of ideal reality in their daily existence. God thus committed them to the care and rearing of their Mother Nature, in whose world every stalk that grows would enlighten them about the principles in whose handling they were to become adept.

It is possible now to see what a profound maxim of truth is embodied in the Latin of an alchemical treatise called *Tractatus Aureus* li, p. 12: *Verum masculus est coelum foeminae et foemina terra masculi.*--"The male is the heaven of the female and the female is the earth of the male." Only through the motherhood of nature is the divine form of the spiritual conception brought to manifestation. Without the gestating function of the mother, the creative Lord would never see his cosmic ideas materialized.

Khunrath again comes in with an appropriate tribute:

This light is the light of nature, which illumines all God-loving philosophers who come into this world. It is in the world as the whole edifice of the world is beautifully adorned and will be naturally preserved by it until the last and great day of the Lord; but the world knows it not. It isÖthe great Stone of the philosophers, which the whole world has before its eyes and yet knows not.

The ancient mythographers included in their pantheons, along with the twelve supreme heavenly deities on Mt. Olympus, the gods of the earth, the chthonic powers. One of the primary family of the Egyptians Gods was Seb, the "god of earth." So we find Jung speaking of the "chthonic femininity of the unconscious." This would bring together in one category the earthly, the feminine, and the unconscious. And precisely that is the connection of these three, if not their identity. Earth, matter (*mater,* Latin "mother"), is the eternal feminine, and it is passive and negative to the polarized activity of the conscious. All its consciousness is, so to say, subterranean to the conscious. It receives from the mind forces of creation the energies they project into matter and simply nurses them into bud, flower and fruit. The Egyptian Seb is etymologically cognate with Sevekh, also a water-earth divinity, and his name is the origin of our "magic number" *seven.* As Pythagoras told us, earth is the domain in which the constitution of things physical is grounded on this number. It is ubiquitous throughout all ancient occult religion and is the basic key to interpretation and understanding of cryptic arcana. Yet in two thousand years, the exegesis of the

Scriptures has shown no signs of comprehending the fundamental relevance of the number. The soul in the Egyptian drama says that it descends from on high to partake of the "bread of Seb," or the "food of earth," and to be renewed thereby. From a higher world of unity it was to descend into a world of septenary constitution, to receive there its instruction in the art of governing the seven archangelic creative powers. All the sanctimonious diatribes that have been fulminated against the world as the enemy and destroyer of the soul receive their fitting rebuke when one reads in that treasure of pristine sagacity, the *Book of the Dead,*--in an address to the soul: "Through Seb thou dost become a spirit, and when through Seb thou dost become a spirit, thou art more a spirit than the spirits." To the descending soul it is said: "Thou art glorified there." It replies: "I come that I may purify this soul of mine in the most high degree."

And Jung descants most lucidly upon the advent of soul upon earth, and its relation to earth and body, as essentially the basic fact underlying all religion. His system or orientation of the conscious-unconscious tie-in would seem to be integrated, he says, with the incarnation in an earthly human, or chthonic, nature of a purely spiritual God, and this is effectuated by an act of impregnation by the Holy Ghost of the womb of the Virgin Mother. In this action we have the higher, the spiritual, the masculine inclining to the lower, the earthly, the feminine, the chthonic, and thus the mother, who was prior to the fatherhood, and who, receiving the insemination of the divine spark of mind, gestates and in the fullness of time produces her Son. The divine Child, being the progeny of the union of the spiritual Fatherhood and the mundane Mother, embodies jointly in himself the hidden potential of soul with the passive nature of the unconscious.

It is thus seen that in its unearthing of the "unconscious" modern sagacity has, after centuries of blindness, recovered knowledge of the compound of positive and negative elements in man's psychic life which the world has lacked ever since the third century, when the Christian hierarchy cast out the Mother from its Trinity and substituted the Holy Ghost. Under the psychological influences of this persuasion, religion in this system was so overbalanced by the unmitigated overemphasis on the functional cult of the spirit, and the corresponding militant negation of the physical and the natural, that Christian devotion was warped into forms of morbidity and corruption. The psychological consequences of this distortion became so patent in the history of the Church that a rectification of the imbalance was perforce dictated by polity and the Holy Mother was restored as a fourth member of the divine Quaternity, as the blessed Virgin, Mother of God. The Son of the Mother thus became the *Salvator Microcosmi,* or Savior of the World, by virtue of his uniting in himself the mundane or chthonic unconscious lower potencies in polarity with the superior conscious divine powers. Through its discovery of this dual composition of both the natural world and of man, modern psychology has recovered the intellectual dynamic of true religious science, and the prospect of a more propitious balance between the two forces of conflict in human life looms brightly ahead.

So engaging became this new insight on the part of the psychologist that he went so far as to declare that even the highest powers of spiritual order, which he equates with the Greek term *Gnosis,* are rooted deep down in the unconscious realm. He deduces that with the incarnation the potential of Gnosis is lodged in the chthonic area of consciousness, the unconscious. We find him saying:

We are moving here in this psychological region where, as a matter of fact, the Gnosis is rooted. The message of the Christian simply is Gnosis, and the compensation effected by the unconscious is Gnosis in an even higher degree. Myth is the primordial language natural to these psychic processes, and no intellectual formulation comes anywhere near the richness and expressiveness of mythical imagery. Such processes deal with the primordial images, and these are best and most succinctly reproduced by figurative speech.

Alchemy, he says, is preeminently concerned with the "seed of unity which lies hidden in the chaos of Tiamat, "--Babylonian mother-principle--"and forms the counterpart of the divine unity."

Jung feels the massive power of the archetypes and symbols so strongly that he attributes the controlling power of the Roman Catholic Church over its masses of devotees to the fact that it never ceases to flaunt these insignia of its mission and function before the eyes of its ignorant following. So that even though there is no "sharp and subtle" intellectual comprehension of their meaning, there is still enough dynamic by way of intuitive suggestiveness and dim apprehensions of hidden force in them to sway the feelings of the communicants. He ventures the statement that even a mistaken idea of the meaning of a symbol or other semantic representation may sometimes produce a tremendous psychic and moral-spiritual effect. This anomalous phenomenon must be obviously possible, since history records no end of the fierce sweeps of massive religious persuasions based on misconceptions and in periods of better vision later abandoned. Many a clergyman and seminarian would freely admit that to a lamentable degree neither the Christian hierarchy nor the laity fully grasp the recondite significance of their symbols.

In this connection the psychologist has impaled himself on both prongs of the two-tined fork of his analysis, as he has laid prime emphasis on both the intellect and the intuition, the clear and the vague aspect of perceptions, giving each just about equally beneficent function. This is a matter of vast importance for knowledge, and the opposing claims made for each over the other leaves philosophical science uncertain and dangerously in the dark over one of the most crucial items of understanding, which should be clear, and can be psychologically a salutary influence only when it *is* clear.

We have glanced cursorily earlier at this widely alleged superiority of "spiritual intuition" over intellect. We hold it to have been the product of unsound religious maundering. It gained a foothold and entrenched itself by default of the influence of the ancient arcane science as perpetuated in the Mysteries and Gnostic societies and cults carrying on the esoteric tradition. with the sages of old, the proficients in archaic wisdom, there was never any belittling of the mind, the intellect; it was man's divinest faculty, an instrument painstakingly evolved by natural evolution over ages of time as the highest light of consciousness for the guidance of man on earth. It was the mark of man's transcendence over the beasts, the badge of his divinity, actual or potential. It embraced the whole of his ratiocinative faculty; there was no distinction of grades and degrees in its function, one rising above the other in power or authority. It was the highest power of consciousness to see things according to reason; it would safeguard the human from plunging into error and point him to truth. The sages never asserted that the most exalted envisioning of truth and beauty was achieved through the more magical development of the intellect itself. The most ecstatic transports of elevated thought and feeling did not discredit the intellect, but confirmed its perfectibility. From slow discursive syllogistic reasoning, its mercurial powers flared out in brilliant mastery of thought processes, giving instantaneous insights in a single flash. This might seem to be a higher power than intellect, but is only its own genius come to maturity and mastership. Slow reasoning in the dark gave place to quick flashes of almost electric rapidity and clarity. It is man's wielding of Jove's lightning, his portion and voltage of it.

Religion's spurning and deprecation of the intellect still prevails in many quarters and has contributed massively and hurtfully to falsities in the psychic and philosophical domain. The acclaim of the mystic viewpoint at times seems to rest on the assumption that a touch of elevated consciousness is all the better and holier for *not* being logically rationalized. But B. A. G. Fuller in his splendid *History of Philosophy,* with a touch of irony, shows that when it comes to the matter of the efficacy and cathartic power of religious experience, it must be a strange perversion of reason not to realize that, however exalting a mystical uplift can be in the realm of feeling, it would generate a still more dynamic benefaction to the soul if it is also intellectually comprehended. Mystery has its romantic charms, but any experience must be the more ennobling for being understood. God's potential of wisdom and beatitude for man may, as the Scriptures assert, be past finding out, transcending our limited thought powers. But man is happier if he can rationalize the import of all his experience, preferably to his standing in ignorance and awe of their incidence. In the end the mind must determine the actual status, the practical value and the handling of all experience, however transcendent. The Scriptures put wisdom and understanding beyond all other values.

The great Hegel comes in here with a clarifying analysis of this problem with an analogue from that final authority, nature. Feeling, he says, is like a wild wind. Intellect is the windmill, or the sail of a boat, the instrument needed to grasp the powerful force and turn it to useful purposes. The wild ecstasies of feeling can, as Jung warns, become devastating scourges of fanaticism, if not chastened by reason. The dissociation of feeling and thought has been a most disastrous cleavage in human life. Hiding in, but at any time springing out from the unconscious, desire, appetency, feeling, would sweep with fell force over the area of consciousness and motivate conduct. Intellect must act like the old draft-controls of a stove, or like any gauge that regulates the force of any motive power. If reason is disregarded, life's ship will have no captain at the helm. Hegel's voice of admonition on this point should not go unheard:

Thought is a rising up from the limited to the Absolute Universal and religion is only through thought and in thought. God is not the highest emotion, but the highest thought . . . The opinion that thought is injurious to religion and that the more thought is abandoned the more secure the position of religion is, is the maddest error of our time. It is only in thought that God is worshipped.

Those who will contend that this expresses an extremely one-sided view of the experience of worship, expostulating that the most intense forms of worship transcend thought, hold such an opinion only because they limit thought to the narrow range of its discursive reasoning processes. In the highest rhapsodies of mystical afflation, the soul is not holding the intellect in abeyance, but is exercising it at such a pitch of keenness and electric freedom and accuracy of mobility, that its ordinary less mercurial function seems indeed to be far transcended. The great German thinker corrects this impression and goes far ahead to assert that, "since the Absolute is intrinsically Thought, the doctrine of thinking must be the doctrine of being." As to that, modern science itself, on its side, is hovering on the brink of identifying the basic force of the universe as the energy of mind. It is time that religion gives over its contemptuous disappraisal of the intellect.

Jung joins Hegel in a succinct statement of this matter. Speculating on the sanifying efficacy of Mephisto's matter-of-fact point of view on Faust's

Finding Truth Without Science   127

emotions as he gazes at the spooks and bogies of the classical *Walpurgisnacht*, he writes:

> *Would that more people could remember the scientific and philosophical reflections of the much-abused intellect at the right moment! Those who abuse it lay themselves open to the suspicion of never having experienced anything that might have taught them its values and shown them why evolution has forged this weapon with such unprecedented effort. One has to be singularly out of touch with life not to notice such things. The intellect may be the devil, but the devil is the strange son of chaos who can most easily be trusted to deal effectively with his mother. The Dionysian experience will give the devil plenty to do, should he be looking for work, since the resultant settlement with the unconscious far outweighs the labors of Hercules.*

If the intellect is this Satanic power that seems to analyze life into the disruption of its wholeness, this holds only on the outgoing arc of the cycle of emanation and return, since a beneficent Providence must itself break its own unity into fragments in order to distribute its largesse to the infinite hosts of its children who are to share its inexhaustible bounty. Each unit of the divine life, starting from the point of its initial ignorance, faces the evolutionary task of reunifying the broken body of the Lord, reassembling the dismantled unity. And this is the work of the intellection. If it is the dishonor of intellect to tear the primal unity apart, it is then its infinite glory to reassemble it, but now with understanding of the dialectical integration of all its parts. A common illustration may clarify this point with finality. Who can be said to know the unity of an automobile better, the man who purchases a new machine without any knowledge of its construction, or the mechanic who does know every one of its parts and the relation of each to the whole, by having taken it all apart many times? How is man, the Son of the Father, to become proficient in his work of cooperating with his Sire in the running of the universe, if he does not become familiar with every part and process by analysis? The philosophy that decries the analytic power of the intellect is banal because it stifles the movement of the mind toward proficiency in its aeonial task. How can the human mind move toward the vision of unity unless it knows how to relate all the parts properly to sense their basic integrity? The Creator, so to say, sets his Sons down in the midst of a world of infinite diversity of its constituent elements, but equipping them with the potential of a genius of understanding capable of discovering the principles that reveal the unity of the whole. This is the province of the intellect, and they render a vast disservice to mankind who decry it. Intellect is not to be surpassed and degraded, but needs only to be perfected. And that perfection, as the sequel will show, must be achieved mainly through collaboration of mind with nature.

A mind as clairvoyant as that of the philosopher Santayana has caught the vision of this transcendent utility of the intellect:

"But when the force of intellect, once having arrested an idea amid the flux of perception, avails to hold and examine that idea with perseverance, not only does a flash of light illumine the mind, but deeper and deeper vistas are opened there into ideal truth.

"The principle of dialectic is intelligence itself; and as no part of man's economy is more vital than intelligence (since intelligence is what makes life aware of its destiny), so no part has a more delightful or exhilarating movement. *To understand is preeminently to live,* moving not by stimulation and external compulsion, but by inner direction and control."

The philosopher, from the other side, may smile at our presumption in inserting the italics. The spirit of Hegel also may nod in approval, as he, too, has told us that true being is Thought. For the expression of a sane judgment that has been sorely needed in philosophy and religion, this passage is beyond praise. It should be noticed that the philosopher says that light breaks on the mind when it grasps and holds an idea with perseverance. Generally it will be only with long and steady surveillance of a concept that the full deep relevance of its meaning comes aglow. God's precipitation of his Sons into the seeming melange of the infinite diversification of his primal unity imposes on them the evolutionary task of studying the relationship of the parts to the whole. We see the parts, says St. Paul, but must become sharply watchful of their action to discern their relation, until eventually the overall Gestalt takes shape. The jigsaw puzzle of the diversity must at last reveal the articulation and beauty of the unity. This brings that intellectual vision of wholes lauded by the Greeks and the synthetic unity of apperception extolled by Kant and the intellectual love of God glorified by Spinoza. The soul's tremendous challenge to raise its vision from isolated particulars to a height of view that will take in a sweep of the whole scene can be likened to the work of an organist, who takes the thousands of dots on a musical composition and by perseverance and nimbleness of mind and hands transmutes them into the ravishing rhapsodies of beautiful movement. The consciousness of unity is only exalting when it embraces a synthesis of the diversity. As Santayana observes, the achievement of the grand view yields a vast enrichment of mind. Prodded by the constant impingement upon it of the outward natural symbols, the soul gradually transforms the external world into an inner intellectual experience, says Hegel. The principle of subjectivity accomplishes the synthesis of itself with the objectivity. On the moot subject of intuition, the German thinker says that "intuition has to join discursive reflection. It has to become reflective itself. The intellect has to transcend itself, not by mere intuition, but in a rational fashion *methodically*." (Our emphasis.) If intuition has any superiority over reflection, it must exert its dominance by effecting a veritable "resurrection" of the unity it has analyzed into its parts. If by analysis intellect has "killed" the unity, it must by synthesis restore it to its living power. As the head executive of a great industrial concern will require his son and prospective successor to master by actual experience every constituent element of the production, so as to know how to govern the whole expertly, so, it seems, God has sent his Sons out into the factory of creation for an apprenticeship in the cosmic operation, requiring of them a pilgrimage through all the ranges of being, in order to become adept in their later work of supervision of the order. So Hegel says that the mind that leaves its heavenly vision of unity must return from its apostasy, but return enriched by its "victory over itself." It is as if God demands that his Sons go out into the universe that he has taken all apart and learn how to put it together again.

    It is almost certainly true that no theologian has ever caught the idea that this is the truth that the Jesus figure dramatizes in his institution of the Christian Eucharist. Having broken his body symbolically into fragments and distributed the pieces to his disciples, with the injunction to eat them to be inoculated with the germ of immortal life, he concludes by exhorting them to do this "in remembrance of me." Theology has unwittingly missed the esoteric significance of this dramatism. The "remembrance" Jesus suggested was not memorial but an actual spiritual transaction physically allegorized. What he asked for was not sentimental memory, but physical reunification of the body he had dismembered for them. The "remembrance" should have been translated "rememberment." "I have dismembered my (spiritual) body," he said; "now it is your task to re-member it." "That each of you may have the essence of immortal life, I have disintegrated my body; now it is for you, by love and brotherhood, to reintegrate it. My dismemberment must be followed by your re-memberment.

CHAPTER THIRTEEN

THE WAR OF OPPOSITES

Dealing further with religion's chronic infatuation with the idea of hastening souls back to heaven by disdaining homely earth, Jung astutely rationalizes the necessity of the soul's unbreakable tie to earth. Man may have lost his Saurian's tail, he muses, but still finds himself bound to a mundane routine that is generally very unromantic and unheroic. But, he reflects: "That we are bound does not mean that we cannot grow; on the contrary, it is the *sine qua non* of growth. No noble well-grown tree ever disowned its direct roots, for it grows not only upward, but downward as well." The onus of our task, he says, is to strike a dead center between the two tendencies, the downward drag, the upward pull. For true poise and balance, the aims of the higher must be accommodated to the mechanism of the lower. His final pronouncement is of crucial import; "These two aspects must never be separated." His rationalization of the cosmic utility and beneficence of the "war of opposites" is magnificent. Without it there could be no experience of wholeness. Most pertinent to our exegesis is his statement that for the evolutionary purposes to be realized through the individual soul, "consciousness must confront the unconscious and a balance between opposites must be found." This, he says, is not to be had through logic; logic must be enlightened by the power of symbols, "which make the irrational union of opposites possible. They are produced spontaneously by the unconscious and are amplified by the conscious mind." The opposite pulls of soul and body generate the powers of consciousness. But the developing powers of the conscious mind would long grope in darkness without a guide if it was not for the prods to intelligence that come from symbols. And nature mostly supplies these archetypes.

The conflict so lugubriously decried by religionists, who would fain consign human life to the peace of the cemetery, brings to birth all positive values in the evolution of consciousness. The animating and presiding spirit-power of life comes charged with its pattern of structure for the physical domain. It must lay hold of the power potential in the atom of matter as its instrument. Mind must seize upon the raw energies of nature and direct them into the preconceived channels. In man's constitution this required the subjection of the wild free forces of sense and feeling to the mandates of the soul's reason and intelligence. This joins the battle. It is the struggle of the two natures in man, higher and lower. "Two souls, alas, contend within my breast apart," moans the poet Goethe. The Old Testament glances at the idea, in the conception of the twins Jacob and Esau in the womb of Rebecca:

In your limbs lie nations twain,
Rival races from their birth;
One the mastery shall gain,
The younger o'er the elder reign.

This is one form of the allegory of the eternal polarity. The one destined to win the battle in the end is of course the conscious mind, which, as the child of the great Mother, the unconscious, is the younger in manifestation. As Jung hints, it will have its work cut out for it in dominating the energies of its mother, to bring them into subjection to the designs of soul. The exigencies of the battle, the tensions of the struggle, open the way for the young divine Child to step out of the unconscious area and assert its right to take its rightful place on the throne of the individual life. Its imperial splendor can then shine forth. This is the background reality that inspired the homely adage that man's extremity is God's opportunity. If potentially higher consciousness "rests in primal unconsciousness," this first domain of life must harbor deep within its womb the seeds of a primal divine superconsciousness. "Only by virtue of psychic existence do we have any being at all," Jung tells us. There must be deep within the womb of being "a sort of unknown *prima materia*," out of which issues the miracle of consciousness. For the sensual perception of this order of consciousness the eye of the senses is needed; but for the apprehension of a rational scheme of meaning in its order symbols are the indispensable requisite. Hegel agrees that this work of synthesis and integration can be done by philosophy alone. This implies that the intellect must in the finale be called in to do what faith, beatified contemplation and mysticism have never been able to do. Hegel elaborates:

Philosophy is no longer assigned to a place below religion; on the contrary, it is destined to replace religion, completing the development initiated by the Reformation. Philosophy is called upon to do what faith can never do: the absolute reconciliation of absolute opposites.

Striking at the false sentimental preachments that the soul's transition back to heaven at death restores its visions of beauty and rapture, he avers that there is no such transition beyond what the divine light in man's own nature can disclose to his cognition in his tensional experience with the natural life here. Mankind contains its own absolute principles within itself, and is equipped with "a fixed and insurmountable finitude of reason" by which to bring its self-illumination into focus. This is its task rather than to attempt to bask in a splendor reflected from beyond his station.

If philosophy is to supplant religion and give a new enlightenment, it must be examined for the principia that will provide the torch for our advance through the darkness. It would seem that Jung's affirmation that consciousness emerges out of the unconscious would ground our understanding on a great basic truth. Nature and physics would seem to endorse the dictum in the scientific fact that the visible universe emerged out of invisibility, passing through stages from etheric and aeriform and gaseous into materialization. The sacred Scriptures affirm also that God caused the light to shine out of the darkness, to which St. Paul adds the sensational assertion that he also caused this light to shine in our hearts. The universe sprang out of the void, declares *Genesis*. The initial Biblical statement that God began with the creation of the heavens and the earth is the first of Jove's two-pronged forks of lightning. The one fork was consciousness, the other, matter. Philosophy, speaking through Heraclitus, declared that the one life initially divides itself into opposites, to unite them again in the cycle's end. And it does this rhythmically, recurrently, cyclically, periodically. The Hindus speak of this as the inhalation and exhalation of the eternal Brahm. Analogy can equally well call it the circulation of the life-blood of the universe, expelled from the heart of being, returning with the diastole of the pulse. Also it can be figured as the alternation of the life of Brahm between sleep and awaking. He throws himself into the conscious effort of creation and returns at eve to sink into repose. The analogy with our experience--since we are made in his image--assures us that back of the grade of consciousness that he discards at night there abides at a higher level that great unconsciousness out of which, according to Jung, all self-consciousness emerges. If it were not so, Brahm would not awaken to another day. In that undying Conscious-Unconsciousness philosophy, from Aristotle, has perforce had to locate the omniscient Cause of all things, the One Cause behind which there could be no other.

The two forces, then, having moved *ab initio* out from the inner core of infinite being, the one essence, the other consciousness, and taken their position at the opposite ends of the polarity, the great battle of Armageddon begins, the war that Heraclitus said is the father of all things. This is simply the tension of polarity. It is the operative modus of creative activity.

The great question toward whose answer we are working is as to how the generative procedure succeeds in disseminating the principle of conscious intelligence throughout the total body of its production. Tied in with this main problem are all those subsidiary ones challenging thought to the limit of its powers. Prominent among these are the ideas of the *tabula rasa,* the innate ideas, Kant's concept of the *a priori* forms of intellection, preestablished harmony between outer forms and inner constructs--in short, all the problems of epistemology, the whole science of philosophy is a derivative of the whole basic fact of polarity between the two modes of being, which are inseparable even when lined up in polar opposition, and merged back into total unity and identity when not so separated. The universe, so the ancient wisdom proclaimed, is suspended on a web of force attached to spirit at the summit and to matter at the nadir. When that tension relaxes, the universe fades out of existence and Brahm enjoys his night of sleep. But he awakes to a new day of tension and adventure.

In the cryptic mode of ancient hagiographic writing, when the intent was concealment of esoteric truth from the ignorant masses, and its release to the initiated through cryptic symbolism, this principle of life's self-renewal through the seed was the hidden meaning of the ark-and-flood allegory. It adumbrated the truth that when at the withdrawal of the breath and blood energies of Brahm from his aeonial embodiment of matter, the *flood of dissolution* washed away his physical fabric of creation, so that the nucleus of life had to retreat within the *arche* (Greek: ark or beginning), out of which it had emanated in the first instance. This makes Noah's ark story pure allegory, and removes it from the pale of history. It is safe to aver that, while there may have been subsidence of continents, as the fabled sinking of Atlantis and Lemuria, to create traditions of catastrophic deluges, the *Genesis* account is not a record of one of them. It is too clearly a semantic construction. When a giant oak is blown down and rots away, its life force retires into its ark, the acorn. In that haven of safety it rides out the flood of dissolution, awaiting the morn of its new cycle, when it, like the seed in April's garden, emerges from its *arche* for a new beginning. And where does it set foot again to root its new ebullition of life? On the "Mount of Earth," as *Ararat* is obviously from the Hebrew *arets,* the earth. It seems at one time to have been spelled *areth.*

The next stage of the creative or emanative process clamors for explanation. The two polarized forces, locked in tensional stress and strain with each other from the beginning, as they swing apart like two dancers who whirl out from a first embrace, yet keep hand-hold, begin to interrelate their influence mutually. So the human individual has his psychosomatic ground problem. As Browning puts it,

Nor soul helps flesh more now
Than flesh helps soul,

so the universe has its basic conflict between world-soul and world-body.

As seed and soil in the garden exchange influences and thereby grow, so consciousness, germinal at first, and matter interact to their reciprocal benefit. Occult mystery though it be, it is the indefeasible reality of living fact. And it is one of the primal *archai* of being, as nature instructs.

But now a legitimate question arises as to how sheer force of consciousness, which can not bodily move objects, can influence matter, which is primarily inert; or how on its side matter can induce changes in consciousness. How is the vast unbridged gap between mind and matter to be spanned for the effective interchange of mutual influence?

For answer we must resort to ancient knowledge, which held solutions that have been lost out of the wisdom-codes of antiquity. The secret cultus of divine mysteries postulated an elaborate system of elements in the constitution of man, so that between pure consciousness at the summit of his life and the coarse matter of his physical body, there was a gamut of instrumentalities composed of matter in varying grades of subtlety and ethereality--such as modern science can now recognize--which form the linkage of a bridge between top-spirit and bottom-matter. At least one of the traces of the survival of knowledge of this inner equipment is found in St. Paul's affirmation that "we have a natural and a spiritual body," Greece had inherited knowledge of such arcana from the earlier Egyptians, who distinguished seven such bodies in the total constitution of man. In the order of grossness to tenuity they were named: the *khat*, or *khabit*, the *ren*, the *ab*, the *ba*, the *ka*, the *sahu* and the glorious *khu*, or body of the resurrection, transfiguring the whole man with shining light.

By means of the electric or vivific powers of spiritual dynamic, currents of living force were transmitted from body to body, both up and down the scale, giving spirit and matter effective intercommunication. As thought to brain cell, cell to nerve force, nerve to blood to muscle and flesh, the creative mind energies operative in the process could course up and down this Jacob's ladder between spirit-heaven and sensuous earth. And if the infinitely fine nuances of this relationship were known, answers to most of the problems and mysteries of living process would be available.

Open self-registering consciousness is manifest only normally in the lowest or most "material" of the seven, through the activity of brain cells. The grades of consciousness that are registered in the three bodies ranking above the physical, too high in frequency and short wave-length to be instrumentalized through the brain, would be operative within the area of the unconscious.

It was the occlusion of the knowledge of the existence and intermediatory function of these psycho-spiritual bodies in man's nature that has left Medieval and modern science bereft of basic data for the resolution of problems in epistemology and psychology. After all, a civilization whose highest guiding light is what can be gained only from a study of the superficies of life's organic forms, will not be likely to discover the secrets that are locked in the intricacies of an internal and unknown mechanism. We are still stunned by our discovery of the seemingly endless "withinness" of the mechanism of the atom; nature gives evidence of being as infinite in minitude as in magnitude. The claims of ancient seers for the existence of psychic bodies within the physical are now no longer either fantastic or bizarre. Science confronts increasing tenuity of organization whenever it looks inward. Nature does not make one leap across an unbridged gulf from gross materiality to pure spirituality. The realm we call the metaphysical is certainly not as metaphysical as we thought. The notion that man is equipped with a psychic mechanism as well as a physical can be ridiculed no more. Man's body is an animate instrumentality for life and consciousness, a dynamo and purveyor of forces ranging from nerve currents to the electronic flashes of thought. Without our knowledge of rays, frequencies and voltages, with the varieties of subatomic structures, a summary dismissal of old Egypt's predication of six sublimated bodies of psycho-spiritual constituency is no longer intelligent. It is nothing but the lingering power of an inveterate religious bigotry, unworthy of the modern scientific posture. That ancient sages knew of man's interior psychic organization intensifies our sense of the direful loss of knowledge which was once held so precious as to be transmitted only to initiated students and tested adepts in a technique considered requisite to safeguard such knowledge from abuse.

From one of the last of the ancient illuminati, the eminent Plutarch, we have a statement that puts in clear light the fact of this intermediary mechanism:

"But in his (Plato's) *Book of Laws,* when he was now grown old, he affirmed, not in riddles and emblems, but in plain and proper words, that the world is not moved by one soul, but perhaps by a great many, but by not fewer than two, the one of which is beneficent, and the other contrary to it, and the author of things contrary. He also leaves a certain third nature in the midst between, which is neither without soul nor without reason, nor void of a self-moving power, but rests upon both of the preceding principles, but yet so as to affect, desire and pursue the better of them."

Here is ground-work on which psychic and spiritual science can intelligently build. Between soul and body stands a living organic structure, with an apparatus of communication of forces from part to part. Each intermediate element is obviously both a receptor and transmitter of messages, which is enough to remove the operation from the realm of magic to that of science. Thus intimations generated at the level of soul sweep clear down to the body and transform it in some way and to some degree; in response soul profits by whatever the bodily readjustment may mean for its economy of life in the body. Thus flies back and forth the shuttle that weaves the web of life.

Clearly this mechanism would implement the function assigned by theology to any principle postulated as mediator between the human and the divine natures in man. The ancients, simplifying their more complex knowledge, referred this mediatorial principle to the mind. Mind was thus the keystone in the arch of "divine philosophy." Intellect thus stood in the place of intercessor between man and the human and his God.

Brilliantly illuminating are the allegorical representations of this "certain third nature" between soul and body handed to us by the semantic genius of ancient Egypt. This middle principle was personified in their dramas by their great Christ-figure Horus, son of the wedded forces of the cosmic polarity, Osiris, Father, Spirit, and Isis, Mother-Matter. In complete fidelity to nature's symbolism, they pictured the divine son as standing on the frontier line separating heaven (spirit) and earth (matter) in the constitution of man, symbolized by the line of the horizon. Standing on the western horizon at evening, Horus dramatized the soul descending with the sun into the underworld of dark night for its much sheer deadlock, many an impasse, and eventually much compromise. The reason and intelligence of the conscious side has the onerous obligation of breaking up the stolid commitment of the unconscious to habit, instinct, appetite and tradition. Jung has called this the work of the divine Child, the Son, against his mother. Plato in the *Timaeus* has informed us that this "Horus of the Horizon" was enjoined by his Father to discipline himself for creative activity on his own independent account, "imitating in your creation the power which I employed in your generation." God has sent his Son (collectively the host of his Sons) into the world to continue at their level his work of creation. But if these Sons are to serve an apprenticeship in the handling of the forces locked up in the atom, they must in turn win, and wed the same negative pole of being as did the Father. Hence they are figuratively dramatized as uniting with their own Mother--Matter.

This brings in the fourth principle, or the second one twice, as first the Father, then the son, copulates with the eternal feminine. In the monograph that represents the fourfold base of all cosmic manifestation, as formulated by the ancient Jewish Kabalists, this mother principle is symbolized by the two V's in the famous tetragrammaton of the Hebrew divinity, J-H-V-H (Yodh-He-

Vau-He). In its seven-letter form it became the Biblical Jehovah. The Yodh is the divine Father, the He the matter principle (or in modern terms the latent energy in the atom) and Vau is the Son (the symbol of Vau is the "nail," the linking or mediatorial power). The second He brings in the motherhood for the productivity of the Son, as in the first instance she was the spouse of the first God. She is eternally the universal Mother, her bosom bared at all times to the embrace and copulation of the forces of spirit, for the perpetual generation of the cosmos. This prodigality of her lavish favors has earned for her in the language of ancient typology the sobriquet of the "Great Harlot." She is Isis of the Egyptian system, and her function is vividly portrayed in the inscription carved at the base of her beautiful statue found at Sais:

I am the goddess Isis, the mother of all the living. No man hath lifted my robe, and the fruit I bore was Helios.

But no longer is her virginity secure; modern man has at least lifted a corner of that sacred robe and now stands shaken and terrified by the glimpse he has gained of that power of Helios, the sun, that lies germinally in the depths of her womb--the more than Jovian might locked up in the atom.

As number is one of the natural categories, the role it plays in ancient semanticism is profoundly significant. One of course represents the primal and eternal unity, and two the duality and polarity. The triad has its basic reference to the first productivity of the primal parenthood, the two parents and their child. But four is the first number that expresses the completeness of a manifestation. This would seem to say that the stability of organic life is not assured until it rests upon a fourfold base, as a table standing on its four legs. In Biblical symbolism the structure representing this truth is the Altar. It was the base on which man could burn his sacrificial offering to deity. And man's life does rest on a fourfold base even in consciousness and organization. For of the seven principles postulated by the Egyptians as the full complement of the compound of forces constituting the human organism, only the lower four are in function. The evolution and exploitation of the upper three powers lie in the future. Through the implementation of the lower four man's conscious life functions at the four levels of sensation, emotion, thought and spirituality. It is truly enough seen that the fires of man's physical and psychic life burn on these four lower levels. His range of consciousness extends only over the area of these four distinct strata.

The four is seen in its relevance to the actuality of man's situation in the cosmos if we trace the origin and evolution of manifest life by the simplest symbolic forms. At the beginning of an epoch of manifestation, life emerges from the void, which must be represented by the circle zero, the most apt symbol of empty space. Then the first appearance of organic existence must be represented by a dot in the center of the circle. Then as God first "moves on the face of the waters," the dot would move across the circle, dividing it into its upper and lower "firmaments." Plato describes this as the divine unity bifurcating in space, and it gives the first idea of the cross. The establishment of the polarity pits the two forces at right angles to each other, giving the four-armed cross. God then squares the circle and life rests on its four-sided base. But the trinity of spirit-matter-child operates in each of the four levels of consciousness, so that the ideal structure of human life is wondrously symbolized by four triangles, giving basic value and significance to the two most prominent numerical symbols in all the sacred Scriptures of the world: seven as four plus three, and twelve, as four times three. Here we have the basis of two such amazing symbolic structures as the great pyramid of Gizeh, with its four-sided base and its four triangular faces, and the zodiac, with its four elements of earth, water, air and fire in three active phases. The zodiac in particular is a mathematical structure of the most amazing semantic significations, almost fathomless in its intimations. And the pyramid (meaning etymologically "a measure of fire") is no less suggestive of the play of the fiery energies of our life in a marvelous cosmic pattern. Of utmost importance for semantic understanding is the fact that the seven resulting from the *addition* of four and three is the number of the basic *physical* structure of the universe, while twelve, the number resulting from the *multiplication* of three and four, is the *spiritual* foundation of the world.

The great and mysterious number twenty-two, called in esoteric reference the "perfect number," gains this character no doubt from the fact that it is the number-value of the circumference of a circle who diameter is seven. The number then would pertain to the outer, not the inner, aspect of being, the divine mind in action and manifestation. The Hebrew alphabet was in all probability limited to twenty-two letters because of this fundamental signification, as the alphabet is the instrument for the *expression* of the universal being. Pythagoras having proclaimed the construction of the universe on number, the Hebrew Kabalists declared that it was founded on the letters of the alphabet. But as each letter carried a numerical value, the two theories coincided.

Then, strangely enough, the basic four and seven, when multiplied, as the creation swept on from initial unity to infinite multiplicity, gives the significant twenty-eight, approximating the days of the lunar month, divided into four Sabbaths, and thirteen such months (13 times 28) giving close to the 365 days in the year, or 364 days.

If the circle zero represents the unconsciousness of non-being, the vertical line, I, represents the conscious creative spirit. It is therefore the symbol of the individual ego consciousness, as the first personal pronoun, the egoic I. As the wedding of the universal consciousness generates all existent being, the union of the I and the O, generating all things, becomes the unit number of all counting--10. Thirteen lunar months in the year, the moon always emblemizing the feminine, negative, matter-unconscious pole of being, gave to this number the character of ill-omen which it has borne. In addition to his twelve sons, Jacob had a thirteenth child, his daughter Dinah. Also there were the five days of the epact, the "extra" five beyond the 360 of the solar year, and they, too, were considered "nefast," unpropitious, with the powers of evil traditionally abroad during their period.

But another number that is featured in the sacred Scriptures with some prominence, and has stood there virtually uninterpreted for an age, is three and one-half. It is next to a certainty that its cryptic significance is only to be discerned in the context of a diagram which takes form in an attempt to draft the outline of the position and relation of the seven interior bodies composing man's total organic existence. As indicated previously, the two currents of force, spirit and matter, take their opposite ways out from the center of primordial unity, reach their opposite positions at the limit of their initial propulsion, then turn to face and battle each other under the law of the attraction of polarity. Each advances toward the other under mutual pressures, and, at the proper juncture, they meet in the middle point of distance from the outer boundaries. That is, they meet exactly on the line of middle distance between spirit and matter, so well symbolized as the horizon line between heaven and earth. On this line stood Horus, the Christ potential, the divine Child, renewing his youth by, as he says, bathing "in the divine pool beneath the two divine sycamores of heaven and earth." The total gap between spirit at the top and matter at the bottom is occupied, of course, by the seven-strata scale of organic bodies from coarse physical up to most "immaterial" spiritual. The diagram shows man, the potential Horus-Christ, standing right on the horizon line both of the zodiac and of existence.

As will be seen, the human kingdom stands exactly midway between the "heaven" of spirit and the "earth" of matter, putting man at the point of balance between the two forces of his nature, the conscious and the unconscious. As well as of the constitution of man, the diagram is an abstract representation of the organization of the cosmos, of which man, said the ancient seers, is himself a complete epitome. Man is in miniature the world in himself. By this rule he would know that his organic life structure would be a copy of the sevenfold design of the cosmos. And in a universe built on the number seven, he would know that his position would be at the halfway station, numbered three and a half.

It is exceedingly significant that in the Gospel drama, the Jesus character, who unmistakably personifies this Horus-Christ principle, distinctly tells his disciples that he is the divine ray that came down from the heights of spirit, to meet the natural man coming up from below. For he says: "Ye are from beneath; I am from above." There we have the lost truth. He might in the scenario have elaborated it a bit, as follows: You are the men of the natural order, evolving upward from planted divine seed; I am the man of the spirit, the ray from the mind of my Father. I have come half-way down from the heights of soul to meet you and share life with you, as you have come half-way up from the earth to meet and admit me into fellowship, as guest in the house you have built. It is the house of an animal, and from time to time needs cleansing, which I shall attend to. I will gradually change the order of things for you, and we can eventually live together amicably and delightfully in the marvelous house of your existence.

Clearly Tennyson had this situation in mind when he wrote:

God lent the house of the beast to the soul of the man,
And the man said: Am I your debtor?'
And God said, make it as clean as you can,
And then I will send you a better.'

If the diagram represents truly the facts of life, it establishes that man's body is the playground of the equilibrated cosmic forces of spirit and matter, the focal point where the unconscious becomes conscious, and he is therefore fully potential and to some degree actual god. He is the compound of the energies of spirit descending from on high and of atomic energy arising from the depths, united in a partnership that is zestful because it is stressful under polar tension. The tragedy of religion, of philosophy, of history is that the once well-instructed knowledge of the elements of this situation has disappeared even among the world's intelligentsia. Where is there this certified knowledge that the human individual is this Horus who stands on the "hill of the horizon," cultivating the crops of mingled wheat and tares on both sides of the boundary, a spiritual crop when he concerns himself with the realities of the order of intelligibles, and a natural crop when he sows the seeds of gross animal sensuality and any form of beastliness? And how rare is the intelligence that, for the happy issues of life, one must cultivate both these crops, must "pacify the two lands" and in the end "unite the two lands"? Pitiably oblivious is the world today of the comforting knowledge that the divine Father dispatched us here designedly that we might be born from and nourished by this prolific Mother Nature, instructed by her as his *alma mater* and reared to adult Sonship of divinity under her beneficent tutelage. Forgotten is Egypt's living intelligence that "his mother suckleth him; she giveth to him her breasts on the horizon." Still the world gazes uncomprehendingly at the image of the Madonna, of Mary, Isis, Venus, Ishtar, holding her divine infant in her arms. So far askew of true understanding has errant misconception led religious fantasy that, most largely in the Western domain of earth and history, for some twenty centuries man's natural happiness has been crushed down under the persuasion that this nature, because it is the polar antipode of the soul, must be trampled under foot and snuffed out. The warped theological infatuations that in the third century exulted in the death of Pan have darkened the sunlight of the world to this day.

CHAPTER FOURTEEN

COSMIC MIND MADE MANIFEST

If God sends out his Sons and future coadjutors in the work of his cosmic enterprise, to be born, bred and adorned *summa cum laude* with the laurels of wisdom in the lap and the school of his fond Mother Nature, the question for our intelligence arises: Whence did this infallible instructress derive the wisdom and the knowledge to serve as her children's teacher? If the right answer to this query can be divined, we shall be able to solve a score of the riddles that have perplexed the philosophical genius of the race for ages. If true knowledge is available here, enlightened thinking processes may proceed to build the house of philosophy more beautifully.

The many philosophical citations that have been marshaled in review in the study have openly expressed or implicitly intimated some aspects of fundamental truth. But to a disappointing degree, they have lacked conclusive demonstration. They so vaguely savor of the character of "pretty theory." The grand fact is that Mother Nature has the requisite elements to instruct her man-child in the essential principia of truth, because she is herself the truth, the actuality of the cosmic Father's mind. And this is so because, as wise ancients have told us, this cosmic divine mind, wishing to behold its archetypal ideas concretely pictured before it, stamped those ideas upon the face and form of the body of nature. There they stand in sculptured forms before our eyes, needing only to be properly read.

If, as our diagram represents, mind and matter both emanated primordially out of the same womb of being, they were both expressions of the same one thing, the one positive, the other negative. The same being was expressed in the one case concretely, in the other ideally. The cosmic mind had stamped its thoughts upon something that would hold their form and image long enough to be contemplated with satisfaction and a workman's artistic delight in his craftmanship. God, as Sri Aurobindo declared, was free to indulge his fancy in the delights of creative activity. If we put God under bondage of any kind, we surrender our own freedom with it, for we are ourselves, in our place and function, involved in God's doing. As this will becomes the ordinance of universal life, it is the business of us his children to catch the spirit of his creative impulse; indeed our happiness depends upon our harmonizing our whole effort with it. This necessarily involves the duty of our learning more and more clearly what the will and the spirit of the Father's Lila is. This objective can be achieved only by our associating ourselves heartily and sympathetically with the actual creative process, as it is enacted before us.

We have, then, the divine mind producing its universe according to the pattern of its wishes and its ideas. Everything generated in the grand procedure bears the stamp of its purpose and its meaning. The naive human sense does not miss the truth of this matter, nor does the most involved sophistication negate this simple judgment. But deepest thought holds that God beholds himself as in a mirror, as he gazes upon the product of his mind and hand. This conception emboldened Kant to say that only God could know the things that he had made. But his children are created in his likeness and image; are they to remain forever incapable of knowing these things also?

Here is the turn or crux of the situation that reflection has not squarely enough faced--or so it would appear. Philosophical speculation has not studiously enough followed the nuances of the problem as it shifted from God's knowledge to ours. High as the heavens are above the earth are God's thoughts above ours, the Scriptures admonish us. Nevertheless those same Scriptures enjoin upon us the necessity of gaining the wisdom and understanding essential to our basic happiness. They even exhort us to a perfection like unto the Father's. The certainly of our ability to achieve knowledge is a postulate of our sonship in God's family. "My Father worketh hitherto, and I work," says the type-figure of our filial relation to God. He has set his children down in the midst of his infinitely diversified creation and made their happiness contingent upon their mastery of its laws, modes and meanings. Hence our task definitely is to gaze upon, to live with, and to absorb into our consciousness the thoughts of the mind of God as revealed in his creation. St. Paul most beautifully says that as we behold the glory of the Lord reflected in his works, we are transformed into the same glory.

But the Western mentality has not caught the benignant glow of God's reflection in nature because errant theological doctrinism turned his gaze away from the mirror where the glory was reflected and fixed it upon a region where it was not to be found. Ideas of the "malignancy of matter," the evil power of the world, contempt for nature, all thrust their darksome shadows between the mind and nature and cut the mind off from the radiance. Religious percussions prevented the Western mind from holding the mirror up to nature; instead sought to hold it up to the void of imagined heavenly realities. If God looked to nature to catch the reflected glory of his own mind and found delight therein, it is obvious that if his children are to partake of their due measure of that same delight, they must find it in looking steadily upon the same world.

And now, with so much of the foundation laid, reflection brings us at this point to a conclusion of the most momentous significance, one based solidly on the premises both of nature and of logic. On the basis of the Scriptural doctrine that God's progeny are made in his own image and likeness, and the validation then of the thesis that both parent and offspring possess similar or at least analogous qualities and attributes, there is every legitimate ground for deducing the truth of the proposition that *the laws of nature are the operation of God's unconscious mind.*

If man is an epitome of the cosmos, if he is a seed unit of God's life, the similarity between Father and Son must prevail throughout, extend to all areas. The inference then that god has a subconscious, as well as a conscious, mind derives from man's possession of two such minds; otherwise the analogy would fail of truth. For God and man alike the law would operate according to what man has discovered of his own psychic processes. This law prescribes that what the conscious mind thinks often enough is taken over by the mechanism of the subconscious and becomes fixed as what goes by the name of habit. The effective factor here is repetition. An act of consciousness repeated often enough becomes a fixation. It, so to say, causes the first impression upon plastic substance to harden for permanency. Even a single impression of a thought upon consciousness, psychologists assure us, is never forgotten. *A fortiori,* mentation that is many times repeated or held steadily or vividly in consciousness, becomes established as a fixed operation of the unconscious. God's archetypal creative thought-forms, then, were stamped upon the plastic protyle of the universe and became the unalterable, the so-called immutable, fixations of the creative will.

Next a corollary of this startling denouement of the rationale leaps into mind with astonishing force for what it implies in the domain of all world religion. It is the realization of the fact that all subconscious operations carry on without the conscious awareness or attention of the conscious mind. This is clearly true for man; it must therefore be true also for God. The staggering conclusion that emerges from this train of logic is that God is giving no conscious attention to the running of the natural order of the universe, with the subsidiary implication that human prayers could not possibly alter the course of nature in any special way for man's behoof. The underlying presupposition of the prayer motive is that God consciously hears and answers petitions.

The alternative question whether God could or would or might or actually does hear his children's prayers and give his *conscious* attention to them and might then initiate changes in the order already fixed by habit is something for religious speculation. Proponents of the prayer cultus readily cite the Scripture's assurance that not a sparrow falls without the Father's notice. But as it appears that the Deity has arranged to take care of all essential processes and details of the salutary natural order through his fixed laws, the sparrow's fall could still be a part of his mental action, though subconsciously. Again, that God manages the natural order through his subconscious habitudes, but gives his *conscious* attention to his dealing with things in the spiritual order, might be argued. And in the theological systematism as formulated by the great Medieval Doctor, Thomas Aquinas, the position taken is that God is free to interpose his conscious mind in the working of the "immutable" natural law, and change it if such is his pleasure or whim.

In one way or another, by logic or in spite of it, the human mind, at least at the "average" level, clings to the belief that Deity hears and answers our prayers, that he can not be deaf to our needs and our pitiable cries. But as far as logic that is grounded on the obvious premises can carry the human mind, it would appear to be futile for man to appeal to God to alter, suspend, redirect his own immutable laws. When the whole question is considered in the context of a larger view, even under the most indulgent concession to the prayer motive, would it not be unconscionably presumptuous on the part of man collectively--and how infinitely more so for one or a few individuals--to beseech God to intervene, to thrust out his mighty arm and hold up, tamper with, switch or juggle with or inhibit the normal established run of his cosmic operation? Even the thought of such a thing shocks any balanced thinker's sense of fitness and proportion.

Yet the prayer cult can still justify itself on the analogy of the God-Mind with the mental nature of man. For if it is possible for a human to bring the power of his conscious mind, will and resolution to change a long-fixated habit, certainly God could not be denied the same power. The pious posture of the religious mind will never endorse the view that God has become a helpless prisoner of his own laws. If he made those laws, and is omnipotent, surely he can change them, is the attitude of religion. But again the positivist can advance the riposte that the present cosmic order is the one God *did* ordain as the expression of his mind and will, and it is so vast and so inextricably interwoven in all its stupendous mechanism that the idea of his being entreated to change a single item or detail at the plea of one of his prodigious family of mortals is preposterous beyond all other crazy hallucinations that have in all ages obsessed the religious mind. Then, too, how can our minds conceive of any power of consciousness that could give careful consideration to millions of petitions that, as world religion stands, are being addressed to it at virtually every moment of time? If the God-mind is not supposed to take care justly of all phases of the operation of his cosmic plans by the instrumentality of his subconscious habitudes and ordinances, then, on the supposition that he does consciously hear and answer prayers, it is obvious that this service to his children would consume *all his time,* leaving him no time for other use of his conscious mind. Unless there is in the case some absolute transcendence that overrides and nullifies all that the word "logic" means for mankind, it is obvious that the prayer addiction runs out into dead ends of the most incredible absurdity and illogicality at every turn. Yet despite all this, it is not an infatuation for the human mind to trust that God is in full charge of his universal order, and that justice rules the order. A sane and considerate philosophical attitude of an intelligent mind, it would seem, would be that it is impertinent on our part to presume to remind God of his obligations.

Had not ancient arcane philosophy been forgotten, occult wisdom would have obviated the predicaments involved in the above discussion. The sagacious Greek esotericism declared that "the gods distribute divinity," allotting to each mortal his due share. The enlightening solution to all the questions posed is found in the knowledge that God has implanted a unit portion of his divine consciousness in the heart and soul of every son of man, itself competent to take care of all the individual's problems. Why bother the central intelligence of the universe with a person's petty interests and woes, when an accredited agent of that intelligence is already and unfailingly at hand for all needed help? The infinite tragedy of most religion has been that distorted theological conceptions have almost entirely turned the focus of human attention away from the presence of the agent at his post in the consciousness of every mortal and directed it out into the vacancies of an egregious hallucination. The tragedy here springs from the sad fact that for the mortal to pray to the imagined head of the cosmos, while neglecting to deal with the agent duly commissioned to handle all exigencies, breeds neurotic instability, even psychotic derangement, permitting the life to grope helplessly in darkness and confusion. The psychologist Jung has certified these disastrous effects of religious misconceptions.

As has been hinted at herein before, religion has regarded the natural order as at enmity with spiritual evolution. Hence its culture of miracle, its demand on God that he obviate the inexorability of nature and set aside his laws for our benefit. But true religion and undefiled should all along have had the wisdom to realize that infinitely more precious to man than any breach of nature for special blessings is the complete dependability he can put upon natural law. Pietism has even carried minds all the way to the delusion that holiness and surrender to God's will can lift the righteous devotee above the reach of the natural law, granting him complete absolution from the order of life under nature and absolute freedom to revel in the "liberty of the Sons of God." But this is a fatuity that would prove disastrous, since it would disrupt the harmonious order of human life and lead directly to the chaotic clash and confusion of individual wills disturbing the balance of things. Human wills do clash at all times, it can be argued; but the natural order tends always to readjust the forces and reestablish balance. If the natural law could be superseded by individual wills, there would be chaos indeed. If the harmonious order of the world were to be rendered subject to interference by individual piety, the resulting chaos would soon drive us back to letting nature take its own course. If all individual prayers were answered, the world would be a madhouse. An observation of Hegel's is of great import here. As he considers all nature as the manifestation of the presence, power and purposes of the divine mind, he says that the divine action in the world is the restoration and expression of the oneness of life, uniting in one association nature, man and God. Hence, he says, "miracle is the supreme disservice." For miracle would break into and disrupt this beneficent relationship.

When thought can be profound enough, it is seen that nearly all questions of epistemology, psychology, indeed of our life as a whole, hinge upon what is the reality behind the common concept of the human *soul*. The ancient mind postulated the existence of an entity or distinctive unit of conscious being which comprehended in itself the essence, the power and the reality of our existence. The modern mind is by no means certain of this postulation, by tradition concedes its existence on the religious side of common thought, but is quite skeptical of it on the side of science. On the basis of the predicated sevenfold physical-psychic-spiritual constitution of man, the ancients could deal with such an entity in a mental schematism that fitted it harmoniously into its place in the seven. As suggested by our diagram, it was a unit of sublimated material composition, that stood at the midpoint of the seven, and became the instrument of egoic consciousness because it equilibrated in itself the forces of both matter and spirit. Only under such conditions could consciousness become objectified to itself.

Working under the terms of this situation, the deep-prying ancient intelligence was able to arrive at many determinations regarding the facts of psychic life to which the modern mind, laboring without a foundation of this sort, has no clues. Such questions as the *tabula rasa,* innate ideas, a preestablished harmony between mind and the world and in fact all *a priori* postulations can be seen to have rational status and explanation under the terms of the ancient arcana of knowledge. If one does not know what the soul is, or whether it is a fresh creation of life at the birth of the present personality, or whether it can exist beyond the demise of the body, one lacks grounds for understanding and premises for thought. If, on the other hand, one accepts the claimed knowledge of the ancient savants and finds that the conclusions to which, on those premises, logic leads the mind comport harmoniously with the living experience of the soul in the world, one at least has in hand a systematism that consistently withstands the pragmatic test. If one has found a schematism that successfully meets the pragmatic test, it is generally considered determinative. We can hardly ask more of any theory than the "practical" demonstration that it "works." And if it works, it must be presumed to have established its validity. Any more finally authoritative criterion that might be demanded would entail an ultimate determination of the terms "it works," and "validity" themselves. This would take us into a regression so deep that all possible question of what constitutes "knowledge" would be well-nigh indeterminable.

If, then, we are discovering that there was extant in what we still regard as "ancient" times of a few thousand years ago a comprehensive system of psycho-spiritual arcana and esoteric knowledge that has in our day at least won the distinction of being acclaimed as the "perennial philosophy," and is definitely seen to have been the primary source of our Scriptures and our most widely accepted religio-philosophical traditions, we are at least challenged to see if the principia of that systematism do not yield to investigation answers and solutions of basic problems more rationally acceptable than those achievable on the grounds of either conventional orthodoxies in religion or the speculations of philosophy or the current predications of science. And in this investigation we are morally challenged to see if, in the context of the great organic structuralism envisaged by the arcane philosophy, the existence and reality of the soul does not receive a plausibility, if not a positive authentication, that would give it a validation in the face of modern scientific skepticism.

The arcana of old embraced a purported knowledge of the cosmos and a bold outline of its history. As to man, it affirmed that he was truly the Son of God, made in God's image and destined to grow into the likeness of his Father. He is a miniature copy of the cosmos all in himself. That unit fragment of his Father's life that constituted him what he is, is his soul. God being imperishable and eternal, this Son-soul must be likewise indestructible. But, being a Son, this entity must be generated *ab initio* by the Father, and sent out into the conditions of existence in which its growth could most propitiously take place. This required its involvement in organic material bodies, its incarnation, its pilgrimage through the cycles of embodiment in all forms and conditions of existence in the gamut of the construction of material universes. It was required to traverse the whole distance from unconscious inertia of matter up to the highest pinnacle of cosmic consciousness. And since the fundamental law of all manifested existence was the methodology of alternate cycles of life and death, or repetition of smaller cycles to compose larger ones, souls were destined to undergo their pilgrimage through the grades of matter in a series of cyclical embodiments alternating with release and disembodiment, in a virtually endless progression. If the total cosmos of Brahm sets the rhythm of eternal out-breathing and inhalation, man in his image must advance by rhythmic succession of lives and "deaths." The idea of one life and death of soul in matter becomes thus an unconscionable fatuity. The law of all life is the "eternal renewal."

The soul-character in the Egyptian *Book of the Dead* exults in the fact that he has come to earth to renew himself by bathing in the pool beneath the two divine sycamores of heaven and earth. "I die and I am born again and I renew myself and I grow young each day." "I am eternity and everlastingness, and I proceed to the confines of heaven." "I am yesterday, today and tomorrow; I am he that was, that is, and that is to be." "All things are in my hand."

Who would not concede that the sweeping majesty, the grand sublimity of such conceptions sink into comparative ignominy and paltry insignificance the barren idea that the soul has a fleeting tenancy of one earthy body and passes into non-existence with that body's dissolution? Under such terms soul could not be said to have a history; or such a history would be meaningless. So the archaic wisdom postulated for souls a history, and in the light of that history, all questions relative to its life and nature could find intelligible and rational answers.

If it was a young god on a pilgrimage through the stages of evolution to highest divinity, it stood at any given moment of its journey at a point where its present status would be the resultant of all the elements of its past experience. As Christian in *Pilgrim's Progress* bore on his back the packet of his weakness and sins, the young deity bore in and on his soul the "karma" of his past. Through weal or woe, this burden of his lot could be reduced and lightened as he, life by life, learned, obeyed and mastered the laws of righteousness and the principles of truth. From wild flinging of his physical energies about in sensuality in the early stages of his progression, he came to dominate these strong forces by the sober control of reason and increasing joy in the delights of rational understanding, as the power and genius of divinity flashed into expression.

Lacking scientific grounds and therefore rational certitude as to the existence of souls as imperishable entities, modern philosophy prolongs its tenancy of the anomalous position of postulating progression for the creature man without either positive or rational assurance of continuity of the entity that progresses. This is its weakness, and it spells futility and dubiety for speculation until it is corrected. How can life progress if the organic beings that carry its values and gains do not themselves persist in perpetuity? Modern concept of progress rests almost entirely on the thesis that values and gains are preserved and enlarged by their transmission from one generation to the next in a chain. The following generation inherits the accruements won by the present one. But this predicates that the entities that win the higher values do not hold them, or carry them on as *their* permanent possession; each generation labors under the heavy stresses and pressures of polarity, wins some precarious advance, only to see its grasp on the hard-won treasure wrenched loose by death. The theorization fails on two distinct counts to accredit itself to reason: cosmic injustice is suggested, yes, specifically implied, by the reflection that neither is the egoic unit of life that struggles to expand the stream and the glory of existence in his tiny cycle rewarded even to the point of being permitted to retain and enjoy the fruits of its effort, nor has the successor to whom it transmits its accrued blessedness and advantage earned this benison through its own exertions. The first worker in the vineyard is robbed of what he justly earned; his successor inherits and enjoys what he has not himself earned, but the fruits of another's stressful labors.

Ancient "occult" science of the soul lifted the mind clear of the fogs and dialectical blankness of this thought predicament by positing, on both natural and rational grounds, the perpetual existence of the egoic unit of consciousness that advanced through the scale of graduated levels of being from lowest to highest and carried all its gains with it. Life itself could make no advance or retain its gains if the units that through rough experience added the gains could not hold them. Philosophy and religion must struggle on in irremediable poverty of rationality as long as they can not fill the vast dialectical gap and vacuum left in their systems by want of a fully rational science that gives both existence and continuity to the soul. If religion comes forward with its pitiable bleating cry that there is a soul and that it carries the values on in a realm of wholly spiritual existence for all eternity, to that rash gesture of despair reason replies that then the human mind has no possible resource that enables it to rationalize one incarnation of soul in earthly body. On the theory of continuity of soul and its progressive advance through successive swings between polarity with matter and rest and recuperation in a return to its primal unity, human life gains rationality and meaning leading on to a transcendent glory as the goal of divinity is neared.

Since, then, the soul is known to be this invincible hero advancing upward through the grades of evolution's curriculum, all fundamental queries of philosophy receive at least elementary answers. If his potential of an eventual godlike order of consciousness was an unwritten slate at the start, each life in embodiment inscribed the record of its experience upon it. Life after life added its scribble, but at any time in the progression accrued insights and wisdom could erase the old scribble and writer a clearer and more legible diary. If the entity started out with innate ideas, they were but potential until experience imprinted them boldly on consciousness. They were innate only in the sense that at each succeeding incarnation they were there subconsciously as the remembered impressions brought over from the past. If there was an established harmony between the soul's mental life and the perceived order of nature, it had been built up by deeper and deeper reflection over many lives. And if any elements of rationality, any categories of thought, could be described as "*a priori*," it could be only in the sense that they were from the beginning there potentially. They were there from the outset seminally. Once experience divulged them to consciousness, they became *a posteriori*.

The postulation of the soul's real existence and continuity puts the needed substantial pillars under the porticos of the temple of philosophy, not to add that it both strengthens and beautifies the temple of human life itself. Symmetry, proportion, balance, the rudiments of beauty and the happiness that accrues from the mind's sense of the fitness of things, all embellish the daily run of human life by their gracious influence. If the present life is understood to be the current episode in the soul's peregrination up the ladder of continuous progression to a glorious goal, the science of psychology becomes the charter of prospective, if not presently actualized, happiness. And a philosophy that fills the yawning abysses left by unintelligent faith and unrationalized hope with a reasonable certitude as to rewards of obedience to known laws will tend to lift the hum-drummery as well as the anguish of life up to the plane of real beatitude.

The science of soul progression could of course stand on valid grounds only if it be found true that the entity called soul possessed the capability of registering and retaining forever the impression of all its experiences consciously imprinted upon its constituent essence. If the soul could not remember its experiences, it could neither make nor hold any gains. Only by comparison of present experience with past can we make a choice for the better. Without memory life would have no pedagogical power. It could not educate us.

The fact, then, that the subconscious mind never forgets an impression is an item of the utmost value for knowledge. It is the guarantee that soul is the ultimate and essential substance of our being, underlying and pervading the whole area of life. While it is permissible to say that we are the body and have a soul, it is doubtless more accurate to say that we are the soul and it has or wears a body. If the body is perennial, it is also true to say that soul dons and doffs bodies as it would a garment. Science is hedging close to the concept that ultimate being itself is mind; and back of mind, it is averred, is soul; and back of soul is spirit. We have the testimony of our revered Scriptures that God, the total, is spirit. Modern science has made us acquainted with the existence of matter in an endless variety of forms, many of which are so tenuous, volatile and ethereal that it is inappropriate to apply to them the term material at all. We now face the reality of such terms as "spiritual." We find the atom composed of many interior bodies of sublimated matter; no longer dare we scorn as puerile superstition old Egypt's asseveration of the human being's constitution of seven bodies.

Deeper reflection on the question of Leibnitz' "preestablished harmony" may take us into the deepest heart of the major thesis of this work, namely the fundamental relation of the three elements, God's mind, man's mind and the mind of nature. On the premises that nature is God's mind objectified in matter, and that man's mind is a seed-atom or unit of God's mind and therefore potentially identical with it, the logical conclusion is incontrovertible that all three minds are akin. On the same grounds it is equally determinable that there is but one Mind in and behind the universe. If we insist upon segregating it into three minds, it is simply that it has presented itself to us under three aspects or manifestations, due to its power to split itself polarity-wise into subjective and objective aspects and to generate seeds of its own nature for the infinite dissemination of its consciousness throughout its objective manifestation. Having effected its own objectification in nature and having generated its infinite progeny of seed-sons, and having set these seed-units of its own being down in the midst of its material objectification, the situation simply requires that the sons of God, standing face to face with God's objectified thought, turn their own thought potential into the realization of its essential identity with that of the Father expressed in nature. As it has been expressed epigrammatically, man is confronted with the necessity of reading God's thoughts after him. And the only book from which he can read them is the open book of nature. Mysticism has egregiously assumed that somehow our minds can galvanize themselves into a vibrational rapport with God's mind and synchronize the activities of the greater with those of the lesser, so to say, in the thin air of pure ideation without the intermediary offices of any objective representations of the divine thought. This presupposes that our minds can "tune in" with the radiations of God's thoughts and pick them up in midair, thus bringing them within the range of our consciousness. This is what mystical religion has ever based its claims upon, a telepathic communion of our minds with the mind of God. It is the basis of most Hindu religionism. Given a sufficiently intensive effort, it is believed that man can sink his consciousness into that of God and become one with God. This is supposed to be the function of the much-extolled "intuition," the capability of which the mystical philosophy always denies to intellect. Our refutation of that claim has already been succinctly outlined.

But how does this "tuning in" theory stand when one scrutinizes it "scientifically"? Our veridical knowledge of the science of vibrations, which seem to be the undersupport of all existences, is quite thorough. We know definitely of the vibrational scale spanning the gamut from a few hundred oscillations a second to incalculable frequencies. Every creature at its station in the order has the capability of responding to its own limited range, whatever it may be. Above and beyond that range it cannot go. The idea, then, that the mind of man, with its specific span of capability of response, can synchronize with the mind of God at its level and rate, must be seen as the grossest misconception. And this is the stupendous possibility that mystical infatuation postulates.

But a conception that is quite scientific and legitimate puts the matter in more acceptable form. If the total of God's creation is the concretion of vibrational forces projected by the Father, why are not all rates and frequencies equally eligible to the divine rating? Are lower frequencies to be put in one category and the higher ones in another? Even if it be that the lower ones give us matter and the higher ones spirit, is it legitimate for us to attribute different *moral* values to the differential? If it be the bent of our minds to attribute evil to material rates and good to spiritual rates, let it at least be understood that this differentiation is but a whimsy of our minds. Our experience with the two rates may justify our figment of thought and feeling. But it can not exist intrinsically in the actual order.

CHAPTER FIFTEEN

UNDERSTANDING THE MIND OF GOD

An earlier elaboration placed such emphasis on the significance of the statement of the Upanishads of India that the true reading of God's thought is to be achieved only by "sharp and subtle intellect" as to make this fact almost the central axis of our work. It is now necessary to explore the potentialities of this thesis if we are to pierce to the heart of the relation between the human mind and nature. If it is the evolutionary assignment of man by his creator to read the creative archetypes as exhibited in nature, and the task demands the utmost keenness and subtlety of which our minds are capable, the nub of the discussion centers upon this crucial matter of the quality of mind that is requisite to yield us the truth. It has previously been asserted that, from Philo down to the present, efforts in the right direction to establish the requisite procedures have failed for want of the special astuteness of mind demanded for the task. The method was never illustrated and exemplified or demonstrated with sufficient completeness to carry conviction of its absolute soundness. The possibility of supplying that lack must now be more profoundly investigated.

In the preceding chapter, the claims of mystical religion for a direct telepathic rapport between man and God were treated negatively. Then, since man is incapable of reading God's mind by this form of immediate intuition, the technique by which this great feat is to be accomplished must be the next theme of discussion. How, in fine, is the requisite sharpness and subtlety to be acquired for the task?

While mysticism mistakenly seeks this quality of consciousness in a veritable entrancement of the mind, the highest genius in the realms of philosophy and psychology has indicated a more rational and eligible technique requiring only the competent refinement of normal mental faculty and using the tools provided by nature for the purpose. The gap between God's mind and man's being directly unbridgeable, the reapproachment between the two minds must be engineered by the intermediary office of a medium instrumentality, a visible something that will confront man's feebler intellect with a sensual representation of the invisible divine thought. This is the symbol. Outside of the mystical area of religion and philosophy, all great thinkers have recognized the indispensable function of the symbol. It is the illustrator, the expositor, the monitor mutely nudging the mind toward understanding. If it can not present a clear picture of a noumenal concept, it builds up at least a shadow-form of the actuality. I carry or suggest clues, it says to mind, which, with the exercise of a little agility, may lead you to the mystery. I belong to, am part of, that real world which is the condensation of the thought of our common creator, and I therefore represent some nuance, phase or aspect of that reality. I represent some portion of the body of truth, and can therefore be to you a guide and revelator. It can not be that the divine author has created a false or a meaningless universe. I am a *veritatis verbum,* a word in the dictionary of truth. My adumbration may appear to be only mute dumb-show; not so, my message glows luminously for the sprightly mind.

Many deep thinkers have penetrated to the inner core of this consummate art of reading God's mind as reflected in nature, and some have come close to divining the mental technique requisite for successful legibility. The almost universal consensus of thought on the subject establishes the fundamental method as that of analogy. What is demanded is a quick and lively sense that discerns similarities and correspondences between the symbol and its noumenal counterpart. And most philosophers and psychologists agree that this is the special work of the *imagination;* and it would not misstate their meaning if one said, the special work of the *poetic* imagination.

It is Santayana who has dealt with this approach with much particularity. Speaking of three great ages of philosophy, he asks:

> *Can it be by accident that the most adequate and probably the most lasting exposition of these three schools of philosophy have been made by poets? Are poets at heart in search of philosophy? Or is philosophy in the end nothing but poetry? Let us consider the situation.*

> *Here I think we have the solution of our doubt. The reasonings and investigations of philosophy are arduous, and if poetry is to be linked with them, it can be artificial only and with a bad grace. But the vision of philosophy is sublime and the order it reveals in the world is something beautiful, tragic, sympathetic to the mind, and just what every poet is trying to do.*

Theoria, he says, is a steady contemplation of all things in their order and worth. "Such contemplation is imaginative." It is unattainable by any one who has not enlarged his mind and chastened his heart. In attaining it, a philosopher is for the moment a poet, and a poet who has focused his passionate imagination on the order of all things, seeing the relevance of single things in the light of the whole, is for the moment a philosopher. If there is a difference, it is that philosophy is laboriously reasoned, heavy; poetry is a freer, lighter flow, "winged, flashing, inspired." "A quicker eye, a more synthetic imagination, might grasp a larger subject with the same ease."

He is never so much a poet as when in a single cry he summons all that has affinity to him in the universe and salutes his ultimate destiny. The light of poetry is to speak the language of the gods.

But poetry can not be spread upon things like butter; it must play upon them like light and be the medium through which we see them.

Certainly there is little to distinguish the philosopher and the poet save the tenor of their feelings and mood and the form of their expression, if they deal with the same problems of thought and seek answers to the same questions. A philosopher could be as passionate as a poet and the poet as soundly dialectical as the philosopher. The requirement in both for the attainment of visions of truth and beauty is the lively imagination, the "quick eye" for glimpses and flashes of sublime meaning and the light that shines when truth is discerned. All this matches the "sharp and subtle intellect" of the Upanishads.

In thus extolling the function of the poetic imagination as the instrument of insight it still can be that we have only one-half of the story. We have here again the dichotomy and the antithesis of thought and feeling. Commonly in philosophy thought, the intellect, is supposed to predominate; whereas in poetry it is feeling that gives wings to inspiration and fires the imagination. But feeling is ever less able to guarantee truth than is intellect, or at least to adduce the evidences of truth. And imagination can offer even less reliable credentials for truth. It has all of heaven and earth to roam through and can dilate on things seen and unseen. It can accept heaven and earth as seen, or it can substitute another world of its own creation. Unless restricted by the intellect, it is irresponsible, footloose and fancy-free. Its vagrancy can take it anywhere and cause it to see anything. It is obviously no safe guide. It can be as wrong as right, as false as true.

If, then, it is to be the handmaid of philosophy in the discovery of truth, its fine service is rendered in its power to goad and stimulate the intellect, to sharpen and subtilize its operation, to lift it out of its ponderosity into an exhilaration that has the extraordinary effect of intensifying the clarity of the mind's vision and the power of its concentration. This is what Santayana means in saying that poetry must play on things like the flashing of a light. It has the happy effect of rendering the intellect more mercurial, more mobile, both more swift and more sure in the lightning movement of its thought. It is a truism that strong feeling intensifies the power of thought. Basically that is all that is here under review, but it is an important element in the unfoldment of the general theme of the essay. It is supreme adeptness in discerning the subtleties of analogy.

The summary truth that emerges out of this item of reflection is the extremely significant recognition that all use of the imagination, whether set aflame by poetic afflations or used normally to recover things in the memory, must be held in close relation to the realities of the living world. If it is not to lose itself in the heavens of fantasy, it must keep its sight on guidepoints on the ground. It dare not stray at random out of orbit into empty and meaningless space. It can render no aid in the discovery of truth if it cuts itself off from its base in actuality. Its consummate function is not to picture things that have no existence, to create fantastic worlds either grotesque or marvelous, but to help the mind discern the unapparent truth and reality of the world that is. As the mind can see more than the eye, the work of the imagination is to make keen this inner vision.

It is of course the faculty that enables the mind to induce general principia from the observation of actual phenomena, or to discern universals from particulars. In the turbulent flux of things and events, it discerns the outline of a pattern, the operation of a law. This process Aristotle called *epagoge,* best translated as "induction." It detects uniformity of process amid the run of variables, and thus reifies "principle." The Greek word for this is *arche,* and its plural is *archai,* the name Plato gave to the primary creative ideas of the cosmic mind. In summation of this whole analysis, Jung maintains that these archetypal ideas exist in the universal unconscious and that the human mind can penetrate to their noumenal meaning through the mediumship of symbols, and these are extant in the realm of nature. And Aristotle is explicit in stating how these *archai* are to be beheld. They do not yield their import to casual observation; they require the power of a sort of "second sight," a light that the physical eye can not give. They are to be apprehended by *nous,* the word back of all Greek philosophy--*mind.* They are discerned by the eye of intellect. Plato considered them the substance and the "forms" of ultimate reality, only dimly, faintly adumbrated by the things on earth. They darkly remind the soul on earth of its memory of them in the supernal preexistence.

Whether in their immaterial noumenal form in the divine mind or in their material objectification on earth, Kant asserted that we can not know them in their reality. But it is time some one asked the question: Why not? Either man has the faculty to know things or he does not. And of things to be known, would he be more likely to know unreal things than real ones? If he is constitutionally incapable of knowing realities, he stands externally condemned to live in deception and blindness. The cecity is not in the things as unknowables;

there they are, they stand naked before us. If there is ignorance of their true nature, it inheres in the limited degree of the exploitation of our divine genius for knowing. As our knowing capability is sharpened and brightened, our knowledge of things becomes more complete and more luminous. And the ultimate guarantee that we can and shall know these realities is implicit in the fact that this knowing faculty of ours is of the same order as the creative mind that forged them in the furnace of its primordial thought. If the mind of the Father comprehended these its productions, it is rational to assume that the mind of the Son will in its maturity comprehend them likewise. It is our prerogative to view the world with at least a rudimentary stage of the same vision which conceived them in the first instance. It seems obvious that God has immersed our life in the milieu of these realities so that our child-minds could not miss growing into a knowledge of these basic realities of being. To impart to us eventually the power of envisioning his spacious creation with something of the thrill of Lila that he experienced in the formative effort, he set the *archai* in objective form over against the consciousness of his progeny, with the inevitable certitude that they would with maturity sense the kinship and finally the identity of the objective world with the order of their developed consciousness.

Students of philosophy are aware that Aristotle went a certain distance in modifying Plato's ideas in the direction of granting more reality to the *archai* as objectified on earth. Is it possible that he would have been warranted in taking another seven-league step away from Plato's position and landing in a realization that would have revealed that his great tutor's theorization was in fact the exact reversal of the truth of the matter? The reversal would postulate that, contrary to Plato's theory, the supernal world of noumena, so far from being the locale where the infant Sons of the Father beheld with delight and comprehension the *archai* of truth and beauty, was on the contrary just the place where they could *not* envisage their reality and their meaning, since mind can become conscious of real being only when polarized with matter. Since these conditions could not be provided in purely noumenal-spiritual heavens, the younglings of divinity had perforce to be sent out into a world where they could find equilibration with matter and undergo the stress of polarity.

It is a fact little known that the Christian creed contains this item of ancient sapience. It is found in three words, in the statement that the second Person of the Trinity, God's only-begotten Son, was "begotten, not created." Clues from ancient Egypt's store of wisdom, where it is said that Horus-Christ was conceived by one mother, Isis, and given birth by another, Nephthys, doubling his motherhood, indicate that the Christian phrase might more clearly be put "conceived (but) not born." Even the Christian version has the two stages of the process separately stated, as it has featured both the "immaculate conception"

Understanding the Mind of God 159

and the "virgin birth." Must birth not always be preceded by conception? And the fact of colossal significance here is that conception, in the cosmic and theological sense, is an act of mind, whereas birth is physical. Hindu systematism called the progeny of Brahm the Manasaputras, the "mind-born," or begotten in mind, as the Egyptian phrase has it. Egyptian sagacity also states that Horus was conceived in heaven, but born on earth. This puts the dual motherhood in its most obvious form, as one of the simplest of truths. Any project carried out by man is conceived in mind then executed in matter. Any child is conceived by the father and given birth by the mother, and in theology fatherhood stands for spirit-mind. The fatherhood of the universe is the God-mind, the motherhood with which it copulates is matter. The almost stunning revelation of truth here is indeed a correction and reversal of Plato's theorization, for these divine soul-entities who, he affirms, had basked ecstatically in the joys of celestial contemplation of the *archai* in heaven, had not yet been born; they had only been conceived there. To be born, they had to be sent to earth. Why? Because a birth has to be where the mother is! "Our Father which art in heaven;" "Mother Earth." Only on earth can souls conceived by the divine mind achieve birth into the kingdom of self-conscious and immortal being. "The tunnels of earth have given me birth," cries the soul in the Egyptian *Ritual*. And Mother Earth is Mother Nature.

If the many statements of eminent philosophers assembled herein have given overwhelming endorsement of nature's educational power, the stage is set now for the citation of one more that should cap the pyramid with a golden apex, the reflected light from which should almost blind our intellectual vision with its dazzling brilliance. As India has furnished us with the shibboleth expressing our central theme--the sharp and subtle intellect--so it is Indian intelligence that supplies us with this other climactic pronouncement. The expression comes from the pen of that eminent Hindu thinker, who, if he gave his splendid powers of mind to the pursuit of "divine philosophy," did not permit it to abstract him from the world of practical and political interests of his native land. For he sits now at the head of the government of the second most populous nation on earth, India's most distinguished sage and philosopher, President Servipali Radhakrishnan. The substance of the golden truth he presents to us is found in the *Upanishads,* those depth-probings of the Hindu soul into the innermost core of conscious being, as commentaries on the Vedas. In his monumental work on Indian philosophy, he expatiates on a discourse between the gods Indra and Prajapati. Based on the gods' statements, he reminds his readers that in the attainment of the assumed consummate peak of blessed release in a dreamless occlusion of consciousness in the Nirvanic state, "there is no self at all." Indra, he says, has the forthrightness to declare that the soul does not exist when it has no conscious content. "It is indeed destroyed." The exaltation that is conceived and expected to bathe it in the ecstasies of *samadhi* and *moksha* ends by obliterating it. "This," he pauses to warn before pronouncing his fateful formulary of the staggering truth, "has an important lesson which is again and again forgotten in Indian thought." Then he pens the eleven words that should irradiate the whole world's darkened religious consciousness with the benignant light of a new day of intelligence: "TO DENY THE LIFE WITHOUT IS TO DESTROY THE GOD WITHIN."'

It can be doubted whether any single utterance in all the realm of religious philosophy carries a more dynamic power to awaken human intelligence to the realization of man's opportunity to push his evolution Godward in the lifespan on earth. Only to be omitted to our loss are the sentences that elaborate the significance of the fateful pronouncement.

Those who think that we reach the highest point attainable in pure subjectivity must turn to the dialogue of Indra and Prajapati. The condition freed from the limits imposed upon the organism from time and space, from the existence of objects, is simply annihilation, according to Indra. This contentless Ego, this abstract Cogito of Descartes, this formal unity of Kant, this objectless subject supposed to stand behind, unrelated to all empirical consciousness, is an impossibility. Philosophical reflection, as well as psychological analysis, leads to this result. Prajapati shows that the whole world is one process of self-realization of the Absolute thought.'

Since philosophers have debated the matter for some thousands of years, we may listen a moment to the debate of two gods with profit. Prajapati had argued that "when the sun is set, when the moon is set, when the fire is put out, the self alone has light." This carries the usual implication that the pure self will shine in all its divine serenity the brighter for the removal of the veil of the lower consciousness.

But Indra was too much of a psychologist for Prajapati. He felt that this self, freed from all bodily experience, from the shapeless mass of dreams, etc., this objectless self is a barren fiction. If the self is not what it knows, feels and reacts upon, if it is divorced from it and thus emptied of its contents, what remains? "Nothing," said Indra. To be free from everything is to be nothing.

Again and again Radhakrishnan seeks to steady Indian religious thought by the reminder that the *Upanishads* do not convey the message of making of the deepest self an abstract nothingness. It is potentially the fullest reality, the completest consciousness, and not a mere negative calm, untroubled by any unrest and unpolluted by any blot or blemish. By a positive attitude and method it has to find its true selfhood in the life and being of all.

A necessary corollary of this affirmation of the living reality and value of every phase of the soul's mundane experience would be the importance of soul's contact with nature. Where could we have encountered in all literature a more inexpugnable confirmation of our central theme than this statement of Radhakrishnan's?

The human self can not think, conquer and love nature, were it unthinkable, unconquerable and unlovable. Nature . . . exists for man . . . nature summons us to the spiritual reality of life and answers the needs of the soul. It is formed, vitalized and directed by the spirit.

Only perhaps in the light of the regained significance of such a clarion reminder of warped religious aberrancies regarding the evil of life in the world, the sinful nature of the fleshly appetencies, and the whole slanderous derogation of matter, can we begin to see the pressing need of a renaissance of reverence for nature. It were a grievous pity and shame on our ignorance, that in our pious yearning for the ecstasies of our Father Spirit we think we have to berate, vilify and besmirch the nurturing embraces of our benignent Mother Nature. It augurs happily for the future of the world that this rebuke to our disparagement of nature comes to us from, of all countries, the President of India! "To deny the life without is to destroy the god within!" Only perhaps through a complete about-face on the part of world religious thought, a drastic revolution in the house of philosophy, a turning of direction from the heaven of mystical allurement back to the beneficence of our life with nature, may mankind be able to gain a steadier footing on earth.

This sweeping assertion that denial of the world without would kill the soul is a realization that would never occur spontaneously to naive thinking or the common mentality, but can only be discerned by abstruse dialectic. It is, however, the natural and direct outcome of principles of truth generally recognized. No one denies that the development of a skill, art, genius, aptitude or function depends upon effort and exercise. A capability, even an organ not sufficiently exercised tends to atrophy. From the start life gives us nothing but potentiality. It never hands us matured and full-grown products. All things would remain in latency unless evoked out of it by the tensions of polarity, when the unity of being squares away and faces itself in duality. And the simple truth here is that the potentiality that is destined to evolve into spiritual consciousness could not so evolve unless it faced the reality of something to exercise its untried powers upon. This foil to its capability, this challenge to its self-exertion, is the "life without" and the world of nature. It reduces to the simple proposition that if latent capacities are to develop into active powers by exercise, they must have something to exercise upon. If consciousness is to rise to the dignity and glory of godlike knowledge and a beatific blissfulness, it must traverse the path of mastery of the actual forces of the universe of which it is a part and product. Says Santayana most pertinently:

Truth depends upon facts for its perspective, since facts select truths and decide which truths shall be mere possibilities and which shall be the eternal forms of actual things. The dialectical world would be a trackless desert if the existent world had no arbitrary constitution. Living dialectic comes to clarify existence; it turns into meanings the actual forms of things by reflecting upon them.

And he adds that were dialectic clearer or physics deeper than it commonly is, the points of instructive contact between mind and nature would be greatly multiplied. We fail in works of imagination, he says, when we swing too far out to what is fantastic and without roots in the world. A free mind and a creative imagination rejoice at the harmonies they can find between man and nature. Were it not for what we know of the outer world and of our place in it, we should be incapable of attaching any meaning to subjectivity. The flow of things in nature would pass by us and mean nothing to us. So it is our knowledge of physics and our reliance upon the world's material coherence and stability that marks our awakening to consciousness and that constitutes our discovery that we exist as minds. Certainly it is our confrontation by the things and the life of the world in which we have to fend for our very physical existence that prods us to perceiving, thinking and eventually knowing. Says the philosopher:

If we consider critically our motives and our ideals, we should find them springing from and directed upon a natural life and its functions, and not at all on disembodied and timeless ecstasies.

This vision of the dissociation of religion from its prime reference to life transcendent and its closer relation to the mundane area is fraught with crucial issues for all the future of mankind. In these elucidations, particularly of Radhakrishnan and Santayana--but echoed by others--there are seen to be implications and corollaries which would appear to be nothing less than epochal and drastically revolutionary for religion universally. As has been sufficiently emphasized already, religion has to a degree of extreme preponderance sought to magnify the predicated values of the spiritual life to the disparagement of the physical, the heavenly life rather than the earthly, glorifying the one, disdaining if not vilifying the other. It has been primarily the cult of otherworldliness, holding the world's interests at minimum valuation.

This is not entirely abnormal and is seen as reaction from and compensation for the engrossment of world life--particularly in the West--in the interests of the sensual and the material. It could even be that the trend toward higher spiritual development might be intensified to actual advantage, if the proper balance with the bodily life could be maintained.

But this is where the dereliction lies; the balance has been inordinately overweighted on the side of heaven and spirit. And, as the idealists would be shocked to be told, the overbalance on the side of spirit, so from advancing the efflorescence of the spiritual nature, has been disastrous to it. For if it is the even balance between the two forces of the polarity that evokes latent potential, any undue disturbance of the equilibration will hurtfully affect the outcome. History reveals the corruption and the evil of this disequilibration. It is indicated, then, that the shifting of the focus of the effort at spiritualization from the mystical to the physical level--as also to the intellectual--would tend to restore the inequable balance and thus give free flow to the forces of the higher consciousness, which might then be thought of as emerging upward out of the depths rather than downflowing from above. If the physico-material energies of the motherhood of matter are choked off, they can not exert their nurturing influence and the soul's development is thwarted. *Mens sana in corpore sano* is ever a vital condition of spiritual growth.

This reorientation of view and approach would proliferate its benefits throughout the whole area of religion, in ways unforeseen and incalculable, but readily imagined. But one specific gain of great significance might happily accrue in the achievement of a sound and fully acceptable resolution of the ever-mooted "conflict between science and religion." Much current religio-scientific literature expresses genuine concern for the possibility of a harmonization of the two. It is not too much to affirm that, in view of the principles of the arcane philosophies of old, as elucidated herein, the grounds of a complete harmonization are in view and need only to be succinctly elaborated and utilized.

It is necessary to start the exposition from Aristotle's predication that there are two states of being in creational operation, *potentia* and act, or *potentia* and object. A thing-to-be emerges out of non-being as sheer potentiality, then begins a process of materialization and finally crystallizes into substantial entification or objectivity. Between the first steps of the departure out of non-being toward becoming and the full consummation of the process, the energies driving it forward express themselves in a scale or gamut of vibrational frequencies from slowest to infinitely rapid, similar or analogous to the mathematically calculable table of atomic weights in the series of the hundred or more chemical elements. It seems undeniable that the unit entities that bear the torch of life, so to say, start at the lowest rung of this ladder of ascent and march up the hill from one grade or frequency rate to the next, destined to mount to the summit. It further seems clear that a point midway in the series--the point indicated by the line in the diagram numbered three and one-half, precisely where man stands in his evolution--the progressing entities step out of the kingdom of unconsciously motivated activity into that of self-consciousness. Up to that point they have been driven by what is called instinct, animated by the superior power of a higher agency directing the total process. But from that point onward, they remain no longer puppets, but begin to exercise self-initiative under the spur of a dawning intelligence of which they become more and more definitely aware. Their future evolution then passes under their own control, and the exercise of this budding intelligence, consciously functioning, strengthens and sharpens it to ever greater efficiency. Man then becomes to ever fuller degree the master of his own destiny, instinct now replaced by conscious volition and decision.

Man, this beneficiary of the great gift of self-consciousness, this highest product of the evolving fires of life, has pushed the development of his higher intelligence to the point at which he knows much about the scale of energic frequencies and wave-lengths of the propelling forces. He can in fact count and measure those quantities. But beyond a certain stage, they surpass any power of his to measure them. It is at this point, broadly speaking, that science and religion sever their harmonious relation. For science abjures any interest in forces or phenomena which it can not bring under the inspection of its powers of observation, measurement and verification by its authentic sensual or intellectual means of establishing virtual certitude. Its concern can not go beyond the bounds of the positively verifiable. When it comes to dealing with forces that lie in the super-realm of the intangible, the immeasurable, the imperceptible and unknowable, science has nothing to say. Hence science and religion part company at the point where, in such terms as have come into usage to express the concepts, the phenomena with which science can deal, the physical, pass into the category of the metaphysical. Here, in a loose form of expression, is where science drops out of the competition and religion steps in.

With regard to the world of the metaphysical, the spiritual, the mystical, science is simply, and from its basic nature, justifiably agnostic. It declares that it has no ground for certitude in exploring that "upper" region. It knows of no laws, no certain principles governing the play of forces in that area of consciousness. The phenomena are undependable and unpredictable, not to say lawless, whimsical, sporadic, bizarre and irregular. Science does not deny categorically that they are real in their domain, valid as experience and authentic, possessing genuine values. But it forswears any judgments upon them because it, as said, lacks the means of verification. Religion is not its province.

Therefore its field of investigation is confined to the lower half of the scale of vibrational energies lying below the mid-point at which man injects his budding self-consciousness into the process, a region which, as our earlier thesis asserted, is the area of the operation of God's subconscious mind. The phenomena of that domain, being under the rulership of the cosmic mentality, manifest invariable regularity, certitude and predictability. So science confines its scrutiny to nature, whose activities can be studied with the assurance of dependable knowledge. Here the operation of law can be discerned.

But religion begins where the unconsciousness, the instinctiveness of nature, becomes self-consciousness in the mind of the creature man, and since the burgeoning of this conscious self-initiative dowers man with the godlike attribute of freedom, and this at the outset is to be exercised, so to say, to the tune of ignorance, all law can be shattered, all regularity ignored, all dependability flies out the window. Where could science get a foothold for law, for immutable principle, in the welter of wayward and fantastic ideas and experiences to which the psyche of humans has given evidence in all history? It is some clue to the unscientific nature of religion that one of its valuable books bears the title: *Varieties of Religious Experience.* Nature itself manifests an infinite diversification, but this seems but to be a flourish of artistic playfulness to grace and beautify the steady working of the regular formulae. Her main modes of procedure can be followed with general uniformity.

It is true that studies in the field of the psychology of religion have not failed entirely to discern certain patterns of uniform and dependable experience. The psyche of man is of sufficiently uniform texture that its modes, postures and afflations do not lack a certain degree of unanimity. The behavior systems of many types of religious expressions show much similarity, and given certain conditions and stimuli, more or less dependable outcomes may be predicted. Ecclesiastical systems have arrived indeed at a proficiency in the manipulation of religious psychology that has enabled them to maintain a rigorous hold on the loyalty of their millions of devotees. This is so true that there may be said to be a science of practical or empirical religionism. But this is still far from an answer to the central question: Can religion ever be brought legitimately into the category of a science? This is the nub of the issue here. The general expression of physical scientists is that there is little hope of so desirable a consummation. The psychic phenomena that constitute religious experience are so multifarious as to defy systematization. Nature, with her invariance, is not in charge here. Man, the young god, has the reins and in the exuberance of youthful adventure, heady with his new-found freedom to initiate action, unsteadied by wisdom, plunges into very attractive interest and reaps the consequences. The possibility of organizing the infinitude of mental and psychic and spiritual reactions flowing from his experience into a well defined science is too remote for hopeful achievement. One might say that in the investigation of physical nature the phenomena run straight or hold still, permitting close examination and increasing the chances of discovery. But in the domain of man's religious behavior, there is no such steadiness; the phenomena, so to say, wriggle all over the place, blurring the outlines of every conceivable pattern, wrecking every attempt at structuralization.

Men of science, however, have been broad enough to admit the possibility that the elements of religious life may still be amenable to scientific status. In the words of Dr. Theodosius Dobzhansky, of Columbia University, there might be such a thing as a "metascience," subsuming all those potential afflations of consciousness which lie beyond normal experience, or even, as mystics and some Hindu systems claim, transcend human experience altogether. Man's experiences at its present stage of capability can not be supposed to be the final product of evolution of consciousness; vast regions extending above man's reach at this stage may become amenable to charting and organization in the distant future. Such a possibility is not excluded from speculative thought, but science has no tools adequate for its investigation. In full corroboration of our central thesis, Dobzhansky says that mans stands with one foot in his biological past and with the other in his divine future. The resultant of his biological past has become the substance of his present existence; his divine future still lies submerged in his unconscious. His progressive experience is charged with the task of bringing these submerged capabilities up to expression in his surface consciousness. The Columbia professor may be quite right in thinking that this divine potential of future manifestation is carried in our physical, or psycho-physical organism by the genes. And he outlines logically the conditions of the great spirit-matter conflict in the polarity in saying that the potential spirituality locked up in the genes struggles with their environment, which, being negative to their positive, presents opposition. The environment resists the formative action of the genes, but it is just this battle between the genes and their environment that unfolds organic evolution. This eminent confirmation of our announced thesis itself carries a scientific principle into the realm of religion.

If science is only now discovering, or certifying, this principle of truth, it should now be duly impressed, if not a bit abashed, to realize that religion itself has formulated and announced this as one of its cardinal dogmas. Tremendous emphasis in the Scriptures is laid upon the doctrine of the two dispensations, the old subjection of man under the "law," and the new freedom of the Sons of God through the prerogative of spirit; man's sin-bound dominance under the old Adamic nature, and his liberty through the Christly oblation that wiped away all sinfulness. At a certain point in his evolution, he would pass over that three-and-a-half line which separates the period of his dominance by unconscious natural forces from his self-conscious rulership of his own destiny. Early Jewish Kabalism which exploited the principles of the archaic esotericism, expressed the conception by stating that in the first period man was under the dominance of severity, rigor, inexorable law, or *Geburah,* then in the second or spiritual stage he came under the benignant rule of *Hesed,* or grace, and even of *Tiphereth,* or beauty. There are many more ways, also, in which science is corroborating Scriptural formulations; so that a greater scientific respect for the claims of religion to scientific character would be indicated.

Santayana has surveyed these problems from almost all conceivable angles and expressed many notable truths about them. As regards science, he asserts that it does not suffice for ideal knowledge and can feel no adequate sympathy for reality. That is, in the whole area of our life in consciousness and ideality, it has no interest and expresses no sentiments. And referring to the body of the world's religious literature, in which the burden of the message of all human idealism and spiritual truth is carried by myth, allegory and symbolism, he avers that until this immense corpus of semantic representation is surveyed *scientifically,* there can be nothing but mutual repulsion and incapacity to understand between religion and science. The issue here is tremendous, the penalties for misconception are heavy in human society and the need for clarification most sore. The sacred Scriptures ostensibly carry the message of divine truth, or so the universal legend of religion has it. If truth is there, it must be amenable to scientific verification, for science is knowledge, and knowledge and truth can not contradict each other. The frightful tragedy of misconception has come into the picture all down the centuries through the misinterpretation of the great accomplishment of ancient semantic adeptship, in representing the archetypal constructs of spiritual truth through myth and symbol. When the genius for esoteric understanding suffered decay and eclipse in the religious field and the divine allegories lost all their occult significance and remained as empty husks of truth, the semantic treasures came to be considered the mere froth of ancient infantilism of mind. It is even yet the attitude of "science" and even of conventional religious belief in its best intelligence, that the Scriptures are the expression of an ancient child-mindedness, and are not to be taken seriously as full-fledged truth. That is, they are regarded as "mythical," with an interpretation put on the word that shows a complete miscomprehension of the true nature of this thing called *myth.* Still lingers in the modern academic mind the conception of myth as the effort of semi-ignorance to portray truth that misses the mark. It is supposed to be the play of fancy and the dance of imagination around the fire of truth, but never fully capturing the light. In brief, myth is still regarded as the libertinism of sheer fancy, the idea that it could be the shrewdest genius of dramatization of impregnable truth being still almost a shocking claim. Science has therefore been aloof to religion largely because of this astounding fact that the mighty truth that the Holy Scriptures of the world expressed in myth and allegory is still considered to be a farrago of childish nonsense. Santayana is supremely right: there can be no reapproachment between science and religion until the sublime semantic constructions of ancient sagacity and wisdom are interpreted at the level of comprehension at which their edifying truths can be seen as scientifically demonstrable.

All this is to say that if the age-old myths of the sacred books were interpreted allegorically, at the level of semantic undermeaning, and not twisted all awry by being forced to fit the Procrustean bed of "history," they would be found in almost every case to be vivid pictorializations of great and completely scientific principles. A statement of this kind will naturally be received in the temple of science with amazement, semi-shock and disbelief, doubtless even scoffed at. It may mean something to these minds adjusted to positivism to remind them that it would not have occasioned the least surprise or eyebrow listing to men of the intelligence of Plato, Aristotle and Philo. And these men were not just novices and fledglings in mental power. Depending of course on the accuracy and felicity of the mythicist's semantic devices, perhaps it is the height of truth to aver that *myth is ever truer than history.* Events of objective history in their single occurrence may reveal something remotely illuminative of the eternal reality of whose expression they constitute a tiny segment; myth builds an immediate formal construction of the eternal *archai,* the truths that are the very ribs of real being. It is said that we have learned little from history; in spite of the atrocious mishandling of the myths of Scripture, they have instructed the general cultured mind of humanity profoundly.

It is not to be doubted that an immense treasury of precious truth is locked up in all that goes with this conception of the subconsciousness of the first or natural order or dispensation and the active self-consciousness of the second or spiritual order. It may hold the key to our more scientific understanding of the law of cause and effect, as to which science itself has had grounds for the expression of some dubeity. It is still probably assumed in general that cause is one thing and the effect another; that effect is non-existent until cause generates it. There is evidence that this crude view has been refined to the status in which the effect is simply the cause itself come to manifestation. If the transition from cause to effect is achieved through a movement or process, the cause may be considered to be the thing in its inception phase and the effect the same thing in its end phase. Now it may be a clearer view of it to say that cause and effect are the two nodes of a polarity, the positive and negative poles of the one thing, the cause being hidden in the invisible world and the effect becoming manifest visibly in the physical world. On the basis of the philosophical principles already adduced, thought could go further and reach the conclusion that cause resides and operates in the sphere of the spiritual-noumenal and effect comes into manifestation in the outer physical sphere. Cause is noumenal, from *nous,* mind; effect is physical, the appearance of cause in matter. In the cycling movement of the forces of life in the spiral of progression, the two states alternate, the swing from one pole to the other increasing the potency of the one and diminishing that of the other. The physical must decrease and the spiritual increase--as John the Baptist expressed it. The ancient sages made much of the symbolism of one star disappearing below the horizon in the west as its opposite rose in the east. So in human history our moral insights are sharpened by the reflection that as the instincts of the animal nature, the sensualities, brutishness, ignorance and grossness of the first dispensation fade out of conscious motivation, the qualities of the higher spiritual order, intelligence, unselfishness, charity, reason and equity, not to say divine love, increase in potency.

The theorization even reaches to the polarization of the two opposites, life and death. It never comports with truth to think that life is the expression of the total reality and death its annihilation. Death is never the destruction, but the polar negation of life. Again they are the two phases of the one reality, which is being, in the act of becoming. "Death" is a necessary foil for the manifestation of life. It is the negative phase, by tension with which the positive becomes manifest. As any organic existence is the resultant of the polarization of consciousness with its material body, we have naively assumed that the dissociation of the two at the cycle's end spelled death. It can be understood now as the cyclical shifting of the polarity. At the middle point of the cycle's activity the two stand each other off in equilibrium, at the cycle's end and beginning the energic force retires into quiescence in one end or sweeps out into activity at the other. As Heraclitus expressed it, the one *lives* the *death* of the other.

Would it need any extended elaboration to accentuate what the application of this scientific principle to the moral-spiritual life of humans would release into knowledge? It would show that good and evil, just as much as spirit and matter, cause and effect, life and death, are the two nodes of polarity, and that the increase of the one necessitates the diminution of the other. This is why the ancient Egyptians weighed the soul of the "deceased" against the feather of right and truth, in the hall of judgment. This sets the inviolable seal of certitude on the truth of the contention herein announced that, from every theological point of view, the judgment posited for all souls takes place in the living phase of the cycle on earth, and not in the after-life, since it is only on earth that the two struggle in polarity to maintain their equilibration. Nature here gives us the scientific key to one of the most basic principles of religious truth.

CHAPTER SIXTEEN

STRUCTURE OF THE ARCHETYPES

The motive that inspires the production of a book is generally the intent to promulgate a theory, and the method followed is to present, formulate and elaborate the theory and then adduce the evidence that might constitute its corroboration. Our work up to this point has been in the main the promulgation and elaboration of the theory, which, stated in briefest form, is that the ultimate grounds of truth are mirrored in nature. Now the task must be to demonstrate the validity or, in blunt terms, the truth of the theory. From this point on, the material can hardly escape the imputation of being an audacious attempt to achieve nothing less than a formulation of the archetypal divine ideas over the pattern of which God created the universe. Nor can it dodge the implication that it is an attempt to divine the architectonic structure of the Logos, the very mind of God. The elaboration of the theory has implicitly carried the expectation, if not the promise, of fulfillment in demonstration. The contention, several times, repeated, that the theory, while advanced and advocated by many philosophers from early days down to the present, has never been convincingly demonstrated so as to win universal acclaim, bespoke at least some measure of performance in the present instance. It does little to palliate the enormity of the presumption involved in this situation to protest that the effort represents simply the intent to elucidate a number of reflections that any thoughtful person with a bent toward the poetic flair would be capable of formulating over the analogical pattern if he had a penchant for that sort of thing. The undertaking will be simply a compilation of many random glimpses of analogical similitude between natural phenomena and noumenal structures. Any pretence to arrange them in a structural form that would constitute them an organic synthesis of the universal *archai* of the world of truth is vigorously disclaimed. They might be presented as just some thoughts on nature, with their intimations of higher truth. Virtually every poet and philosopher makes some sort of pretence in this direction. They must themselves demonstrate whatever validity and worth they possess.

It is indeed a bewildering matter to choose the point of departure for the enterprise. To pinpoint a "beginning" of creation is a precarious undertaking.

But if the creative God force projects itself in cycle after cycle, one must think of what goes with the beginning of the present grand cycle. The primary realization here is that God begins his exertion in each cycle with the operation of splitting his unity, first into duality of spirit and matter, then on into infinite multiplicity as the resistance of matter to the projection of noumenal force fragments the primordial energies into smaller units, much as a quantum of water in one body falling from a height is fragmented into multiple drops. On the statement of revered Scriptures, God's purpose was to enhance, augment and multiply his life. If we may judge by nature, which is his own work, his method in this procedure was to break up his unitary being into infinite units, each carrying the potential of renewing his entire life, planting them in matter, where through growth each would reproduce his being in toto. The fact and the truth of this methodology is seen in every ear of corn or spike of wheat. Each grain is dowered with the potentiality of reproducing itself many times. And how does it achieve this miracle? By its inherent capability of generating its seed. All living vegetation shouts this wonderful truth to us. Its universal and unexceptional character attests its veracity. All units of abounding life follow this law of multiplication of their kind by generation and planting of seed.

The prime instructive force of this natural fact for religion is implicit in the realization--so completely overlooked by theology--that seeds must be planted. Any one knows this, what makes it so significant for theology? The answer to this is that orthodox theology seems never to have known that the divine soul in man is a seed of God's own life, therefore his Son, and that for its growth and glorification it had to be incarnated in human flesh. The whole dialectic of the incarnation is flashed into our intelligence here, but theology has never seen it as the rationale of the incarnation. God could conceive these Sons of his in heaven, in his mind; but for their birth, growth, and evolution to godhood, he had to plant them in the soil of earth, in the garden of the world. If they were to cooperate with him in his creation, they had to gain competence through mastery of the laws of matter which they would have to manipulate.

The seed production, planting and germination are at the same time the open sesame to the central sacrament of the Christian faith, the Eucharist. What could the breaking of the bread into fragments signify but the dismemberment of the deific unit force, and the distribution of the pieces to each and all be but the planting? Each higher animal entity received his seed portion of the divine potential, which it was to nurture in the womb of its physical organism and bring to birth therein. Lacking the clarifying insight that analogy with the natural seeding process would have brought to bear on the doctrine, Christian mental dereliction stultified the whole science of theology. Seen through nature's eyes, the whole mystery of the incarnation would have retained its illuminative intellectual character as well as its dynamic cathartic spiritual power. And what psychic motivation could have exerted more influence to lift the human spirit to heights of beatific exaltation than the positive knowledge that every son of man bears deep within his constitution a seed of the imperishable splendor of the infinite and absolute Life? What could be a more sanifying and salutary influence than the realization that he has the obligation to bring to birth, growth and maturity this child of God?

Much of nature's intricate and involved procedures in the accomplishment of her purposes was known to the hierophants of the ancient Mysteries and occult brotherhoods. They retained a quantum of explicit data and arcana of knowledge that clarified the understanding of the modes and mechanism of the incarnational procedure. This knowledge reveals that as the stream of evolving life moves forward, it organizes the substrate matter with which it must work into a series or scale of gradations determined by the density, substantiality or vibrational rate of the force at each place. It does this for the formation of material structures through which it can manifest its powers and its modes of the divine being. We know these formations superficially as the planes, levels or kingdoms of life, and they confront us openly and palpably in many forms, but most universally in the four kingdoms of the natural objectivity, the mineral, vegetable, animal and human orders or stages.

The Greek wisdom lore postulated the projection of the stream of creative force "from on high as far as to the last of things." This means from the apex of spirit to the nadir of descent into matter. But on the way "down" the rhythmic and cyclical plan of emanation brought temporary stops at these movements, where the outgoing force of the creative energies was exactly counterbalanced by the inertia of matter at the point, and at each such station the spirit force and the material stability united to structuralize organic life in its expression appropriate to that stage. These formations constituted, as said, the planes and kingdoms. The progression of life downward into matter proceeded under the modus and mechanism of a law by which the energic force stepped down from one of these stations to the one below it until it reached the nadir of descent in the mineral kingdom, or the subatomic kingdoms beneath it. Still in the sphere and aura of the seed generation and dissemination analogy, this has been called the Law of Incubation. It ordains that since the life of a being whose world is one of these platforms of nature is to be reproduced in its succeeding generation, and this process always entails the production of its seeds and their planting--since in homely terms its eggs are to be hatched--it must enwomb its seeds in the soil of the kingdom just below it in the gamut. So we have the seed of a vegetable incubated in the soil of the mineral kingdom; the seed of animal reproduction mothered in a body that if it is not ostensibly vegetable in texture, is at least composed of the vegetable matter ingested into its body as food; and we definitely have the seed of the human nature incubated in bodies which are of the animal order. We have noted Plato's statement that man is a god inhabiting the body of an animal.

Well, then, it requires only the extension of the law's jurisdiction just one step higher to discern in one flash of analogy a fact of stupendous importance for all theological science: this marvelous truth that man harbors the Christ-child within the precincts of his humble domicile of flesh. As the law applies to man, his physical body is the soil of the plane lying just below the "divine," and it must therefore become the planting field in which the seed-germ of the divine life of that higher plane must be incubated. That unit life of divinity is the lowest of the divine orders; Plato speaks of its units as "junior gods," "minor gods," the Innocents whom Herod tried to destroy, the "younglings in the egg" in Egyptian terms, the Kumaras of Indian systematism, at any rate fledgling gods, infant deities, Sons of God. But it is the order of divine life that occupies the plane just over man's head in the scale of the kingdoms. So man is incubating, hatching, in his body the seed-germ of the first of the supernal deities. On his physical side, he is the mother of the Christ-to-be. We prate of the dignity of man, in spite of his abject relapses into brutishness and savagery. If the term has any appropriateness--and it truly has--it is by virtue of the incubation of the infant god within the womb of his physical nature. It is our animal task in the end to join forces with the growing god and help him to redeem us.

With such a goad to inspiration, imagination, seeing how the multiple grades of life's manifestation stand linked in living connection all the way from first emanative impulse down to near statisticity in the mineral kingdom, or matter's lowest depths, buoys the mind into a whole gallery of semantic realizations in the sphere of religion and philosophy. The sheer fact of the operation of such a law acts like a magic wand to open up vistas of understanding and vivid ideas carrying entrancing meaning. All questions of immanence or transcendence of nature and life by postulated deity, and the relation of man and nature to each other are at once linked in a mutually congenital affinity. What theological blindness has left in obscurity and perplexity is clarified by this analogy with nature. In one flash of vision, the vast gulf that in lieu of this discernment has been unbridgeable by intelligence between man standing far down in the scale and his God at the summit, is spanned by the knowledge of the law which shows the interconnection of all intermediate stations stretching over the interval.

The Egyptian mind, nature-wise as ever, fixed the symbol of a stairway between man and God--echoed in the legend of Jacob's ladder--and placed man at his proper station upon it. Each gradation of the volume and power of the life force in its outgoing from first deific projection, is thus linked with the summit of all through its immediate connection with the superior grade just above it, which grade, by virtue of its higher voltage of the divine fire, becomes for its immediate inferior its god or daemon or "higher self." In its turn it enacts the same role for the order below its station, to whom it passes on the further dismembered seeds of its order of creative essence. Hence the vegetable is the god for the mineral, the animal the deity for the vegetable, the human is the genius governing its own animal appanage. And now we can see that the young deity, variously styled as our Ego, Soul or Christ nature, is the divine entity more or less consciously awakened to its aeonial task of playing God to our humanity. He is the God potential, the God seed, assigned by the Father the commission of becoming the God actual, that is, the God consciously expressing his divine nature through the brain organism of the animal in whose fleshly domicile and for whose evolutionary uplift he has been sent to earth. He remains an element of our unconscious until we, the humans, evolve and sensitize the bodily apparatus of brain and nerves to the capability of registering at our level his higher vibratory waves.

Nature thus irradiates our mind with the grandiose conception of how the God force disseminates itself throughout the entire domain of its manifestation. Just as in human physiology, the life-giving oxygen must be carried to every region of the body by the red corpuscles of the blood, so in the whole body of creation the formative and sustaining power of the God-life impregnates the entire corpus of existence. And is the instructive lesson for theology to be missed here? Since there is but the one stream of the God-force that proceeds from the throne at the summit and animates the whole creation, it is a certain truth that the life of the universe is in all parts and at every elevation, low or high, intrinsically divine. One part is not beatific and divine, in contradistinction to another segment which is earthly, sensual, devilish. There is but the one life and that is essentially divine, at whatever level it manifests. However our minds must take account of the gradations in the scale of manifestation, and through misconception of the law of polarity, the lower half of the gamut's stations, the expression of God's automatic subconscious, have been stigmatized as hostile to the higher stations, or the spiritual life and so have incurred the contumely of evil. Every part of the universe is instinct with the presence and its appropriate rationing of the mind and spirit of God. Every creature embodies and expresses as much of the God-power as the grade of its organic life enables it to instrumentalize.

As the divine creative impulse thus subsumes the corollary of infinite multiplication of primal unit being, nature again furnishes the paradigm by which we may rationalize the diffusion of primal energy into endless diversification. In the outward-downward sweep of creative force through the operation of the Law of Incubation, the seed-planting of higher dynamic in the soil of the kingdom below, the multiplication of seed from higher parentage looms as a necessary corollary of the process. For the life of the higher parent plane vibrates at a more dynamic rate and frequency and wave-length than the life of the plane below it, so that if a unit of the higher potential is, as seed, to be buried in the matter of the kingdom below, which functions at a far more sluggish tempo, it is obvious that the voltage of the unit life of the superior plane must be stepped down, if it is to accommodate itself to the slower rates of the plane below. This demands the breaking up of the heavier charge of the upper plane's dynamic into smaller units, just as electricity must be transformed into smaller voltages according to the size of a smaller light. Thus the Eucharistic doctrine applies to life at every stage of descent, higher voltages of living energy having to "dismember" their larger units to synchronize with the more inert forces of the planes in the lower segment. Thus life achieves its infinite multiplication through the paradox of infinite division. Unless the One divided itself endlessly, there could be no multiplication. The ability of one grain of corn to produce several ears is the mystery of life that it always will be, but at least nature displays it to us. What theology has not seen in ages is that the mystery furnishes the paradigm over the pattern of which we can grasp the sense of the doctrine of the incarnation, the Eucharist and the existence of souls in mortal bodies. Arcane wisdom allegorized this principle of the breaking up or "mutilation" of the higher units of soul dynamic for incubation in secondary orders by the doctrine of "dismemberment" and "disfigurement" of the bodies of the gods. The gods were cut to pieces, and it was the work of the fragments to restore the primal unity through the integrating force of love and brotherhood. "That ye may all be one in Christ Jesus," the higher consciousness. It remains only to say on this subject that the farther the creative power proceeded from the summit source into matter, the weaker became the voltage and the more multitudinous and smaller became the units. The unity of God atomized itself.

In all ancient religion the central legend was the mutilation of the body of the God, his shedding his blood for the redemption of mankind, and his "death" on the cross of matter. Nature again holds the key of interpretation. Always in the rhythmic alternation of the two nodes in the swing of the cycles, in incarnation spirit-soul goes "dead" that matter may live, and at the cycle's end, matter goes "dead" that spirit may live. The two exchange life and death. This truth is of absolutely paramount importance for religion, as it elucidates the fundamental principle of all religion, the idea that the deific power sacrifices its life for mankind, higher orders die for those below them.

It is therefore a revelation of absolutely crucial import for, particularly, the Christian religion, that the "death" of the Christ for the salvation of the world can not connote the physical demise of the body of an assumedly living God in the flesh. It can mean nothing but the "death" of the spiritual principle when it is buried in the inertia of matter. The bodily demise of any personalized figure playing the role of the Christ nature dying for mankind could be nothing more than dramatization of a great truth. For the positive node of polarity must "die" if the negative is to live, and vice versa.

The light which this arresting natural principle casts into the dark region of theology is of such illuminative power that it fairly dazzles mind and imagination. It is in effect the one great central beam that lights the understanding of all religion. The whole of the relation of God and man to each other is prefigured by the analogy with nature in the relation of seed or young plant to soil. The soul stands in precisely the same relation to body as seed to earth. A seed of godhead is planted in our bodies. The body is Paul's "natural man," the soul is his "spiritual man." The two are polarized. It therefore becomes permissible to assert, on grounds which nature is doubtless prepared to supply, that every aspect and nuance of the living relation between soul and body will be found prefigured by the phenomena of the relation between seed, or plant, and soil. If we would comprehend the spiritual life and history of man, we must set up our study in the garden. For there the paradigms and analogies will be found in evidence. Some of these may be caught and noted.

As ever in polarity, there is a mutual exchange, a maintenance of balance, or a diminution of one force for the expansion of the opposite. If a physical organism, the negative pole, is to live and mature, the soul of its life must be poured into it and go *in abscondito,* or "dead." The physical frame of the expression absorbs the energic force. Here once more is the natural key to a Biblical structure. When Jesus symbolically broke his body into pieces and distributed them among his disciples, he adjured them that for the gift of immortality they must "eat my body." He might have said: You must incorporate the sublimated essence and living dynamism of my spiritual body into the texture of your nature. My divine substance will go into obscurity in your bodies, but it will be your life. In the form of Heraclitus' expression, he could have said: I will die unto your life, as later you will die to restore my life to me.

As, also, it is the tensions of polarity that advance the life principle, the God-force, to new and greater expression, the interrelation must work to mutual advantage. While the soil gives nutriment to the seed or plant, it receives benefit for itself from the power in the latter. It is a fact of agriculture that the roots of alfalfa deposit nodules of nitrogen as deep down as fifteen or more feet, the chemical power of which is absorbed by the soil for its enrichment. The analogue of every such interaction must be discoverable in the mutual interchange of influences between soul and body.

Again, religious philosophy gains immeasurably from the implications here involved. In view of the inveterate drive of religion to detach souls from the influence of earth and the flesh as the enemies of the spirit, the stern rebuke to this errant persuasion is forcefully administered by nature, which so clearly shows that there could be no growth for souls apart from their "marriage" with matter. If religion is to serve humanity helpfully, henceforth it must reduce the emphasis on the mystical lures of "heaven," and accentuate the beneficence of soul's attachment to earth.

Greek astuteness had embodied these basic concepts in symbolic and allegorical forms. Since it was known that soul goes "dead" for the life of the body, yet renews its own life through the experience of incarnation in it, the body thus was poetized as first the *tomb* of the soul's "death," and then in turn the *womb* of its new birth. So their word for body was *soma* and that for tomb was *sema,* while in English tomb and womb make the equation.

The ancient semantic genius played all around this central idea and constructed many a metaphorical figure for the body and the earth as the home of "death" for the soul. The earth was first the "underworld," the deep, dark dungeon, the pit, the cave, the grave, the sepulcher, the coffin, the wilderness, the desert, in which soul spent its dark night and winter hibernation, to emerge renewed and resurrected in the spring turn of the cycle. From the first, all the ritual forms and the annual round of festivals of religion were dated and symbolically structuralized in celebratory form according to the relation of the sun, earth and moon (and several prominent stars and constellations, as Sirius, Orion, Spica, the pole star and others), all to analogize and pictorialize the elements and phenomena of the interlaced life of soul and body. All semantically bespoke the occult meaning of our human life, soul and body in polarity.

Obviously the two solstices and the two equinoxes had to be given great prominence for expressive intimations of relevant significance. The sun, crossing the horizon line downward at eventide and rising afresh each morning, became ineluctably the symbol of divine soul-fire descending in the west for incarnation. This emblemism made the September equinoctial date the time for the memorializing of the meaning of soul's descent to earth and body, which is now the lost significance of our wild and semi-licentious revelry on the night of October thirty-first, Hallowe'en, the eve of All Souls' Day, November first. The relevance of the October thirty-first date is that it comes just forty days after the September equinox, and forty is the number symbolizing the incubation period between "death" and resurrection, or planting and germination.

Just as inevitably the winter solstice (advanced three days to conform to the legend that life must lie in the tomb three days, to December twenty-fifth) became the time that ended the descent into matter and the beginning of new birth for the soul. And just as inevitably the spring equinox had to be the epoch of the resurrection out of body into the life of "paradise regained." The whole fabric of ritualism and semanticism lies charted before us, and leaps into meaning as we survey it from its basic analogy with nature. All of religion's dark and mysterious rites and usages are to be resolved into relevant meaning only when they are referred back to elements inherent in the natural apologue. In most of the festival semanticism the sun, as spirit, and moon, as dead matter, replace the seed as central symbol of the divine power that incarnates. And this is most appropriate, as the soul is in fact constituted of the same spiritual essence as the energy of the sun. The moon, being dead, symbolizes not that divine light, though it does bear witness to that light,--the same as does the body of man to his spirit. One need not be reminded of the prominence of the analogy of the sowing of the seed in the parables of the New Testament.

CHAPTER SEVENTEEN

THE FOUR POWERS OF CREATION

Throughout all the operations of nature, the formation of objects, the run of phenomena, and the rhythms and durations of periodicities give prominence to the play and significance of numbers. The Pythagorean system made number the basic element in its philosophy. This is not strange when one recognizes the immense part mathematics plays in life.

Some aspects of the significance of the number *four* have entered incidentally into an earlier discussion. But the way nature features this particular number and the function it serves in the business of the interpretation of the Scriptures entitle it to much fuller consideration.

These Scriptures inform us from the very outset of the creation story that four is the number, so to say, on which the world rests. They say that the stream of creative force issued from the "throne of God" and divided into four heads. It does not elaborate, but leaves us to presume that these primal four branches further subdivided and finally carried the constructive streams out into infinite proliferation and ramification.

As is evident to sense in our dimensional world, four is the number that bespeaks stability, firmness, secure setting, as in a table of four legs. The things in the world must stand four-square for steadiness and permanence. The four divisions of the river of life put under the world the four supports of existence. They were, to be sure, only the lower four of the total seven that, the Egyptians said, compose the structure of life. They were conditioned to lay the physical foundation on which the superstructure of man's metaphysical triad of conscious spiritual principles could rest and flare into manifestation at the summit of the order of evolution. These three exalted states of being may be described, or merely named, as the abstract mind, enlightened consciousness (as that attributed to the Buddha) and an ultimate consciousness of transcendental being beyond thought or imagination. The lower four thus established the lower platform on which the trinity of conscious life could parade or dance to the tune of existence. How meaningfully this numerical basis of life has been wrought into the architecture of the Great Pyramid, as also inscribed with fathomless semantic genius in the figure of the zodiac! The foundation of four sides, supporting three-sided faces! In the zodiac, a sphere of twelve segments grouped in four elementary divisions, each with three aspects! Such is the recondite artistry of the archaic genius of semantic representation of cosmic truth to human mind.

Of the primary seven substances, four, then, were sufficiently progressed in atomic evolution to emerge into material substantiality in the concrete world, while the upper three remained in invisible static essence. We must look closely now at these four in the world. They can not be readily missed, as all things are composed of their material substance. They are *earth, water, air* and *fire*. (Aristotle posited a higher one as the fifth, which he called *aether,* as the ultimate sublimation of the essence of the three. It is beyond human cognition, except abstractly. Being the fifth, it has come to be called the *quintessence*.) These four lower substances must be examined, not from the standpoint of physical science, but semantically for evidence of their valence in the structure of the world of life and for the endless analogues they provide between nature and ideation.

All students have known that the ancients claimed that all things were constituted of the four primary elements. What perhaps few know is that the ancient esoteric insight considered the four not from the angle of physics but from their perception of the analogy subsisting between them and the nature and constitution of man. This parallelism having long been a lost secret, it appears that nobody in the history of philosophy since ancient days has essayed the task of tracing the lines of the correspondence. It will be found to yield the most thrilling run of accordances at every turn.

It must be seen that the identity that demonstrates the paralogue can not be a matter of coincidence. The four in nature will be seen to run an exact parallel with the operation of the four in man's psychic makeup. Man, himself a creature of nature, shares nature's constituent ingredients. In outer nature the four operate in lower matter; in the human, their play is at the level of psychic forces and sublimated essences, in the realm of sensation, feeling, thought.

The genius of analogical sense made each of the four elements in the outer world the counterpart of a corresponding psychic mode of consciousness. Earth represented sensation; water matched emotion; air symbolized thought; and fire was the universal ancient emblem of the spirit-soul. At the mere listing of the chart the mind senses a fitness, if not some phases of actual suggestions of identity, of these correspondences. Earth is appropriate to the fact of sensation, because this psychic state is generated in a body composed of earthly elements, the physical. Paul reminds us that the natural man is of the earth, earthy. And how kindred seem emotion and water! Both are lightly mobile, fluid, unstable and readily changeable, shimmering at every turn of sun or wind. Likewise how close in affinity are air and thought! Both are invisible, yet alike they reveal their character by what they affect outwardly. It is a testimony to the reality of this correspondence between air and mind that virtually every people in the world, in casting about for words suitable to convey the idea of mind-soul-spirit, has simply appropriated for this concept the words for air, wind or breath. Mind and air are definite poetical counterparts of each other. Then fire; universally this chemical phenomenon, subsisting on air and some more subtly potent elements above it, gave man his most realistic conception of the fiery nature of the creative energy. "Spirit" is itself from the Latin *spiro,* I breathe. The breath keeps the fires of life burning. The Greek has it as *pneuma,* which again means "breath." To deeper reflection, the energy of life creative assumes the concept of a fiery potency, both able to build up and to dissolve. The light of the sun, naturally conceived to be the fiery energy of the creative power, was antiquity's universal symbol for the life-giving power of the Logos. It was the great god Re in Egypt, whose hieroglyph is the sun. Expressing a recondite item of ancient esoteric knowledge, and one which modern science seems to be on the point of confirming, stands the statement of the Greek Neoplatonist Proclus: *The light of the sun is the pure energy of intellect.* Not man's intellect, to be sure, but God's, of which man's is a miniature and potential copy.

This is verily a concept to stop one's breath with its astounding significance: the suns in infinite space would then be the glowing fiery brain cells of God's mind. When God said "Let there be light!," he carried out the command by the exertion of his mind. The light of the universe has been generated by the thinking process of the cosmic mind! Even at the human level, it is a fact that the act of steady thinking generates in the brain a quantum of heat and light, measurable by delicate electrical apparatus. Thought is known to be a product of the flash of electricity from one brain cell to another oppositely charged quite analogous to the lightning in a thunder-storm.

It is not surprising, then, that we find the so-called "Fire Philosophers" of the Medieval period expounding the theory that "every man has a little sun within himself." He would necessarily have a central dynamo of life and "light" within himself, on the cardinal principle of his microcosmical relation to God, the macrocosm. If God has brain cells glowing with ineffable splendor, man in his image would have tiny suns of intellect similarly glowing within his organism. If this seems too much poetry and too little fact, it is to be remembered that the atoms and cells in our bodily structure are proportionally as far apart as these sun-brain-cells of God in the abyss of space. And again much that modern fact-minded mentality has put down as ancient myth and puerile fancy turns out to have been very subtle and recondite scientific reality. Modern science seems to stand close to the conclusion that the ultimate "stuff" of the universe is mind force. Matter has resolved into pure energy, and this energy seems to be akin to the force of mind. Recovering such basic facts of knowledge, the religion that shouted in wild and drunken triumph two thousand years ago that "Great Pan is dead," must now, in humiliation and contrition, acknowledge that in cutting itself off from nature, it severed its connection with the very fount of life.

As the four elements constitute and operate as a gamut in the outer world, their four corresponding grades of consciousness in the life of man will be seen to act in the same serial fashion. A change in the condition of any one will by close association induce changes or initiate effects in its neighbor above or below. As we are more familiar objectively with the outer world, the action must be viewed there first. Following Hermes' maxim that "that which is above is that which is below," we look at natural fact first, as it is visible. The invisible can not be the clue to the visible; the opposite must be the workable formula. The close and affective relation the four bear to each other in the outer world may be well viewed in such a phenomenon as a thunder-storm. We may say that the causative factor in the action is the topmost element, that is, fire, heat. The latent potency of *fire* in the *air* is released in the form of lightning, with the effect of condensing the aeriform particles of moisture in the *air*, which again results in the precipitation of *water* down to *earth*. The phenomenon is an action involving all four. The sunheated *earth* helps to *fire* up the *air*, and all tends to precipitate the *water*. Fire, air, water, earth; all participate in the interaction.

Is there anything comparable and analogous to this in the psycho-spiritual realm? The fidelity with which the correspondence holds will prove illuminating. To begin with, the four coefficients of consciousness, sensation, emotion, thought and spiritual vision are as interdependently associated in action as are the four external elements. They are related even more closely than are the base, tenor, alto and soprano of a singing quartette, though quite analogously. If either of the four notes in the voiced harmony is off key, the harmony of the whole ensemble is jangled in discord. So if sense, as a toothache, if emotion, as anger or hatred, if thought, as a wrong idea or concept, if a misguided spiritual aspiration, is active in the area of consciousness, the equable balance of the psyche as a whole is disturbed. As in the thunder-storm, the impulse precipitating action seems to start at the top with fire (heat from the sun), causing pressures in the air, which in turn send down the rain to nourish the earth, so we have precisely similar communication of energies from top to bottom of the scale. The dynamic power of the highest inmost spirit pushes out to seek expression in and throughout the organism. Out of the unconscious region of the oversoul there flashes the vision of some exalted truth, an impulse of good, a touching sense of beauty, a new, more cognition than any experienced before.

This is comparable to the lightning of the storm. A flash of the fire of spirit, it impinges on the stratum below it, the mind. In this it stimulates vigorous new thoughts of dynamic voltage. From mind it impacts upon the next level and arouses emotions of gladness, happy elation. The well-known psychic effect of such states of feeling is a vivification of the life force through every nerve and fiber of the body. A vivific impulse of spiritual character can thus start at the summit and run down the scale. But an impulse can also originate at any of the four gradients and send its mantling influence both upward and downward, the impact being likely to affect all four levels.

The interrelation of any two of the elements when scanned with a poet's reflective sensitivity, yields most fascinating intimations of significant meaning. Holding strictly to the four-aspected symbolism, what could more vividly analogize the power of an idea to agitate an emotion than the impact of a breeze, gentle or violent, striking upon the surface of a pond or other body of water? Here is nature dramatizing before our eyes the power of a thought to bestir an emotion. Every degree of the force with which the wind strikes the water surface bespeaks the benignance or the virulence of the emotional repercussion. A raging gale in the air, a rage of feeling in the mind; a gentle breeze, a gracious placid feeling. Then if thought is controlled, steady, luminous, how perfect the reflected image on the water! But if thought is of the irrational order, how unclear and disturbed the feelings!

The phenomena resulting from the intercommunication of the four elements yield in all cases significant intimations of moral-spiritual instruction. As fire takes water out of the air, so spiritual intensification eradicates emotion from thought, leaving pure intellection. Then if air dries up water, thought clears or purges, purifies and sublimates emotion, as when calm reason is exerted to stop anger, passion, violent emotional storm. The Biblical allegories of both Jonah and Jesus stilling the storm on the lake by the power of the spirit, or the Christ-mind, reflect this analogue. Plato picked up the symbol of mire, and the Bible that of miry clay, to emblemize the carnal nature of man. Well, mire, mud, is the mixture of earth and water, and carnality is the mixture of sense and emotion. Pure water will cleanse the dirt and muck of a garment or a surface; pure emotion will purify the grossness of animal tendency. The drying up of the Red Sea and again of the Jordan River for the facilitation of the Israelite crossing is the amplification, is the mythicization, of the power of mind and soul (heated air) to extinguish the elements of sensuality and emotion, as impediments to the soul's progress across the sea of life.

Can we miss the impressive force of the analogical instructiveness of the fact that water is the deadly enemy and conqueror of fire? Do we need any cogent "proof" that an overcharge of sensual emotion can kill the divine spirit in man? St. Paul's "carnal mind" and "concupiscence" and "fleshly lusts that war against the soul" and asceticism's misguided drive to subdue the flesh in the interests of the soul acclaim this relationship.

The correlations between the four within and without stand in still more striking suggestiveness when we take the ancient sages' bifurcation of the nature of man into its two upper-lower components, the natural man and man spiritual, man of the body, man of soul-mind. "The first man is of the earth, earthy; the second is the Lord from heaven," says St. Paul. "First that which is natural, then that which is spiritual." Obviously it must be so, since patently the body must be here before there can be a brain through which an intellecto-spiritual nature can function. Just as obviously the natural man is composed of the two lower elements, earth and water, by actual physical constituency, about seven-eighths water, one eighth earth. So he has the conscious powers of sense and emotion. Just as certainly the second or spiritual man from heaven is composed of mind and spirit, with air and fire as their symbols.

The realizations which come to us through reflection upon this symbolism give us an insight of the most vivid character into the significance of the great doctrine and fact of the incarnation. If the spiritual man is composed of fire (spirit) and air (mind), and the natural man of water (emotion) and earth (sensation), the incarnation of the higher in the body of the lower carries every suggestion of the phenomenon of the introduction of fire into water. And precisely under these terms the arcane scientists conceived it for purposes of graphic representation. It vividly portrays the entire moral-spiritual conflict in the life of man as an analogue of the struggle between fire and water. Gross sensuality will as effectually douse the pure fire of spirituality as water will quench fire. From the other side the superior chemical power of fire can dry out and evaporate the dank, moldy "moist nature" of the carnal impulses. It is this latter symbolism that is the interior sense of all the allegories of God drying up the rivers to effectuate the passage of his children across their period of immersion in bodies that are three-fourths water. The power of the sunlight of mind and spirit to purify and cleanse the foul corruption of the flesh is the ground-base of the theological hypostatization of "purgatory." This is indeed the catharsis of the Greek conception, which was rightly applied to the struggle of the soul on earth, and not, as in Christian misconception, reserved for the after-life. The soul-figure in the *Book of the Dead* distinctly says that he comes to earth to purify himself in the most high degree, and to effect this purification by bathing in the pool beneath the two divine sycamores of heaven and earth.

Also he says that he takes his position on the line of the horizon because there he stands directly on the line that separates the air and fire of his divine nature from the earth and water of his lower bodily life. Strikingly illuminating too is the idea that the soul finds purification from what in the symbolism must be thought of as verily a mud-bath on earth! This emblemism is found in some systems.

But most significantly of all, the symbolism depicts the esoteric purport of the rite of baptism. It never could have carried any other connotation than the dipping of the soul into the water of the body. However, in the warped ideas of theology, it has seemed incongruous that an innocent soul issuing from the "pure" state of heavenly life should have to plunge into the muck and mire of earthly sensuality to be purified. The paradox disappears when the terms of the situation are known and the rationality discerned. The *Book of Revelation* portrays this transaction under the metaphor of a mountain of fire from heaven going down into the ocean which is on the border of the earth and, as it were, setting the sea on fire. It is the tragic fate of poetizations of this sort to be transmogrified by the ignorant masses always into arrant nonsense through literalization, so that the occult sense is traduced into gibberish. Lyrically inspired philosophical genius conceived the figurative purification of man by his being washed in the blood of the divine nature shed for him. Under zodiacal symbolism it was the blood of the lamb slain from the foundation of the world, of the bull in the Mithra cult, or the sacrificial goat, or the wounded lion or the ram in the Moses story. But from the other side the young god needed to undergo baptism in the earthly pool, the body's blood. This is made expressly clear in the New Testament allegory of the baptism of Jesus by John, his forerunner. John defers to the superior evolutionary rank of the Christ nature, and hints that it would be far more fitting that he, the lower, should be baptized by Jesus, the higher. Jesus demurs to this, protesting his necessity of being baptized by the lower element of water. His baptism is only that of water, and for evolutionary purposes, this is necessary for the infant deity; the baptism which he will later give the lower human will be that of air (*spiritus*) and fire. The youthful god, however, is to walk on the surface of the water and not sink into it.

We have but to reflect a moment on Paul's animadversions on the power of the carnal mind to drag the soul down into the dank and corrupting mire of sensuality.

How marvelously nature confirms the reality of his fears by its own symbols! For *earth and water fall!* By natural gravity, they move downward. What, on the other hand, is the tendency of air and fire? Just as naturally they *rise*! Does any reflective mind need any further confirmation of the theological doctrine that the Christ nature came to earth to lift the human race toward divinity? Our humanity degrades us; our divinity exalts us. The conflict of these two opposing tendencies is depicted in the figure of the Solomon's Seal, the six-pointed star formed by the interlacing of two triangles, the apex of the one pointing upward, the other downward. Man lives his life at the point of the clashing of the "upward and the downward ways," as Heraclitus said.

Then theology receives another quite astonishing corroboration of one of its chief psychological forces from the side of nature, the redemptive power attributed to the experience of what is called "conversion." To be redeemed and exalted, man must be converted. He must inhibit the downward drag and turn and move with the upward attraction. If his "watery" carnal nature will not rise by any power of its own, does nature suggest any possibility of its being converted into a form in which it will rise into the air? And what power would effect this transfiguration? *Mirabile dictu,* nature comes forward with the instant answer: There is a force that can transform water into a form in which it, too, will rise, and that force is *fire,* the fiery power of spirit-soul. The entry of the soul into the body in incarnation puts its spiritual fires under the kettle of the water of human life. If the soul-fire can not elevate the carnal nature in its unconverted state as water, it can do so by first converting it into vapor, steam. Steam stands just midway between water and fire, thus representing the union of emotion and spirit. Here is forever established the truth that if man will mix his emotions with the fiery energies of thought, he will rise in evolution. Here is the gist of most religious science, condensed and thrown on the screen of the mind by one nature symbol.

Shakespeare drew this analogy for us in the scene of the witches' cauldron in *Macbeth*. This word "witch" is from the German *wissen,* "to know," and the knowing principle is the work of the divine spirit, the trinity in man that matches the trinity of the cosmos. So the three "knowing ones" dance around the steaming, stewing kettle, in the water of which the poet has placed a mixture of elements all symbolizing the dark, gruesome nocturnal side of life. The fire beneath the cauldron is the fire of spirit doing its work of converting the hellish brew into the steam that will "cause the principles to rise," as Egypt puts it.

But nature has more than one way of symbolizing this principle of conversion. One of the most compelling forms is seen in the great religious symbol--the candle and its flame. The verisimilitude of the two sides of the analogy is perfect. You have first the body of the candle, and then what might be called its spirit, the flame, and the two are mediated by the wick. If the flame is to remain in connection with its body, it must exercise its power to *convert* the elements of its body into the likeness of its own fiery nature or texture. Again the converting power is fire. Through the process of first converting the tallow into liquid, then into gaseous form, the flame effectuates a perfect illustration of all that can be conceived as what theology calls transubstantiation of the elements of human nature into those of the divine status. Some murders of delegates to early Church councils, where the heat of creedal passion burned more fiercely than the fires of reason, might have been avoided if mind has taken counsel directly from nature.

Again a light shines from nature into theological darkness when one looks closely into the aspects of the hell-fire doctrine. Heavenly light and glory have been universally symbolized by the element of fire. But so also has the hypothecated experience of souls unfortunate enough to fall into the hell of religious conception. But occult science has in its symbolism always distinguished between two kinds of fire, the one of spirit burning in its purity, the other of spirit enmired in the carnal life of the flesh. The one is the pure clear light of the spirit, the other is the murky, smudgy, sulphurous dark flames of purgatory, generating lurid flares and noxious fumes to asphyxiate the hapless inmates of the underworld. Since there is no hell lower than our good earth, the suffering in hell's fiery tortures must be experienced in the life here. It needs only a flare of active imagination to carry the mind from symbol to reality if one will reflect on the connotations of the emblemism here under the eye. It is fire fighting water again. The fuel the spirit is trying to convert into sublimated form is damp and moist with sense and emotion, and when fire has to contend with damp material, the product is smoke, foul acrid fumes, heavy offensive odors and dull turbid flames, in dark contrast to the bright translucent flames of soul. To purge and purify the murky fires of the soul's experience in hell, the moist elements of such psychic states as hate, passion, violent emotion of all kinds must first be eliminated. Then the flame of conscious life can burn brilliantly even here while still attached to the candle of the body.

Clear insight into further illuminating revelation comes with consideration of the datum that each of the four elements standing below its upper neighbor, contains the essence of the one above it. Earth contains some water; water contains air, as is seen in the bubbles raised in boiling; air contains fire, and fire no doubt harbors in its interior composition the potency of still higher-pitched energy in sublimated form. This would seem to intimate that the primal basic "ultimate" stuff of the universe contains within itself all the lower manifestations and extrudes them out of its unmanifest unconditioned essence in the process, so to say, of unfurling its flag of being out into limitless space.

The ancient sages do speak of matter as being the dregs, the lees, of the wine of life. This symbol of matter as a sedimentary deposit at the bottom of the vessel of life gives the mind an apt hint of profounder reality.

The concept of fire emanating out of water was ubiquitous in religious semanticism of the early day. In the first place all birth issues from the primal motherhood of water. Life on earth issued from the sea. The blood in man's veins is sea water, though somewhat transformed by the air in lung breathing over long ages. Shall we think it strange, then, that many of the various mother-goddesses of mythology were actually named from the sea? Mary is of course the Latin *maria,* the seas. In the Berosan account of creation, the primal mother is named Thallath, which is the Greek word for "sea." Mother, matter and water are metaphorically one.

Moreover our Christian Bible definitely uses the figure of the fire of soul descending and kindling a flame in the ocean, setting the sea on fire. Several verses in *Revelation* speak of the fire going down into the earth or the sea and "causing a burning within the sea," which, incidentally, turned the sea water in man's body into blood. It is established beyond cavil now by present erudite scholarship that in fact the "Red Sea" does not historically refer to the geographical body of water on the map, but to the blood of the human body. The translation of *iam suph* (Hebrew) as the "Red Sea" was a hint of ancient esotericists to that effect, as the original sea water of the biological evolution had become red. As a matter of straight fact, the translation as "Red Sea" has no other warrant, since *iam suph* does not translate as "Red Sea" at all, but as "Reed Sea," several later Bible translations having made the true translation back to the true one, the "Reed Sea."

The ancient semanticists pointed to all vegetation as emanation of life out of earth and water. One of the most favored symbols of this kind was the lotus. It stems from the mud and water and rises to fructify in the air and the sun-fire. As human life is impossible in or under water, life was pictured as coming out of or floating upon it. Even the kingdom of the heavens rested upon the water: "He hath founded it upon the waters and established it upon the floods." The coming of soul (air symbol) down to rescue man immersed in the water of the body was referred to in several chapter titles in the *Book of the Dead*: "May air be given unto these young divine beings," the incarnated young god-souls. "Of sniffing air in the waters of the underworld." "Of breathing air and having dominion over the waters of the underworld."

But nature can show us another symbol of the sevenfold constitution of man in her display of glory in the rainbow. In its coloration we read again the septenary Gestalt of the universe and of our own construction. The one primal essence of being, symboled by white light, being refracted as it passes through the grades of matter--whose symbol, be it remembered, is water--is broken into its seven constituent rays. In the supreme cosmic reference, these are the seven Archangels of religion, the first subdivisions of the primary unity of God. All manifest form must therefore be septenary in structure. Every cycle runs its course and attains its culmination in seven sub-cycles. Hence the rainbow comes at the end of the rain, in shining token of the fact that never again--in that cycle--will the life of soul have to be immersed in the water of incarnation. Also it is clearly delineated in the rainbow phenomenon that creation can come only through the passage of the creative fire through the medium of water, i.e., matter. How mutely instructive is our schoolmistress, Mother Nature!

Then there is the phenomenon of an optical nature which seems to endorse the theological doctrine of the Trinity, as well as that of the seven-aspected form of creation. How singular it is that when a ray of sunlight is passed through a three-sided prism, the image thrown on a screen is that of the seven colors of the spectrum, the rainbow! The stream of energy emanating from the one, passing through the trinity, is precipitated out into a septenary manifestation.

In addition to the concern that the soul should have air to breathe in the waters of the underworld, there was expressed also the danger of its being burned by the smudgy fires of lust and passion. So we find other chapters of the *Ritual* with such titles as: "Of drinking water and not being burned by fire in the underworld;" and "Of not being scalded with water." The noted Egyptologist, A. E. W. Budge, comments: "as fire and boiling water existed in the underworld, he hastened to protect himself from burns and scalds by the use of chapters 63-A and 63-B." We find the echo of this in *Isaiah* (43): "When thou passest through the water I shall be with thee; and through the rivers, they shall not overflow thee; when thou walkest through the fire, thou shalt not be burned; neither shall the flame kindle on thee."

This underworld, then, must be the place where fire and water are joined in affective relation. And the history of mankind over the last two or three millennia would beyond all cavil have presented a more felicitous, certainly less horrendous, record, if intelligence had been sharp enough to inform the religious mind that the only place in evolution where fire and water are mingled in such a relation is in the human body on earth--which, then, must be that underworld. For while fire has been variously associated with heaven, and the very name of the celestial region is the *empyrean* (*pyr* is "fire"), never in all religious literature, either actually or figuratively, has water been located there. That element has always pertained to the lower world. Ancient semantic perspicacity represented the soul, the young god, as in danger of drowning in the water of this nether world. And when to this water there was applied, like an alcohol flame under a test-tube in a laboratory, the fire of spirit brought down by the Promethean soul in incarnation, and the flame elevated the temperature of the water to the boiling point, the metaphor depicted the soul as in danger of scalding.

A common form of air and water mingled with some violence is foam or bubbles. Froth arises when air is forcefully associated with water. Here beyond doubt is the clue to the esoteric riddle of Greek symbology, which represented the birth of the goddess Venus from the sea-foam which was stirred up about the knees of the great God Jupiter as he strode through the sea. Here is the beautiful poetic figure hinting at the truth that Love is born in the evolutionary process when the energic injection of the god's power of fiery mind into the emotional life effects the blending of air (mind) and water (emotion) in the consciousness. Can analogy that runs as true to fact and life as all these things do be thrust aside as too flimsy for intimations of the living truth? Is not love the product of the conjunction of mind and emotion? Froth would indicate the elevation of emotion to the plane of thought, the injection of mind into feeling. The emergence of bubbles of air to the surface suggests how thought is generated out of the mud (sensation) and water (emotion) of the bodily experience. Scriptural exegetists should not forget the name "Moses" means "drawn out of the water;" and the legend had him picked up as the infant floating in a basket of reeds, calked with bitumen, among the marshes at the river's edge. The same tradition went with the semi-mythical Sargon of Assyria before him. Life and consciousness do take their rise out of the mingled earth and water of the worldly, the human underbase.

In this connection it is most fascinating to find a legend that clung to the symbolical baptism of Jesus by John in the Gospels. According to the second-century Christian exegetist, Justin Martyr, at the baptism of Jesus, "a fire was kindled in the waters of the Jordan." In a human birth, the new unit of fiery life is born out of a sack of water.

It should not demand a special poetic genius to catch the trenchant force of the realization that mind truly is born out of the elements of sense and feeling. By incarnation the fire of soul enters the watery realm of the body, and water is already permeated by air in hidden form. Heat from spirit fire raises the water into vapor, which, being an airy form of water, typifies the generation of mind. How amazingly true to this symbolism we find the figurism of old Egypt's portrayal of verities when we read in the *Ritual* (chap. 164): "Oh, the being dormant within his body, making his burning in flame, glowing within the sea by his vapor. Come, give the fire, transport or transform the vapor of the Being!" The very breath of life, air containing moisture, is the symbol of the fiery soul now linked with emotion. This exhortation was a plea to the god, with his fire, to enter the lower human nature and sublimate the emotional element, water, by impregnating it with the air of mind. Each higher element is able to raise the potential of the one below it and refine it. By the single application of this principle of understanding, a hundred subtle discernments of abstruse meaning hidden esoterically in myth and Scripture, are apprehended with the force of a luminous clarification hardly dreamed of. There is cathartic dynamism in these conceptions of psycho-spiritual realities when they are seen in the analogical light of nature's inescapable realism.

In the range of the symbolism of water and air, it was impossible that so conspicuous a natural thing as the existence of creatures like fish in the water could fail to be caught and elaborated for semantic figures. It is doubtless of great significance that in the arcane lore of the mythologists, all world saviors were represented as being born in one phase of zodiacal emblemism--in the sign of Pisces, the Fishes. The birth at Christmas, or the winter solstice was rather the quickening of that which had gone "dead" at the lowest point of fire's immersion in matter. The final delivery of soul-fire out of the water was consummated at the end of Pisces, the spring equinox, when the sun crossed the line separating the underworld from the heavens. For here the soul graduated finally from its schooling in this underworld of matter and body into the kingdom of spirit. Symbolically this occurred at the end of Pisces, and is the base of all Eastern ritualism. In the understanding of the seers of old time, the first of the two mothers of the Messiah-Christs was matter in its inorganic, invisible, subatomic state; the second was matter organic, visible and atomic. Hence legend gives to the Savior-gods two mothers, Isis-Nephthys, Sarah-Hagar, Leah-Rachel, Aholah-Aholibah and Elizabeth and Mary, to bring the Sun-gods to birth. The first conceived them, the second gave him birth. And so, as Jesus said, the first birth is of water; the second is of spirit.

How significant it becomes, then, that both in Greece and Rome the early Christians were given the appellation denoting "little fishes." Both Augustine and Tertullian compared Jesus to the Great Fish in the sea, and his followers to the little minnows. They were dubbed the "members of the fish-cult." The Greek word for "fish" is *ichthys* and its five letters were made the initials of the designation: *Iesous Christos theou uios soter:* Jesus Christ, Son of God, Savior. This was all because the early esotericists in the movement (who were soon silenced) made a play on the zodiacal symbolism. In Indian religion, there had been the Fish-Avatar of Vishnu, and in Babylonian the coming of Ioannes, half-man, half-fish, and in the old Hebrew tradition there was Dagon, whose image was broken (*dag* is Hebrew for "fish.") It is not to be flouted as without significance that in the "miracle" of Jesus feeding the five thousand in the desert, fish and bread were the two elements of nutrition. And Bethlehem, where figurism placed the Christ-birth, means the "house of bread," with the birth in the fish-sign. The Christ is figured as the divine food, as bread and fish, to be eaten by humanity. As symbol the fish points to the submergence of the god life in matter (water), who yet does not drown there, who can still breathe under the elements. Even the fish's bladder came in for suggestiveness, as the means by which the fish can rise higher or sink deeper in the water, hinting at the power of mind (air) to control life in incarnation.

Then how readily the fish symbolizes the forms of organic life floating in the medium of the inorganic! As was shown above, the two states of matter, first inorganic, then organic, give birth to the ultimate divine product in evolution, the Christ mind. These two mothers, first matter and second matter, are usually two sisters, but sometimes are mother and daughter, as the first must give birth to the second. Isis, first mother, says that she gave birth to the suns; naturally enough fish floating in the water suggests the infinite hosts of suns floating in the sea of space. Several of the Mother-Goddesses, notably Atergatis and Semiramis, instead of being named for the sea, bore the designation of "Fish-Mothers." And how few would know that, as Jesus was the son of Pisces, the fish in symbolic legendry, so his Old Testament paralogue, Joshua, was the son of Nun--and *nun* in Hebrew means "fish."

There will be the feeling on the part of many that all this semantic flourish is strained, far-fetched, irrelevant and proves nothing. What it does prove is that the ancient genius, in its effort to portray the deep cathartic power of spiritual truth, turned to nature for outward pictorializations of the cosmic thought.

CHAPTER EIGHTEEN

EXPERIENCING THE DIVINE FIRE

As the sun injects the rays of its dynamic into the body of its system, so the little spiritual sun in each person's life irradiates the body with its energies. One special exemplification of this process was in view everywhere in such a vegetative operation as is seen in the production of the grape. And in respect to the fruit of the vine being the main source of the intoxicating efficacy of wine, this natural symbol gained the widest prevalence. To minds seeking semantic parallels, the production of the grape was viewed as an analogue of the god-power of the spirit-sun in man turning water into wine. In the most direct view of it, this is just what happens. The energic life of the vine seeps up water through the roots and the sun turns it into wine. In so doing, it injects into it a fiery potency to raise the "spirits" of the one who drinks it. Even naive imagination caught this imputation so strongly as to give rise to the vulgar name for wine or intoxicants--fire-water. It is water with fire in it. Also the law could find no more suggestive descriptive term for it than "spiritous liquor"--liquor with "spirit" in it. So it is said in an Egyptian papyrus addressed to Horus, the god: "Thou didst put grapes in the water that cometh forth from Edfu." The Quiche name for lightning is Cak-ul-ha, "fire coming forth from water." The symbolism of Jesus coming as a wine-bibber has been badly distorted to suggest his loose mingling with the lowly sinners and the outcast. On a higher level, it means that he came like Horus of Egypt, "full of wine" or "the Jocund," or as in Greek ideology, as Bacchus, God of Wine. The ancient semantic tendency seized on intoxication itself as a not inapt symbol of man's apotheosization, his being raised to a divine exhilaration or ecstasy. The spirit elevated his consciousness to a divine mania, as Plato called it. "Heaven is pregnant with wine," is an Egyptian fragment. The natural man, with his body seven-eighths liquid, furnishes the raw water, and heaven puts the grape of divine exaltation into it.

There must therefore be a similitude between the natural chemistry of fermentation and the spiritualization of the elements of the psyche, that effects a transubstantiation of lower consciousness to higher. Fermentation generates air in a liquid, faithful paralogue of the generation of mind from emotion. What is imparted is literally an inflation--better, afflation--of feeling into subtler apprehensions, a higher mysticism. Matching it is of course the figurism of yeast in the dough of bread which "raises" it. Leaven is like a seed with potency to expand to higher dimension.

The power of air in motion--mind at work--to dry out the "moisture" of the subordinate sensuality was picturesquely illustrated by the figure of the god with a fan in his hand, in the act of winnowing the wheat on the barn floor. It was a type of spiritual purification, achieved by the work of the intellect operating to sweep out the dross of sense, the chaff, and thus free the golden grain of the divine food for its proper nourishment of man. The initiates in the ancient Mysteries were washed with water, then fanned as evidence of their purification by spirit. "Let air be given to these divine beings in the underworld."

The incarnating soul, being typified as a nucleus of fire in the sea, can be poetized in scores of suggestive ways. It all dramatizes the ruling, converting power of intellect in every relation to the lower life. The *Chaldean Oracles* declare that "the artificer of the fiery world is an intellect of intellect." The mortal who approaches to fire will receive a light from divinity, it was said. The brightening spirit of man "becomes refulgent with the radiations of ineffable and implacable fire." Men were begotten, was the statement, by the mingling of the fire of the gods with the blood of women. Hence the sacred books affirm that "in the blood is the life of the soul."

Inescapable from the semantic mind seeking analogies was the light of the firefly. It seems to glow best in moist grasses, a typical emblem of our divinity flashing in the emotional atmosphere of our lives. Then the presence of phosphorescent fish deep down in the dark of the sea! How vivid a token of the power of the light of mind-spirit to reach far down into the sea of matter!

The general idea behind the sacrifice of animals on the altar was that of the conversion of mortal flesh into higher forms by fire of soul. The glory of the Lord was pictured as a consuming fire on the top of the mountain. Even the lower smudgy fires of Hades and Tophet were purgatorial. Most suggestive, then, is the descriptive name given this earthly underworld by Egypt's hierophants: "the crucible of the great house of flame." That the burning is always in connection with, or having to overcome, the soul-deadening power of water is attested by the idea of the soul's keeping its flame intact "through three days of navigation."

The idea of the need of the human to keep the divine fire alight in the house of flesh, the temple of the soul, was, as is well known, carried out ritually by the Romans in the institution of the vestal virgins, who maintained the fire on the hearth, and by the Greeks with their eternal torch. The fire on the household hearth was another form of the same thing, and gave rise to the significance assigned to the chimney in the Santa Klaus legend.

When Moses was to receive a communication from deity, he ascended the mount and the voice of God spoke to him out of the flashes of lightning mingled with smoke on the summit. The fiery glory of the full presence of divinity was so overwhelming to mortal sight that it had to be dimmed by the intervention of a cloud. So the figure for it was a pillar of cloud by day and a pillar of fire by night. By day man can see his way by his own inner light, but in the darkness of incarnation, the soul's night, he must have the aid of the divine light.

And how can one miss the beautiful poetic intimations of such a metaphor as is seen in the Bible's figure of the burning bush seen by Moses? A green moist raw product of nature, yet burning with a fire that did not consume it. Here we have man's vegetative life aflame with the fire of divinity, yet able to sustain the illumination. The fire arises out of the natural order, though the torch that lights it descends from above. "Our Lord is a living fire."

The Egyptians it was who took the Babylonian word for "fire," which was *ur*, and added the initial "p" which made it *pur (pyr)* as "*the* fire," and gave it to the world's most massive structure, the pyramid, as "the measure of fire," and they are also the authors of the symbol of the fiery serpent. Ubiquitous in their iconography was that little figure of the *uraeus,* a serpent of fire. This was Satan, the son of divine fire turned demoniac by the forces engulfing him on earth, "that old serpent," the reputed stoker of the underworld furnaces. It is he, our lower sensual emotional self, that keeps feeding the fires of lust, passion, greed, hatred, and all iniquity and uncharitableness. The Chaldean *ur* was that original creative fire out of which all things were first created. The first father of life, which was A-Brahm (*not* Brahm but the first emanation from Brahm--*a* meaning "not"), issued forth from *Ur* of the Chasadim, the first seven radiations of the archangelic fires of life, who made creation sevenfold. The cleansing power of fire is marked in our word *pure* and the many derivatives from it. "Wickedness burneth as a fire. It shall devour the briars and thorns and shall kindle in the thickets of the forest, the animal underbrush of man's bodily life," says *Isaiah* (9:17).

The ancient religious figure of the sea-serpent, or fiery dragon of the waters, breathing out flames from his nostrils, portrays the potential divinity of man, mingling the potency of spirit (fire) with the moisture of his breath.

Revelation dramatizes the seven angels as pouring out their fires upon the sea and upon the earth. The net effect was to set the sea on fire--need one say, allegorically?--as well as to turn the sea into blood, in which is harbored the fire of spirit. When the biological evolution which originated in the sea was shifted to the land, by the exchange of gills for lungs, sea water was turned into blood.

And as blood is red, here at last is the solution of a Biblical conundrum that has defied elucidation for over two thousand years.

How apt is Heraclitus' definition of our nature: "Man is a portion of cosmic fire, imprisoned in a body of earth and water." Just as a babe at birth transfers from the kingdom of water to that of air, so by evolution man comes out of the sea and has a new birth in the kingdom of air. All this states the scientific fact that the evolution of consciousness brings man first through the level of sensation and emotion up into the kingdom of (air) mind, and fire (spirit). Hermes says: "I am gone out of myself into an immortal body, and I am not now what I was before, but am begotten in mind." Man bathes, said the sages, in two pools, the pool of water and the pool of fire. "I purify me in the southern tank, and I rest me in the northern lake," says the soul in the underworld.

In ancient Egyptian scripts, the twelve followers of Horus, the Christ, were, according to the varieties of the figures used, called masons, carpenters, potters, harvesters, reapers, fishermen, herdsmen, shepherds, husbandmen; but were in all these characters the "twelve saviors of the treasure of light." For divinity was destined to come to a fiery glow in the human constitution in twelve modifications of the innate divine flame. That is why all world saviors came accompanied by twelve supporters.

As souls made their journey across the turbulent sea of life in physical bodies, these were inevitably represented as boats that crossed the lower main, the "lower Nun." As "nun" means "fish" in Hebrew, the semantic origin of the Jonah story is clear. On board were Horus and his twelve rowers or sailors. But having crossed this lower sea in the boat of the physical body and being destined to cross the expanse of the heavenly life after the dissolution of the body, there was required for the heavenly journey a boat of a "spiritual" texture, the fabled "ship of the sun." When man at death drops his physical corpus, he is not bodiless, for body of some substance, coarse or tenuous, the soul must have. So at what we call death, the soul disembarks, say the Egyptians, from the boat of Horus, the physical body, and reembarks on the bright ship of Re, the boat fabricated of sublimated sun-essence, and in it majestically sails across the heavens to begin its next descent on the western side. This is that "spiritual body" which St. Paul says we have, along with a physical body.

This run of natural features forms a large and distinctive body of the analogical material utilized by the authors of the sacred books to dramatize spiritual and cosmic verities. Our effort with it has been to correlate it significantly with its actual scientific references. The fact that the mentality that conceived and expressed the literature most highly and universally accredited as oracle of truth in human history, found nature symbolism to be the most graphic and dynamic mode of expressing this highest grade of truth, should solidly attest the affinity between nature and the principles of spirituality. It can on this ground alone be assumed that in the minds of those ancient sages nature was held as the highest tribunal, the court of final authority on all matters of truth.

But there is an immense, almost measureless, area of nature's essences that relate to general philosophy without particular application to religion or the Scriptures, although an indirect relevance to spiritual law may be discovered. Much of this grade of typology will be seen to throw a brilliant light on the principles of general science, or life's universal laws.

As introduction to the next appeal to nature for verification or illustration of universal formulae of truth, it may be instructive to review the most fundamental of those primal *archai*. First there is the bifurcation of original unity of being into the duality for the necessary action of polarity, then the further division of the stream of creative energy into infinite multiplicity. The outward creative movement proceeds, as seen, not in a continuous smooth flow, but in the wave-like motion of rhythm, periodicity and eternal alternation of activity and rest, life and death, and all the shuttle movement. The conjunction of life and spirit with matter gave rise both to the tension between them and the alternate exchange of predominance, now of one, now of the other, the balancing and then the rotation of the forces of life and death. Notable also was the principle that life expresses itself in the active arc of each cycle in manifest organic existence, then when time dissolves the organism, it retires into its *arche* or beginning form, to bide its time for renewal of its active expression in matter. Perhaps the greatest mystery of life for the mind of man is the miracle by which life can dismantle such a gigantic structure of its creation as a great oak tree, condense the entire particularity of its organism in some sort of durable essence, and pack it all up in the body of a tiny acorn, preserve it in that form for its period of quiescence, then at the turn of the cycle, bring it forth again with every part intact. by its ability to perform this living legerdemain life proclaims itself as the alpha and the omega of being, the first seed and the last fruit, the beginning and the end. Finally we have the phases of the struggle between the two forces, positive and negative, between spirit and matter, matter moving upward from first inertia and spirit descending to wrestle with it.

The purpose of this brief sketch of the most obvious basic *archai* was to make impressive the statement now to be made, that in truth every item and element of these principia is to be found demonstrated in the life of perhaps the most wonderful of nature's productions, the majestic thing we call a *tree*. Yes, the tree is the fit object of our wonder and adoration. At the same time it becomes the most illuminating teacher of the great basic laws of our life and that of the cosmos. It preaches to us its gospel, flaunts in our eyes its message and dramatizes for us the living formulae of truth.

We have for a moment to go back to the diagram illustrating the sevenfold staging of the approach to each other of spirit and matter and their meeting in the middle on the line of the "horizon," to engage in their aeonial battle to achieve eventual union. We must contemplate closely the phenomenon of the two forces moving toward each other in opposite directions. Suddenly in the light of what the tree shows us, we get a keen and subtle comprehension of what Heraclitus meant by the movement of the upward and the downward ways in the living process. The tree displays the life force moving in the two directions and carries thought on to astonishing further revelations of hidden truth.

The great "vegetable" stands rooted in earth, yet with its organic body reaching up into the heavens. From the earthy watery depths through roots and trunk rises the life-bearing current, the sap, and spreads upward to the topmost and outermost branches, distributing the vivifying nutrients for physical being to the entire organism. That is the movement upward; is there a creative power from above descending to meet it? And would such a power come through the agency of air and fire? Sure enough; down from the celestial heights through the air streams that splendor of the light of the sun! Having lifted the material elements up as far as they can go, the upward movement is met by the magical converting power of a heavenly essence, sunlight. And the miraculous process of photosynthesis takes place. In scientific terms, this results in the production of chlorophyll, green leaf substance. The fact of greatest moment here is that the conjunction of the vivifying power descending from above and the watery substance ascending from below brings the generation of a new birth of life. Just as in man the divinity is born from the union of body coming up from below and soul descending from above, so the tip of every branch of the tree becomes that mid-point where sun and sap meet to procreate new life.

From this phenomena mind leaps to the determination so clearly symbolized: that new life is generated and given birth always out on the periphery of creation, on its remotest frontiers. Not in the interior recesses of being, but out in the open sunlight of its organic existence do the two nodes of the eternal polarity travel to find their rendezvous. The unity of being can not breed renewal; only when the two forces of the duality swing far out from their point of emergence to meet each other halfway between summit and nadir is new birth possible.

Only one allusion to this *arche* has come to the notice of the author in the Bible, but the reference to it is a very pointed one, and that its deep significance for theology has seemingly been missed for centuries is again an evidence of the blindness to esoteric truth which exoteric literalism has thrown upon spiritual vision. In addressing his audience, presumably of Jews, in the temple, he said: "Ye are from beneath; I am from above: ye are of this world; I am not of this world." (*John* 8:23). He means to tell them that they are of the order of the first or natural man, born physically, but not reborn spiritually. His reference to himself is of course as the type of that divinity that despised not the virgin's womb in bringing the seed of the divine life down for implantation in animal man.

All arcane wisdom of the past is at one in affirming that while the evolution of atomic matter could generate brain consciousness to the level of sense and emotion in animals, there was required, as it were, a spark of ignition supplied by a higher development of mind dynamic to impregnate the natural order with the potential of future divinity. For everywhere it is asserted that this power "came down from heaven" and was made man. "The first man is of the earth, earthy; the second is the Lord from heaven." It is said to be a light to enlighten the unregenerate and that it came from the Father of all lights.

Again it is our universal mentor, nature, that can turn what is outwardly poetic figurism into meaningful significance even in the province of science. In the meeting and marriage of spirit and matter in man's development, the forces operative under--be it remembered--God's subconscious mind work to evolve the physical bodily functions and instrumentalities through which the higher dynamic of spiritual force can express themselves in open consciousness. What, then, is spoken of in the Biblical allegories as the descent from heaven of the Lord of life to become the new leaven in the being of lower man, can be more realistically seen as simply the building from beneath, by natural evolution, of the organic functionalism for the flowering out of the divine expression. The development of this mechanism for the manifestation of the divine seed potential in man is what is meant by the natural life coming up from below.

An illustration, crude but patent enough, is at hand in any radio or television apparatus. The air is vibrant with the waves of a symphony, which would remain in the upper gamuts of the vibratory area if our mechanical genius had not contrived an instrument which by synchronization brings the effect into the room.

So when the natural man, coming up from below, has through the stress of experience developed a brain and nervous system of requisite sensitivity, the higher octaves of the celestial music resound in the area of consciousness. This certainly is the meaning of the Promethean myth; this is the method by which Jove's fire is stolen off the empyreal altar and brought down to man on earth. Mortals will receive all the supernal power for which they can provide receptive apparatus.

Quite likely, if the minutiae of the processes of photosynthesis were completely under observation, more than one highly instructive analogy with the interfusing of soul and body would no doubt be discernible. For the fire of the sun in the air and that of spirit in the mental realm must work analogously.

Natural and spiritual processes must be generally commensurable, since the spiritual is in fact a proliferation at a more advanced stage of the natural force. The upgrowth of spiritual seed in human soil must be the more highly organized analogue of the vegetable growth. The process would reveal spiritual mind calling to the unconscious to awaken to its grander conscious potential. Even the resistance of matter provoked the latent divine spark to glow brighter by exertion. And this kindling spirit-fire in the lower man is the match that lights the candle of life.

A strange fact which comes to light in the science of agronomy carries certain intimations as to the relation of seed to soil that would parallel and clarify the relation between soul and body. It appears that the action of the sun's rays falling upon the ground have the effect of breaking down the elements of the soil and releasing carbon in a form assimilable by plants. But, wondrously it is found that the lightning of a thunder-storm is the higher voltage that releases the nitrogen element in the earth for plant nutriment. A matter of this kind spurs thought on to rare apprehensions. It gives validity to the inference that, in the scale of energic forces, the higher reach down to exert influence and pressures upon the lower, thus to transform and raise their status. The superior potencies elevate the lower. It is not fanciful poetry, but a quite scientific concept which religion has asked us to accept, that the spiritual man reaches down, flashes a ray of his richer dynamic of love into the compound of our sensual life and releases its elements that will then work for an accelerated upward movement. The flashes of divine spiritual lightning that are generated in the storms of life definitely transform the lower into the higher order. And once again a fact from the natural world enlightens a religious doctrine.

And how can one miss the significance of the earthworm and other lower lives? Without this lowly creature's ministry man would be far less able to derive his sustenance from the earth. It refines soil for a richer product. In a handful of earth there are countless living entities that raise its level. So religion stands on scientific rock-fact when it exhorts us to let spiritual motivations have rein: they will transform man from bottom up.

Another meaningful fact is that the science of chemistry is seen to work at three distinct levels. First there is the reaction resulting from the commingling of any of the many elements in a test-tube. This is chemistry at its lowest level, its purely material state. Then there emerges a different reaction when the same elements are brought into interrelation within the confines and processes of a living organism. This is called biochemistry. The purely "chemical" reaction is now modified by the play of the higher energies that living organisms generate. But there is a still higher category into which matter is lifted when its elements are subjected in the human stage to the impact of such a more potent force as that of mind, and even more when forces that may be called spiritual impinge upon the chemical processes. These forces, the Greeks said, emanated from the twelve gods on Mt. Olympus, spearheaded by Jove's thunderbolt. They are the mind energy of God, in general religious terms. The regular play of these forces in nature, as has been shown is the fixed activity of God's subconscious.

There is yet more instruction in the tree. It bespeaks the divisibility of life's unity into infinite multiplicity. Its one ground trunk divides and subdivides. In the light of this salient fact, the religio-philosophical debate as to whether life is monistic or multiple is gratuitous. It is a unity unfolding into multiplicity. The division of the blood leaving the heart in one vessel to nourish all parts of the body exemplifies the principle again. But possibly the blood's return through the arteries has not been seen in its analogical pertinence. Nor has it been discerned for its full value in indicating that a current of involution from source must precede a return to base, the latter movement being what we call evolution. Science is too prone to start investigation of living phenomena in matter without asking how matter was endowed with these potencies to begin with. The essence of all truth here is that the prime source of all things rhythmically involves itself in matter in order to deploy its creative energies and manifest itself, and then withdraws. The function of matter is to implement the consciousness of the eternal force.

A brilliant light on this rhythmic cycle of outflow and return is caught when one views its natural analogue in what may be called the round of the water cycle in nature. It is seen in any rain. The fall of the water from "heaven" and its return to the skies to fall again offer points of significance. There is the condensation of invisible vapor in the upper air, which brings it to visibility as a cloud, and then follows precipitation. Reascending it returns from individuality to unity; likewise in falling it passes from individual drops into lake or sea. But how does it get back again to the sky? Here is an item that can speak volumes of meaning for religion. And it can even pronounce a decision on the eternal question whether, when the human body returns to dust, the soul does return to God who gave it, as *Ecclesiastes* declares. Religion has affirmed that the soul does return to the heavens of spirit; science is dubious because it can discover no empirical evidence of such return. But science can no longer remain so naive as to limit evidence only to empirically verifiable form. It itself takes the stand that the existence of sublimated physical energies and their activity are not amenable to empirical verification. No one will probably ever see an atom. Yet the reality of atoms is logically demonstrated by the phenomena conforming to prediction and logical inference. In the same way the imponderable realities of visions of high truth may be substantiated.

So it is with the features of the water cycle. Rain does fall and just as surely returns to the skies. But it falls in one form--as visible liquid--and returns in another and more sublimated form, as invisible vapor, borne aloft by the convection of heat. It visibly descends, but invisibly returns. Again nature gives religion a lesson. For it testifies that soul, which descends to earth or arrives there in visible body, completes its round of outgoing and return in invisible but still existential form. Exactly as that of the atom, its invisibility can constitute no disclaimer of its existence and reality. The rain that invisibly returns to the sky assures humanity that souls, too, must complete their cycle. The invisibility of evaporation gives the mind the conviction that soul likewise gets back to heaven. Nature here enters the court to refute the denier of the continuity of the existence of her elements, merely because they change their outward form. Life's forces move outward to construct their physical tenements, then dissolve them and retire.

Nor yet has the tree exhausted its oracular preachment for our edification. In every new leafage in the spring, it mutely proclaims life's ordinance in answer to the most pleading interrogation that the human heart sends up to the supreme intelligence: If a man die, shall he live again? And the categorical response from this deep source of truth is a ringing affirmative. In what language does the tree utter this assuring pronouncement?

It presents a living formula and pleads to us to read it with intelligence. Can we not see, it cries, that I am a creature that has in my existence two parts, one that is permanent throughout my existence, but another that comes and goes? In roots, trunk and branches I maintain my life through all seasons and vicissitudes. But this other part of me is transient; it comes forth from my body each springtime, flourishes in the genial summertime, but looses itself from me each autumn. As I am under the eternal rule of all being, this phenomenon announces to you the decree of the law of life: that nothing exists but does so by virtue of the universal root-principle by which every existent organism periodically thrusts forth a projection of its force to afford it the experience of Lila in the exertion of its potentia, without which exertion and its delights and pressures it would remain oblivious of its own nature and capabilities for glorious progression. By divine impulse the inner soul seeks aggrandizement of its selfhood, and this is only to be achieved by projecting rays of its power out to reap a harvest of growth in conflict with material inertia. "Having impregnated the universe with a portion of myself, I yet remain," affirms the deity in a Hindu scripture, and it speaks the law of all life behind the screen of invisibility. Even in the human organism, the inner genius expresses itself in outward action and reaps the reward. But under the law of periodicity, each outward exertion is temporary, a foray out of being into the streams of becoming. Souls put themselves forth into action, but withdraw at the end. They return, "bringing in the sheaves" of their harvest of experience.

And now for the supreme illumination of dull mortal mind, the tree reaches the pitch of its eloquence in its final revelation. By the law of rhythm, as well as by the eternal decree of supreme mind, the tree gives itself this repeated experience of baptism in the soil and water of earth, this thrilling joust between earth's moisture and sun's rays, because thus only can it grow. Without this beat of the pulse of life, systole of effort and diastole of repose, the life of the vegetable would remain in static inertness. Miracle of all miracles it may be, but so it is: The permanent part of the organism can expand its potential of being only by its exertions put forth periodically in its production of the leaves and the utilization of the sun's transforming power appropriated through their agency. The inner life's expression through its temporary extension in the leaf gives the permanent part its growth.

Here indeed is one of life's crowning mysteries: Life expands from within outward, but does so by periodical repetitions of exertion through a temporary extension, a tentacle of itself, as it were. What it protrudes from root and trunk comes back to it with increase. One grain of wheat planted in the soil multiplies itself manifold. What transpires as the result of the polarized relation of sap and sun at the branches' ends makes a deposit of permanent increment in the whole of the organism. Life multiplies and increases by exertion in the outward movement. Corruption and decay ensue from stagnation and failure of effort. By the innate urge to renew itself, periodically, life maintains itself in wholesomeness, purity and integrity. So our sacred scriptures beautifully say that the *leaves* of the tree shall be for the healing of the nations. They liken the righteous man to a tree planted by the river of waters, whose *leaf* shall not wither. Again, it is said that blessing comes when the tree is planted on *both sides* of the river. This evidences the ancient recognition of the principle of polarity, the soul standing in necessary relation to both poles.

The no less than amazing outcome of this parallelism is the revelation to all intelligence that if reincarnation be the order that life has prescribed for the effectuation of its cosmic purposes, it is the periodical leafing of the tree of life. The "leaves" of life's tree are its successive incarnations. How disastrously erroneous, then, must be that philosophy which makes the life of man the only manifestation of being that does not continually renew itself? "I die, and I am born again, and I renew myself, and I grow young each day," exults the soul in the Egyptian *Ritual*. "I am yesterday, today, and tomorrow. I am that which was and is and which shall be." "I am eternity and everlastingness."

Philosophers have speculated that God is not a being of absolute perfection but is the total universal life itself in process of evolution. Religious theory has also asserted that since we live and move and have our being within the context of his life, he grows through what we, who are in this figure the "leaves" on his permanent tree, do in our individual and collective evolution. As cells in his body, we increase his glory to the degree that we cause the tiny portion of his life aglow in us to more radiant shining. It may be blasphemous to pietism to speak of God as short of "perfection," or less than absolute in any respect. Problems involving the Absolute, infinities and ultimates are beyond the scope of human intellection. But it may be permissible to think that God is that part of the Absolute that is adventuring into finitude and conditioned existence. So thinks Sri Aurobindo and other profound scholars. God is thus the first emanation from the Absolute. In Indian systems, he is Ishwara. The Gods are emanations from the Absolute, generated by it in the first place as seeds, or seed-atoms capable of infinite growth who now have risen through the grades of matter to become mighty powers in control of vast natural energies in the cosmos. In so far as we are gods in the making, we are the leaves on the tree of eternal and absolute being planted in the garden of material existence.

Implicit in all this symbolic figurism is the great principle that becomes the redoubtable assurance that the relative and conditioned existence--so harshly reprobated by monist-absolutist theorization--is the expression and embodiment of the Absolute. The life of the eternal is expressing itself in the rhythms of the temporal and the transient. Here is the vindication of Aristotle's "entelechy," Heraclitus' permanent in the changing, and the general teleological view of purpose in the world order.

CHAPTER NINETEEN

THE RULES OF NATURE CONNECTED TO MAN

If any natural object evokes more of man's homage and adoration than the tree, it is the flower. Gazing at its vivid coloring and varied structures, the sensibilities are gripped by a seizure of awe and a strong upsurge of the sense of beauty. What must be marveled at is the virtual miracle that nature has produced in bringing this glory of color out of that crude green stem just below it. Although the common mind does not rationalize the analogy, nevertheless some modicum of its psychic import seems to seep through from a higher area sufficiently cogent to bestir the sense of a numinous shadow of divine intuitions and intimations.

For even more incredibly than does the candle flame, the flower proclaims our divinity with the unimpeachable authority of God's own utterance, his monograph in nature itself. Yes, the red, red rose atop that coarse green stem is the utter certification of our credentials for divinity. For any one who can grasp the wonder of nature's transfiguration of the green sap into the brilliance of the flower, there can be no question that by it God proclaims the certitude of our spiritual transmutation. It is a keystone affirmation of deeper religious conceptualism that our animal-natural life is destined to be crowned with a radiant light. The burning bush is a figure of the descent with Prometheus of the empyreal spiritual flame that is to set the natural world in man on fire. The flesh is to ascend back to deity in the smoke and fumes of the altar sacrifice. It is most patently pictured in the Scriptures in the drama of the transfiguration, when the final burst of divine force in man's life caused his face to shine as the sun and his garments--his inner spiritual bodies--to gleam white as the light. In Hindu religious science, it was expressly averred that in literal fact in the higher stages of our transubstantiation into divinity there would blossom in the area of the head a lotus of a thousand petals, each a radiation of celestial light. This is the glorification of man. In only a variation of detail, the Yule pine tree, adorned with glittering ornaments or lights, emblemizes the same idea. In the body there are what the Hindus called *chakras,* or "wheels," nucleated centers of a force generating light, which in advanced evolution will come aglow with a spiritual light, as naturally as the phosphorescence of certain fish in the deep sea, or the flash of cold light in the fire-fly. Man's little sun of righteousness will then have risen with healing in his wings, and man will be forever henceforth the Lord of Light. The bedizened Christmas tree is so close to an actual pictorial representation of what man's glorified body of his resurrection will be that it might be said to be a facsimile thereof.

The emblemism of the rose or other flower was so forceful and piquant in its suggestiveness that it became the accepted symbol of our burgeoning divinity. And the rose blossoming on the axis of the cross became the mystic symbol of the Christ-legend. The key significance was lost for its full cathartic efficacy when the cross as emblem was deadened to the hardness of wood, its esoteric relevance and power thus killed. The cross was truly the signature of *life,* not of death; so that the allocation of the rose to the cross carried the true dynamic of the realization that our divinity was won in life and not inherited in the after-life. Accentuating this earthly localization of our transformation, the legend added the semantic detail that the divine rose burgeoned at the solstice of winter. In England it was the tale of the Glastonbury thorn-tree that put forth its flower at midnight of the solstitial date, "when half-spent was the night." Figuratively this was the witching hour when the old year passed into the new, suggesting the end of the old or natural dispensation and the rebirth into the kingdom of spirit. Beyond question, the flower testifies that man, a product of nature, will flower also in light and beauty at the summit of his being.

In and of itself, the vegetable kingdom is vocal and articulate in its moral-spiritual preachments. To catalogue all the ways and forms in which the many interactions of the four basic elements; earth, water, air and fire; with sensational fidelity analogize their four conscious counterparts; sensation, emotion, thought, and spiritual intuition; would constitute a convincing demonstration of the theory of nature-mind correspondence. These would further harmonize amazingly with the facts and features of the four kingdoms, mineral, vegetable, animal and human. Thousands of phenomenal data of natural history would provide the material for thousands of such analogies.

First it is clear that, in blunt terms, the kingdoms above their subordinate brothers feed upon the life of the latter by natural ability to appropriate and assimilate their substances. The vegetable, clear down to moss and lichens, feeds upon the mineral, consuming the very rocks. The animal consumes the vegetable, and the human the vegetable and sub-animal life. In numberless respects animal life takes advantage of the habits, periodicities of vegetable species in order to promote their own welfare. A notable instance is the connection between the night-blooming cereus and some other plants whose fertilization depends upon the visits of certain birds which fly only at night.

Phenomena of this sort by the hundreds makes natural history a source of endless fascination. The four kingdoms, like the four elements, are inextricably intertwined in a network of relations that make the life of all a unity. The effort here is committed to the task of showing that these interrelations provide vivid analogies with the interactions between the four elements of psychic life. Perhaps in all this field of interest nothing yields more trenchant admonition to the mind than the characteristic phenomena of that extraordinary creature, the bee. Whole books have been written and not exhausted the marvel of the story.

One Egyptologist, Gerald Massey, may be right in claiming that the name of this busy denizen of our fields comes from the name of one of the seven bodies of sublimated essence in the constitution of man--the *ba*. It was of psycho-etheric nature and was one of the several "souls" of man, an intermediate one between higher and lower ones. Much as a soul extracts the sweet nectar of spiritual value from every "flower" of experience in the broad field of life, the bee becomes a fit type of this agent of integration in the moral-spiritual field. Again the bee and the *ba* stand in a striking similitude in that both perform the function of the priest as marriage officient. As the bee, by introducing the fertilizing pollen of the male organs of the flower into the female organs and thus marries the two for the birth of seed, so the *ba*, by his intermediary offices in the psychic economy of human life, marries the two forces of the polarity, soul and body.

Then in its great avocation of collector of honey, the bee is provocative of the most enchanting reflections. Poetic instinct may readily be charged with imaginative libertinism; yet could anything be more beautifully suggestive than the comparison of the bee collecting the sweet product of the life of every flower and depositing it in a central treasure-house, with the work of the soul, which similarly extracts its scintilla of sweet wisdom from every living experience and collects it in the central bank of spiritual memory? The ego-soul of man is the bee that collects the spiritual honey from all life's efforts at growth.

Furthermore there is a positive sweetness of the treasures of mind exactly matching the sweetness of the material nectar, and to this all great philosophers have testified. Honey's properties and working efficacy in the human dietary bear as close a parallel as could be demanded for the validation of analogy. Honey is long chemically incorruptible, is the most delectable and sustaining of human foods. All this holds true when transferred to the honey-sweetness of truth, or man's assimilation of it. Our venerable Scripture lauds the supreme virtue of mental nectar: "With all thy getting, get wisdom and knowledge; sweeter are they than honey and the honeycomb." Egyptian perspicacity chants the prayer of Pepi, one of the type-names of the soul. He pleads for the bread of eternity and the beer of everlastingness; the bread that will not go moldy and the wine that will not go sour. The soul does pray for the honey and nectar of eternity.

Three things, the sages declared, were not products of earth, but were brought by the gods with them when they came to earth from Venus, as the most pungent symbols of divinity. These three were wheat for bread, the grape for wine, and the bee for honey. Be the tradition myth or charming fantasy, there is ample ground for all the play of poetic perception that discerns how fittingly the analogies hold. Egypt speaks of the incarnated divinity as the "collector of souls." The honey of each flower may be considered as the sweet soul of the plant. The divine ego, collecting this distillation of sweetness--moral and spiritual--out of the experiences of each individual, garners them all in a central place. This typifies the eventual unity of all souls. The bee and the soul, alike in their several spheres, are the collectors of the sweet values that life distills out of its activities. Perhaps the most potent lesson from honey is its prod to mind to realize that out of the effort at existence every creature distills a drop of sweetness of a spiritual thing that will never "go sour."

At least one touch of the honey symbolism was retained in the Old Testament, in the Samson dramas. The hero--his name from the Hebrew *shemesh,* the sun--slays the young lion by the way and casts its body by the roadside. On his return he finds the bees have made a nest of honey in the decaying carcass of the animal. Then he propounds the riddle of the eater bringing forth meat and the strong generating sweetness. Are we so crass that we fail to discern the magnificence of the theology hidden in the construction? This divine nectar which life must distill for eternal preservation is produced amidst, and as it were, drained off out of the muck of our sordid life in body, the sweet byproduct of life's tribulation. Another figure makes it the oil of gladness that is squeezed out by life's pressures. So the allegory pictures it as being nested in the very body of animal decay. Bees have often made hives in the hollows of dead trees.

The tree has taught us that it is the fleeting and transient that generates the permanent. Nature's intimations are all to this effect, as some of our illustrations have shown. The eternal values issue from the flux and are aggregated in spiritual storehouses for the eternal behoof of souls. Nature repudiates at every turn philosophy's disparagement of the values accruing from the changing, flowing stream of living events. Nature refutes these negative conclusions by showing that the seemingly meaningless eventualities of the daily activity head up finally in rich and abiding blessings.

The golden treasure garnered from life's fields of effort has been figured under different symbols. As in the *Book of Judges* and in some Greek myths, fleece is used as a symbol. This has reference mainly to the zodiacal Aries, the ram, and his son, the lamb of God.

But another most interesting emblem is the manna with which it is said that God fed his children of Israel in the desert. The significant feature here is that it was precipitated on the ground and is described as being as light and thin as hoar-frost. If we drop poetry for gross realism, we face a fabrication which is downright impossible as factuality. How does one scrape a substance as thin as hoar-frost off sand or grass, for edible purposes, without also scraping up the muck of earth with it? How would enough be collected to supply the commissary department of a host of two and a quarter million of people for three "squares" every day? Perhaps history records no more lamentable hallucination of the human mind than that directly due to the literal-historical reading of the "Scriptures."

As the bee, roving in all directions from the hive, unerringly finds his way back home, this may be nature's assurance that our *ba*-soul, roaming afar in fields of incarnate life, will be guided by its homing instinct back to the heavenly palace.

Amazing imagery of the same drying-out of sense-emotion by spirit fire comes to view in one feature of the life of the bee. As the industrious insect on a wet day will bring in honey admixed with a bit of moisture, rain or dew, it is necessary that the water be drained off within the hive. One reads that for this purpose two platoons of bees poise on the wing, the one just inside the open door at the right, the other at the left, keeping a steady vibration of their wings, the one acting as a ventilating fan drawing in air, the other propelling it out on the other side. A circulation of air is thus produced to dry out the moisture. Here is the drying-up of the "Red Sea" and the Jordan River in the Bible. The soul, the bee of our life, will dry up the watery elements of sense and sin out of our lives.

The principle that enjoins upon gods the obligation to come to earth and give their life blood for the redemption of humanity is enacted in living form by the king bee. Male spiritual essence must be sacrificed for the production of new life. The spiritual force must die for the life of the physical order. If ever nature dramatized the play of this principle, it has done so with staggering literalism in the case of the bee. The king bee, pursuing the queen in her flight, copulates with her and--falls down dead.

Nature is replete with parallel illustrations of the same rule for life's renewal. Graphic instances come to view in the life of certain insects of the aphid family, plant lice. The female breeds the eggs, and as a provision for their coming need of sustenance when hatched, she digs a cavity in the fleshly portion of her husband's body and there deposits the eggs. When the larva awake and look about for food, they simply consume the surrounding substance of the father's body. "Unless ye eat my body and drink my blood . . .' said the son of divinity in our New Testament.

Nature of course infinitely varies the play of her general principles. The palolo worm of tropical waters puts on a show of strange character. It consummates its reproductive history annually on one fixed day of the year by a spectacular procedure. It thrusts out from the rear of its body a structure of softer material until at a certain stage, this separates from the body. It floats up to the surface and there runs the course of its existence, while the original segment retreats to the depths. Here is the bifurcating into duality, the one portion going "up," the other "down." Any one who has witnessed a tiny paramecium split its single body apart into two while you watch will know of life's breaking from unity into duality, for the endless multiplication of creatural existence.

Sharply pointed in its hints of meaning is another of nature's products, one that shared the semantic interest of old Egypt's theological romanticists even beyond that of the bee. This other insect is almost a cousin of the bee and almost bears its name. He is the scarabaeus, the beetle. Primarily its type reference is to the sun. It is observed to follow the sun so as to be directly under its radiation. On a grape arbor which stands over a garden walk, it will be found consuming the east-side leaves in the forenoon, on the top area at noon, and on the western side in the afternoon. In temperate zones it emerges from the earth in summer, then bores back into the ground for the months of hibernation. The sun's rays glisten on the metallic back of the insect, as a type of divine glorification. With the snake and other animals, its emergence in summer and retirement in winter typifies the soul--our sun--in its descent to mundane life and return to the skies.

But this creature, in some special and very mysterious way, manifests a unique trait in its living economy. The esoteric significance of this strange phenomenon could have furnished a light to Christian theology at a crucial juncture in the formulation of its dogmatic system, and this happy development could have drastically changed all Christian history--and for the better. In this connection the lowly insect's habitudes and traits take on an importance of the first magnitude. It gives us an absorbing revelation.

A start toward this key elucidation must be made somewhat farther back in the exegesis. In fact we take off from *Genesis*. In the Egyptian figurism, creation was generated by the Gods, through the self-projection of their power from head source into the field of space, and a main idea of the natural formula by which it was typified was the self-ejection of the life-blood of the deity; or, bluntly expressed in occult terms, the ejaculation of their seminal essence, which, falling upon the earth, generated mankind. The sun is the source of the life energy in the blood and hence also of the seminal essence. In fecundating the female, a man actually sheds his life-blood for new birth.

So the Egyptians represented the creative Lord, Tum, Atum, as pouring forth "the blood of his being" for the generation of mankind. In a variant version, it was the God Kepher, the "beetle-God." Under symbolism that does not flinch the bluntest realism, these gods were represented as drawing forth their creative fluid either by "mutilation" of their bodies, or by projection of their essence with their own hand, and sprinkling it upon the earth. So flatly is this typology exploited that these gods, Ra, Tum, Atum or Kepher, were dubbed the "masturbating deities." The central item is that they thus expelled their creative essence without conjunction with the female. That is, the divine Fatherhood, the solar light of cosmic mind, generated the seed of world creation without the aid of mother matter.

The first conception of the world originated out of the energies of mind. "This is the sun within us," said the semanticists of old, "the seminal source of life. Do not dim its luster or cause it to suffer eclipse. Save your soul and do not sin against the treasure of light."

Imagery makes it a sowing of their seed upon the land, fertilizing it. The Greeks distinctly say that the gods scatter divinity upon earth, or sow the divine seed. Jesus does essentially the same thing in the ordination of the Eucharist. So the world was created from the drops of seminal solar essence that were ejected from the phallus of creative deity. The male creative fluid became the type of creative deity. It was said that the holy emanation that proceeds from Osiris vivifies gods, men and cattle. This was the blood-shedding of the Gods. In the case of Bata, the younger of the twins with his brother Anup, the phallus is torn away and thrown into the water and devoured by a fish. As the fish is a type of organic life floating in the sea of inorganic life, its swallowing of the emblem of creative power suggests the incarnation of soul in body.

What should be seen here is that this figure of masturbating deity matches on the male side the "virgin mother" and the "immaculate conception" on the female side. The so-called "Innocents" whom the dragon of mortal life tried to slay immediately upon their birth were in Hindu, Greek, and Egyptian symbolism figured as masculine, as well as feminine. The "Kumaras" of India, the Hamemmet Beings of Egypt, who had not yet united with matter, were styled "Virgin Youths" or "celibate young gods." They were as yet "innocent" of intercourse with matter, having been generated by mind alone.

It is here that the beetle enters the scenario. A fertile source of much arcane imagery which bases theological thought on nature, is an obscure early writer, Hor-Apollo. Plutarch is our main source of quotations from him. He says:

> *To denote an only-begotten the Egyptians delineate a scarabaeus as a creature self-produced, being unconceived by a female. The scarabaeus also symbolizes generation and a father, because it is engendered by the father solely.*

To this Gerald Massey, English Egyptologist, adds: "Kepher, the beetle-god, buried himself with his seed in the earth; there he transformed, and the father issued forth as his own son."

Before the primal unity bifurcated into the duality of polar opposites, it was androgyne, hermaphrodite, epicene. Hence it was as much father as mother, being father-mother. But when the spirit side was foremost in thought, it was masculinized. Hence the beetle was a kind of male-mother. (Gods were often represented as male-female, even Jupiter being named Ju-mater. Likewise, goddesses were pictured with beards. Plato in the *Timaeus* says that "all things are contained in the womb of Jupiter.)

The *Litany of Ra* contains an apostrophe to the great sun-god: "Homage to thee, Ra, the beetle that folds his wings, that rests on the empyrean, that is born as his own son."

This regeneration of the God of life through projecting himself, in the form of his life-blood, into the womb of matter, and his coming forth again as his own son, is a key necessary for understanding what involved the early Christian movement in acrimonious controversy that has not yet been adjusted, but remains in an impasse in theological polemics. Nature now stands with the key formula in hand, and the beetle is the umpire whose verdict is final.

It is possible that the provenance of earliest Christian theology, which at first held to much of the occultism and arcane wisdom lore of remote ancient times, especially that from Egyptian crypticism, was mainly responsible for the ejection from the Trinity doctrine of the mother principle and the substitution of the Holy Ghost. The Egyptians stressed the mind-born origin of the cosmos, before it included the polarized parentage of the Father and the Mother. The clear original comprehension of the elements involved gave way to imperfect conceptions, and it all eventuated in a sad wreckage of the truth. Consequently Church Councils wrangled with almost tigerish ferocity, inspiring the Emperor Julian to declare that "there is no wild beast like an angry theologian." the controversies culminated in a deposit of a legacy of warped theology and false dogma that verily has twisted the psyche of the West into tragic illusion for all the centuries since the fourth. And this falsity and mental corruption were embodied in one fateful word in the Christian creeds. That fate-laden word is "only-begotten."

In the Latin it is *unigenitus*; in the Greek, it is *monogenes*. Its translation as "only-begotten" may transliterate or paraphrase the wording, but it fails utterly to render the true meaning. Far from intending to connote the limitation of God's progeny (which Scripture declares is multitudinous) to one son, its reference is to the limitation of universal progenation of his offspring to but a single, instead of a dual, *parentage*. In short, God's spiritual sonship sprang from one parent only, not from the copulation of two. The Son was generated by the Father alone, from God as Kepher, who brought forth his young without the aid of the female. It connoted the primal conception of the creation of *mind, as yet not polarized with matter,* still epicene. The proper translation might be achieved by changing "only-begotten" to "onely-begotten."

Had Egyptian subtlety in semantic artistry been rationally envisaged by the delegates at the earliest Church Councils, and in all that vicious cycle of controversy over the fourth century, the grievous disputes that rent the movement in twain over the Arian-Athanasian issues could have been obviated without a ripple. Man, as Adam, means "red earth;" that is, earthly clay reddened by the injection into it of the vivific life-blood of the Gods. The God who shed his blood and mixed it with earth, and the beetle that similarly goes underground to renew himself in a new birth, would have stood as the two luminous symbols of bright angelic spirit incarnating in human bodies. Divine life had to undergo a baptism in the stream of earthly existence to be born again. These two symbols stood prominently in that long-sealed mass of old Egypt's wisdom-lore ready and at hand to resolve all the fury of theological disputation. Alas! those tomes of buried light had lain unreadable for five hundred years even then. And fifteen hundred additional years had to elapse, while mental darkness reigned, until the Rosetta Stone in 1799 opened the door to the renaissance of ancient light. The beetle could have enlightened the minds of the warring theologians as to those basic questions concerning the relation of the "three persons" of the Trinity, as well as the *homoousia-homoiousia* conflict and the famous *filioque* disputes.

The question arose between the Church factions of Arius and Athanasius as to whether the Father and Son of the divine Triad were of identical substance (*ousia*) or of different *ousiae*. As by descent but one step removed from the being of the Father, the Son was held by the Arian party to be of a substance differentiated by at least one step of gradation. But the Athanasian party held firmly to the complete identity of the *ousiae* between the two. When the question is viewed in true light, it is at once apparent that the question itself is gratuitous and more or less inane. It only arises at all out of a wrong conception of the problem itself. The beetle holds forth, if not the answer--for none is needed-- at least the full light of understanding in which all the issues of the matter are resolved. For, declares our self-renewing insect, I and my father are one; my father has renewed himself in me. How can we be different, if we are one and the same being?

The Egyptians held Osiris the Father and Horus the Son to be identical. Horus was Osiris *redivivus*. It was Horus the Elder and Horus the Younger. At the declining stage of each cycle he was Osiris old and dying; at the start of the following cycle he was Horus youthful and resplendent. As to *ousiae* how could there be any difference? Young or old, decrepit or virile with new life, both were of the same *ousia*. If the still involved dispute may be said to have been compromised, it was at any rate left in dubious and equivocal status and so remains. Is the Son of the *same* or only of *like* substance with the Father? On the answer to that question, the issue hangs today. If *like* is not equivalent to *same*, who knows the difference?

As to the filioque dispute: the Latin word means "and from the Son." The debate was over the matter of whether the Third Person was the product of the Father *and* the Son; or of the Father *through* the Son. There should have been little room for question, as virtually every Christian prayer ends with "through Jesus Christ our Lord." All benison comes to us from the Father, but through Christ, the Son. But what says our oracle, the scarabaeus? As all projection of spirit into matter proceeds from the Father through the descending gradations of matter-energy formations, any subordinate rank of being receives its allotment of vivification both from and through--how else?--the powers immediately above it in the scale. At the same time it is, is not, untrue or misleading to say that the vivifying powers flow down also from the grades still higher than the one just overhead. So again, as in the other dispute, it is true in either case; and all a matter of comprehending the true relation of the elements in the graded hierarchy of being.

CHAPTER TWENTY

SPIRITUAL TRUTHS IN NATURE

Could nature symbolism, anymore than Biblical, overlook the semantic potential of the serpent? Its significant intimations match closely those of the beetle, or any form of life that hibernates in earth. Still as nature infinitely varies her procedures, different creatures or phenomena are likely to adumbrate variations in the spiritual principle analogized. Imagination catches suggestive resemblance, in the form of the snake's body, to the two ends of polarity and the seven ranks of being between them. The picture of a lengthy reptile coiled, with his head projecting from the center and his tail erect at the end, with the three or four (theoretically seven) coils of his body between, is an apt enough mimeograph of the same meaning structure. The coils, too, give a verisimilitude of the cycles through which life must swing between head and tail of evolution. Also, when pictured with its tail in its mouth, it graphs the idea of the eternal cycling of life, round and round from alpha to omega.

But, further, this creature manifests a characteristic feature in an especially glaring form, although it is shared by many in less striking fashion. If the scarabaeus renews himself in his seasonal regeneration through his own son, the serpent has his resurrection from death in his own person. He casts off the outer body of an old nature and comes forth sleek and shining in a new embodiment. As the retirement of any creature into the earth in the autumn suggests the soul's incarnation and descent into "wintry death," so its vernal emergence bespeaks with clarion voice the resurrection of the "dead." The snake accomplishes this in thoroughgoing fashion, by actually throwing off his own skin and coming forth in new and radiant garment. In a social way, humanity has come to imitate him in blossoming out with new and brilliant raiment on Easter Day. But the serpent's garish Easter parade is self-generated, whereas man's is artificial. The snake indeed puts off the old man and comes forth in the body of the resurrection. He can show us an empty tomb on Easter. In somewhat different form, the locust, casting off his old shell in August, illustrates this same life procedure.

In Egypt the dog and jackal were made the types of the god Anup, the Anubis of the Greeks. By no means could the typism of an animal that is able to follow an invisible Ariadne's thread through field and forest and in the dark of night escape the eye of those searchers for nature's clues to eternal truths. Anup was the god to whom was attributed the function of guiding souls through the darkness of wandering in the underworld of earthly incarnation. Does it do nothing to strengthen our assurance of divine guidance to have nature validate the presence of a divine bloodhound deep within our constitution to guide us unerringly through the shadowy forest of sensuous existence? Anup was the type-figure of our inner divinity that senses the straight road through the dark night of human life, when the god is in the *Goetterdaemmerung* on earth.

Sharing aspects of this ideation was the cat. He, too, can browse abroad in the dark and catch the unwary bird or the field mouse; or perhaps attend to his mating. It is in the darkness of the night of incarnation that souls find and mate with their wives, their physical bodies. Ancient sacred tomes abound in the legendry of the Sons of God taking unto themselves wives from the daughters of men. Nearly all soul-parentage unite a god-hero and a daughter of earth. Even Love (*Eros*) came down from heaven to kiss into joyous wakefulness the soul of the human psyche. Egyptian art pictured the divine cat standing with foot on the head of the serpent, or with a knife cutting off the reptile's head. In the person of the goddess Bast, the feline was an object of ritual worship, not as a fetish, but as symbol.

In his short poem *To a Waterfowl,* the young American poet Bryant caught the image of a beautiful analogue in one of nature's impressive phenomena, the seasonal migration of birds. It is to be explained "naturally" enough, to be sure, as simple instinct, to follow seasonal shifts of temperature. But, as one writer remarked, "Nature is not altogether as natural' as it may appear to be." As one penetrates to the depths of a mysterious and quite incredibly submerged intelligence in lower orders, the almost overwhelming conviction is that indeed a keen mind power is marvelously at work almost everywhere. The bird weaves his nest and not without adroit planning. The beaver builds his dam. Creatures take measures revealing prevision of future contingency. The chameleon changes color to remain unseen. The male flaunts gaudy plumes to attract the female. But the "instinct" that tells the flying geese when to migrate, and guides them back to the same locality they haunted the previous season, is enough to quicken our senses of providential leading, the assurance that we are souls "Lone wandering, but not lost."

Souls, too, migrate periodically from a spiritual clime to another, a physical one. We somehow must have the instinct of the homing pigeon.

The ichneumon, or mongoose, was a companion type with the cat in overcoming the serpent from its amazing ability to throttle the deadly cobra.

An observation which the present writer has noted may have a bit of pertinent significance for analogical suggestion. It would appear that nature carries out a principle of philosophical truth in the habits of birds. The paradigm that finds expression here is life's methodology in fragmenting primal unity in the beginning, that is, in the springtime of a cycle, and restoring it in the autumn of the round. Inference here may be faulty, but we do not recollect ever seeing birds flying in great flocks in the springtime, whereas in the autumn this feature will be observed everywhere, as one strays over the countryside. The gods distribute their powers in the outward migration into elementary nature, but reassemble--remember--the separated units in the cycle's end. Jesus enjoined that his people recollect and re-member the scattered fragments of his dismembered body for his resurrection. As the first movement toward creation is the breach from unity into multiplicity, birds come forth in the spring, not in flocks, but in single pairs, for mating. In the autumn they return to unity, also having multiplied life bountifully.

In Egypt the town of Anu (Annu) was localized as the place where Osiris went to his death and in the turn of the cycle had his resurrection. It was described as the "place where thousands reunite themselves;" also as the "place of multiplying bread."

One of the most keenly suggestive features of noumenal relevance is a gesture instinctively exhibited by at least one species of the ape family, the cynocephalus, dog-headed ape, or gibbon. This animal affords mankind a most singular example of sympathy with nature, the luminous implications of which can stir the deepest wonder. There is a wide-spread ancient tradition that groups of this species of ape assemble at sunrise on an elevation facing the east, and as the solar orb spreads its light over the earth, the animals prostrate themselves as if in worship; then with cries and a strange effort at jibbering speech, which Gerald Massey calls "clicking," rise to salute the lord of day, with hands raised on high.

Who can fail to read in this scene one of nature's most striking evidences of a fairly patent intent to play the role of dramatic poet? As Proclus has prodded our intelligence with the knowledge that the light of the sun is the pure energy of intellect, and as philosophy agrees that the development of intellect came *pari passu* with and by the implementation of speech, this animal species, closely approaching the human, somehow senses that the birth of the sunlight of intellect in their lives would unlock the faculty of speech. If this is natural history and not a bit of mythical play on the Platonic model, it testifies to nature's ineluctable bent to dramatism. If a baboon can have an inner subconscious prescience of the rise of the sun of intellect and connect it with the effort at speech, merely from sight of the rise of its outer symbol, and this strong enough to send it out on the bank to salute the appearance of the symbol, he is the paragon of all natural philosophers. It will be claimed, of course, that the cynocephalus, for some reason unknown to us, is instinctively led to enact this spontaneous ritual, and that not he, but we, read into it its analogy with mind. It is the habit, if not the divine necessity of our minds, to search for meaning in all natural things, and this may be our supremely divine necessity. That being granted, the important point is that we do find in nature items of the most gripping analogical significance.

But this near-human species challenges our disbelief with another and perhaps even more sensational demonstration of its kinship with nature in a form that proves that he is far more acutely sensitive to nature's occult forces than is man himself. Gerald Massey cites this excerpt from the writings of that ancient narrator previously mentioned, Hor-Apollo. It seems necessary to give Massey's quotation in full:

Hor-Apollo says the cynocephalus, the personified speaker, singer and later writer, that the Egyptians symbolized the moon by it on account of a kind of sympathy which the ape had with it, at the time of its conjunction with the god. For at the exact instant of the conjunction of the moon with the sun, when the moon became unillumined, then the male cynocephalus neither sees nor eats, but is bound down to the earth with grief, as if lamenting the ravishment of the moon. The female also, in addition to its being unable to see, and being afflicted in the same manner as the male, ex genitalibus sanguinem emittit; hence even to this day cynocephali are brought up in the temples, in order that from them may be ascertained the exact instant of the conjunction of the sun and moon. And when they would denote the renovation of the moon, they again portray a cynocephalus in the posture of standing upright, and raising its hands to heaven, with a diadem on its head.

So majestic and impressive is the semantic cogency of this extraordinary phenomenon, that any attempt to vindicate its instructive compulsion would weaken its histrionic force. It was the last of ancient occult seers, Plutarch, who asserted that man derived his "astral" or emotional body from the moon, as he got his spiritual body from the sun, his mental body from Venus, and his physical body from earth. Is it silly illogical credulity to assume that these counterparts of the two orbs man has incorporated in his own constitution still retain an affinity with their source? Power currents and rays as we know them, from their parent bodies, must vitally effect their descendants even down here. Our magical modern science has only begun to acquaint us with the might and marvel of nature's *finer* forces. The day for sniffing at the dynamism of the most delicate radiations is now past. Distance itself is melting away when rays of finer character are sent out.

While "elucidation" of the gibbon's sensitivity to soli-lunar influences--the conjunction of the two orbs symbolizing their "sexual intercourse"--may come as anti-climax to nature's superb drama, it will likely be missed, if not pointed out, that intercourse between sun and moon (spirit and matter) prefigured the incarnation. Not until it is either poetically or in gross actuality realized that the soul's incarnation in body *is* the impregnation of female matter with the seminal seed of spirit, will these similitudes be cogently perceived. That incarnation should *naturally* or *logically,* or even *semantically,* be a cause of lamentation and grief, casting the imputation of catastrophe upon the natural order, is a segment of theology against which the pen of the present writer has inveighed consistently in protest. He contends that in effect the "fall of man" was not in any sense a miscarriage of divine schematism, but a natural procedure in divine operation. It is as clear as anything can be that the doctrine of the fall, in the sense that it was a dereliction on the part of earthly humanity from obedience to God's injunction, and thus the cause of all disaster to the race, is simply an ignorant misinterpretation of the allegorical constructions aimed to dramatize the descent of the soul into incarnation. This cosmic procedure was wholly within the scope and province of natural law, and entirely beneficent. Souls are sent to earth for schooling, for education. Ignorance in the realm of Christian dogmatic theology is responsible for involving the soul's descent for incarnation in all the lugubrious miasma of sin and retribution. It has overlaid the Christian conscience with a totally gratuitous and depressive morbidity.

In Adam's fall
We sinned all.

This Puritanical dictum has no grounds in evolutionary economy.

Whether the analogical intimations of another challenging natural phenomenon match those of the migration of birds, it is a fact that fishes, such as the salmon and the eel run the round of a remarkable cycle of outgoing and return. It is found that the eels hatched in the headwaters of the rivers of the eastern United States from Maine southward emptying into the Atlantic make their way downstream and strike eastward across the sea to the Sargossa Sea west of Portugal. Fulfilling here some essential function in their living ecology, they return in due season, find and enter the mouth of the same river from which they had debauched, and made their way up to the region of their previous spawning. The Prodigal Son was not the only soul that was brought back to source of its life by the imperious force of the homing instinct.

Fruitful in analogical hints is the tremendous phenomenon of the waterspout occurring in the Indian Ocean. How completely it exemplifies the mutual attraction of the upper and lower of the four elements in their interaction! By the force of a fierce fiery energy, the heated air hovers over the waters with such a power of convection as to create a nearly vacuum-like suction that is able to pull up the surface water from below, and unite it with the whirling maelstrom of superheated air. The same semanticism is manifest in the land tornado and hurricane. All are natural evidences of the law of polarity between rarefied energies above and gross ones below.

Some further aspects of bird symbolism are singularly impressive. A creature so naturally intriguing to poetic fancy could not escape the notice of the sages looking everywhere for analogues with nature. As a denizen of the air, the bird became the leading zoo-type of the soul, which can divide its life between "heaven" and earth. It can soar aloft or nest on the ground, and in the latter position, it typifies the soul in incarnation; building its home in a tree it suggests soul that rather hovers over the earthly personality than descends fully into it. And this sort of connection of ego with the personality *is* spoken of. The unfortunate fledgling that falls victim to the stealthy cat or the wily snake bespeaks a soul caught and imprisoned, as St. Paul says, in "the body of this death."

The Greek esotericists created the myth or legend of the cavern of Avernus, the mouth of the pit of the fabled "underworld," and the bird is the representative figure in it. This name, Avernus, is of most interesting etymology. It is made up of "*a*," meaning "not," and *ornis,* Greek word for "bird," with the "n" thrown in between "a" and "av" to interpose a consonant between the two "a's" for the sake of euphony. The meaning then would be "no birds," but with the mythical intimation of "not a good place for birds." In fact the legend had it that it was a deadly place for birds, as in flying over the orifice in the earth, birds--and by analogy souls--were certain to be overcome and asphyxiated by the noxious exhalations arising from the corruption in the underworld, so that they swooned away and fell helplessly into the cavern--incarnation. Here is a perfect mythologization of exactly what the Buddhistic doctrine alleges as the way the souls falls into this region of deadened spiritual sense. And other Hindu figurism directly asserted that the soul actually swooned away in a sort of preparatory stage to the Platonic loss of divine consciousness in incarnation. And Virgil's famous line from the *Aeneid--descensus Averno facile est,* (the descent to Avernus is easy) has been turned into the ribald jest: "It is easy to go to hell."

There is, of course, the great legend of the fabled phoenix, which every five hundred years migrated from the north of Egypt and there died in its nest, but out of its ashes came the worm that renewed its life in a new cycle. This is strictly not a natural representation, rather a fabrication of mental ingenuity and artificial. However it does naturally depict the law of reincarnation in repeated cycles of "death" and renewal. One feature of the legend was that this bird became black in its northern migration, but regained white color on its return to Egypt. The raven and some other black birds stood for souls besmirched by the soil of earth; the white dove of course suggested the purified soul, washed white in the blood of the gods. In Hebrew the raven, evening, and darkness are virtually one in the word *ereb*.

The cow and bull were the base of much symbolism centering around the zodiacal sign of Taurus, the Bull. As the bee provided the supreme type of divine food with its honey, the cow furnished the companion nourishment, in milk. The ram-lamb, the lion-whelp, the goat-kid, the whale-minnow, were other types deriving significant semantic relevance from their incorporation in the zodiac.

CHAPTER TWENTY-ONE

READING THE STARS

The heavens, too, partake of the life of the natural, and in their celestial domain, night and day, season for season, earth's two nearest stellar neighbors, sun and moon, enact a romantic drama that again stirs the gazing human on our globe to wonderment, if not awe. The sun, as masculine (spirit, fire) and earth's satellite, the moon, as feminine, and associated symbolically with water, symbol of matter, play the roles of a monthly mating and generating process with a fidelity to analogy that affects one with an uncanny sense of design and dramatic planning. Could anything more faithfully dramatize the aggressive character of make fervor of courtship than the sun's complete flooding of his paramour's body with his attention and his light at full moon? Or the passivity and receptivity of the feminine party as manifested in the moon's deadness and "privation of initiative?" He, the generator and prodigal lavisher of creative power, she the passive recipient. Then, from the angle of phallic symbolism, his attention to her, starting from the three dark days of the moon--her period of negation, as Hor-Apollo graphically depicted it--and visiting her night after night with growing ardor for fourteen nights, until at the stage of half-month he has glorified her entire body with his favor. If his light, reflected from her surface be thought of as his impregnation of her womb with the seed of his radiant being, then the fourteen days of its increase is fancied as the swelling of her body in gestation, with its culmination on the fourteenth night. If their meeting for copulation once each month, so closely watched by the Egyptian priests that they called in the cynocephali to fix the exact timing, took place in the west in the dark arc of the cycle, out of sight of the world in the privacy of the night, then the delivery of the child at the light of the full moon was the work of the mother in the glaring light of the whole world. The fatherhood of life is ever enacted in the darkness of night, for spirit and matter are in contact for intercourse and mating only in the dark underworld of incarnation. "It is only there in the darkness of body that the twain ever meet," says Gerald Massey. The light that is born in his body after the meeting is their divine child, and the nightly increase is his growth to maturity at full moon.

But the most trenchant significance of the luni-solar relationship is poetically divined in connection with a statement in the *Gospel of John,* where it is said that the forerunner and baptizer of the Christ was not that true light of divinity, *but bore witness* to it. This concept of the pure spiritual light is so remarkably dramatized by our planet's satellite as to strike the deeply cogitating mind with the almost sublime wonder of it. The sun, being for us our true light, its reflection on the moon and its indirect transmission to earth make the quite perfect paradigm of the light of spirit that comes to us from the ultimate source, the sun, the Father of Lights. How precisely this comports with the Scriptural asseveration that man can not bear the full splendor of the Father's glory, but must receive it dimmed and paled by its reaching him secondarily and in reflected form through a medium that reduces its glare. In *Exodus* there is that badly misinterpreted statement of Jehovah to Moses (man), when the deity says that he will place the man in the cleft of the rock, and the eyes of the man will not look full into the face of the blinding effulgence, but will be shielded from it. Following the passage of the glory, the Lord will remove his hand, and blindness will have been averted.

Even here nature matches the allegory with astonishing fidelity, as our eyes can not gaze into the full glory of the symbol of the supernal light, the sun, without danger of blinding. And along with this there is that statement of sage insight which tells us that "The Lord God is a sun *and a shield* from its light. If we were exposed to the untempered glare of pure spirit, we would be incinerated in short order. We can endure spirit's stupendous radiance only in forms mitigated by its transmission through the various media of matter of requisite densities. Matter is our shield from the sunlight of God's insufferable glory. St. Paul puts this in quite explicit form: "For God, who has caused the light to shine out of the darkness, hath shined in our hearts . . . but we have this treasure in earthen vessels." It comes to us, who, standing far down the scale of evolving life, are capable of giving play to any but a limited voltage of the divine radiation. And luna in the sky speaks to our semantic sense the same piece, as she receives the full complement of solar light, but relays it to us in pallid moonlight. That philosophy, then, is truly wise which affirms that the light of God's life that can shine in our organic being, is not the full splendor of the deific glory, but bears witness to it. Yet it is that ineffable light, turned low for our blessing and protection. Our whole theme is the concept that nature is the reflection of the light of divine truth.

Out of the blending of astronomy and nature, building on the reflection of the heavens upon the earth, was born that mimeograph of recondite meanings, the zodiac. It was in fact the first of Bibles, if only pictorial and semantic, the word of God written upon the earth and matched in the sky. It is a hieroglyphic photograph of the interrelated life of man and the world. Said the sages, man is destined to evolve twelve facets of Godhood, which will slowly emerge into manifestation in his being as he, like the sun (in appearance), makes its long series of cycles of life and death in shuttling back and forth between heaven and earth. The six houses above the horizon line represent heaven, or discarnate life; the six below are the mansions of earth which it fleetingly tenants during incarnation. The Greeks depicted this in the myth of Ceres and her daughter, Persephone, the latter being caught and dragged down into the underworld (not below the earth, but on it), and only by her marriage with the king of this lower region, Pluto, did she win the right to return to heaven during the other six months of the year. It is the sun's journey back and forth between Capricorn and Cancer; rather--for this is what religion has forgotten--it is the solar analogue of the soul's migration back and forth from heaven to earth. Ignorance of hagiographic semantics has warped the human mind into the very reverse of the true occult significance. This means to say that tribal rituals were designed to implement or facilitate the movement of sun and moon, as well as the spring rebirth and autumn fecundity of earth, whereas it was these natural phenomena that were memorialized to quicken man's communal realization of the fact that he harbored within himself a sun and moon whose interaction made his life. The subtle ruses of sagacity resorted to the phenomenal to bring home realistically to consciousness the noumenal and spiritual verities. It was too much for the capabilities of general mental acumen; stupid inertness of mind could not transpose the significance from the physical to the metaphysical, but left it there, to harden into gross misconceptions.

Imagine the absurdity of what has been called in anthropology "sympathetic magic," involving the actual assumption that tribal ritualism could persuade nature to attend properly to its functions, which it might fail to do if the tribe did not strengthen its hand. The misconstrued actuality behind these ceremonials is simply the fact that more ancient enactment of symbolic dramatic structures to make vivid outward and visual representations of spiritual realities of mind. They were ignorantly believed to be magical operations affecting nature's operations. When a civilization deems the preservation of structures designed to preserve the durable images of supernal truth a sufficient motive for the erection of a great pyramid, or sphinx, the carving of a zodiac in the landscape of Somersetshire in southern Britain covering one hundred square miles, erecting the round towers of Ireland, the twelve-pillared temple of Stonehenge, the great mounds, obelisks, and streak the plateau of Nasca in Peru with an elaborate design of stone-filled trenches to indicate the position of the sun at solstices and equinoxes, it is tragedy when following ages can only gape in uncomprehending wonder at the meaning; or, worse, regard these hoary relics of past intelligence and semantic art as the product of infantile superstition.

Studied comprehendingly, the zodiac yields a fairly comprehensive chain of meanings that seem endless and fathomless. It is somewhat like the modern mechanical computer or brain machine which, fed with the elements of a problem, will turn out the answers. Each of the twelve houses marks in the solar system a segment of the total spiritual influence, and the soul (the sun) as it passes through each sign assimilates into the texture of its make-up a portion of that influence, until eventually it has absorbed the entirety of the divine transforming power. "I am a soul and the soul is divine; I am divinized in every part," chants the ego of man in the Egyptian *Ritual.*

The circle of the figure, with Cancer (not Capricorn) at the top, represents the course of the swing of the soul round its repeated cycles of incarnation. Also it stands for the whole evolutionary cycle. The figure emblemizes the experience of each cycle or of the summation of all cycles. One minor cycle is a miniature of the whole cycle. The soul's position on June 21 in Cancer represents the apex of return to spirit and reabsorption in its essence. Then the next cycle of outgoing begins the descent toward matter, and at September 21, it crosses the horizon and sinks down into the earth and water of the body, its planting in matter. Losing its spiritual light as it descends, it reaches the nadir of outgoing and at the December solstice it *turns to return.* Gerald Massey, competent Egyptologist, is authority for the statement that the very idea of swinging around on a hinge and turning from involution to begin evolution is precisely the meaning of the Hebrew "Sinai," which he traces to the Egyptian word *sheni, shenai,* meaning "turning to return."

The dying light obscured in matter is at any rate rekindled from the point of the winter solstice, and on March 21, the soul that began its plunge into matter's darkness in September is resurrected out of its material tomb to shine again in brighter glory than before. The thousand corollaries of meaning that flow out from the soul's actual experiences in the rounds, are implicit in the structure, and the arcana of Scriptural writing are cryptically embedded in the fabrication, in the signatures and nomenclature of the twelve signs. The discovery of these relevancies and intimations is indispensable for comprehension of the rational and intelligible meaning of the Bible, the *Book of the Dead* and many other ancient esoteric documents. This is made necessary by the fact that the divine spark in our nature, the Christ-Messiah grade of mind, is represented under the figure of the sign of each house in turn, as the sun moves around the circle of the ecliptic. That is, in Taurus, he is the bull, or golden calf; in Aries, the lamb of God; in Pisces the Fish Avatar, as food to be eaten by man; in Aquarius, he who pours out the water of life in two streams, blood and water; in Capricorn he is the sacrificial goat, led submissively to the slaughter; in Sagittarius, the archer, half-animal and half-human aiming at the bull's eye directly across the zodiac from him; in Scorpio he is the sexual nature that stings the divine soul into a coma on its descent into its "death" in incarnate life; in Libra he is the Lord of the Balance, weighing all hearts in the pan against the symbol of truth; in Leo he is the lion of Judah, the "Lion of the Double Force" of spirit and matter; in Cancer he is the Good Scarab, the symbol of the fiery soul of the sun; and in Gemini he is dual as the two brothers, soul and body.

In the first Christian century, or just before it, the sun was in the sign of Pisces, and this fact gave prominence to all the emblemism of the fish; fishers of men, twelve fishermen as disciples, the miraculous draught of fishes that tore the net; the fish symbol of the Christos as Ichthys; and the name Pisciculi ("little fishes") given to the Christians themselves by the Romans; and other piscatorial references. Still lingering from the two previous periods in Aries and Taurus were the poetisms of the sacrificial lamb and the bull of the Mithraic cult. "Washed in the blood of the bull" had been as common a slogan in religion at an earlier time as "washed in the blood of the Lamb" became later.

The heavens adumbrated the life of spirit, and the north polar star was the symbol of the eternal fixity and stability of the universe. Those stars nearest the pole star were the highest orders in the spiritual hierarchy of the cosmos, and those that never dipped below the horizon were such logoic spiritual powers that nevermore descended into incarnation. The axis of the earth was, as it were, the backbone of the creation, the support of all. In Egypt it was the Tat cross, an upright stout pillar. The point of September 21 was called the Tuat, or Gate of the Underworld, where souls plunged down into the night of incarnation. It seems to be repeated in the Hebrew name Delilah, for *lailah* means "night" and "D," the fourth letter of the alphabet, *daleth,* means "door," the Door of Night.

Of two stars standing for the poles of duality, as one rose in the east, the other would be setting in the west; this was nature's portrayal of the alternate succession of the predominance of the spiritual and physical epochs in the soul's history. As the spirit gained, the power of the flesh diminished, and vice versa. A similar polar opposition was graphed in the structure of the sphinx; for when Aquarius, the one man in the zodiac, is at the forefront of life, that is, in the head, directly opposite and behind him is Leo, the Lion. So he is depicted with the human head and the rear body of the lion. Some symbolic dramatization of this imaginative sort perhaps pertains to every one of the twelve zodiacal constellations and the thirty-six other figuratively conceived in the sky. Orion prefigures the divine soul, as the mighty hunter, pursuing the Seven Sisters, the Pleiades, while his animal soul, in the character of the great Dog-Star Sirius, follows him. For the body, our lower animal self, is following behind soul on the upward path. Most interestingly the Great Bear is the seven-starred mother of all that lives, and eternally circles the pole star close at hand. Mother Nature operates on the number seven, the geometrical base of the physical world. Massey suggests that she is the Great Bear in the sense of the Great Bearer, the prolific mother.

A most intriguing etymological signification arises here. In the old Egyptian, the original word for the "fire" of spirit was *ur* (found in our *uranium*); and the original term for matter (its universal symbol, water, the sea) was *sa*. The conjunction of the two made the parentage of all life and birth. Thus the combination giving this parentage was therefore *ur-sa, ursa,* the Latin word for "bear." So the Great Bearer is Ursa Major. As man is a triad of the conscious qualities of spirit-soul-mind, joined in incarnation on to the four lower elements of physical body, so the three stars of the handle of the "Big Dipper" (so called because at the lowest point of its round, it touches the ocean and dips up some of its water) represent the trinity of spirit, and the body carries the quatrain of the physical life.

In the lower six signs lurks the great water serpent, Hydra (in the Egyptian he is Apap, in Syrian he is Herut), symbolized as the deadly dragon that captures the young soul. Its elongated body trailed over all six lower signs, with its head and open jaws coming directly under the feet of the Virgin, who is standing in her sign with the Christ-child in her left arm and the great star Spica--a head of wheat--in her right hand, prefiguring the divine babe as the coming of the Son of Man, in the symbol of that divine bread whose consumption will redeem humanity. If she should let the babe fall, he would be devoured by the monster of the lower nature. Away down in the southern heavens far below the horizon of the northern sky rises the astrological river of life, the Egyptian Iarutana (the Greek Eridanus and the Hebrew Jordan), which flows north and empties its stream right under the feet of Orion, the Christ. This depicts the natural evolutionary current, arising out of the atom, the lowest depth of matter, and flowing up (north) to the point where it joins the descending spiritual current to implement the birth of the mind power of Christliness. When semantic fancy will write the legend of human life and evolutionary science in such graphic terms on the surface of the sky, we can realize in a strange new way that in very truth "the heavens are telling."

If the area of sense and emotion is the lower hemisphere of man's conscious life, thought and spiritual aspiration are his heavenly kingdom. If, then, it is true, as all religion asseverates, that in heaven we see the verity of things that were opaque to us on earth, is it not possible that in our celestial home of mind and soul we can now see the veritude that eludes us when we use no higher lens of vision than the sense?

Viewing all things from the high point of heavenly vision, we can discern why the thirty-seventh Euclidean geometrical theorem was an exemplification of one of the instructive divine principles. The square of the hypotenuse is equal to the sum of the squares of the other two sides of a right-angled triangle. And a bit of reflection of our seraphic faculty lets us into the mystery of this illuminating realization. Life is doubly aspected, as spirit and matter, and four-square as constituted of the four conscious processes of sense, emotion, thought and high aspiration. Therefore the soul must traverse in evolution a course from one corner of a rectangular plane to the corner diagonally opposite. That is, it can not move only in the horizontal direction, that of sense, or only in the vertical, that of spirit, since the two forces about equally impinge upon him. Therefore his course, with reference to his maintaining his balance on that Egyptian horizon line, is the diagonal across the rectangular square of life. If, say, his course is upward from lower left-hand corner to upper right corner, his direction parallel to the base and top lines represents sensual experience, and his upward direction spiritual advancement, the analogy reveals exactly what lies behind ancient discernment, to give this figure its deep significance. The perception of this diagram's intimations yields understanding of great import. With each step soul takes across the plane of life in lateral direction, i.e., in purely physical life and effort, at the same time it advances vertically upward--spiritually. Thus by the sheer logic of geometry our lives are certified to be moving upward even in the most barren and dreary days of mundane existence. So that, however mystical the conception, the sum of the square's diagonal must equal the squares of the other two sides. In our "heavenly" discourse that says that the product of our horizontal physical experience is at the same time a gain in spiritual progress, so that the final squaring of our life circle brings us to the unity of the two elements. For religion it offers a conception of consummate reassurance that if our progress here below seems to be moving sidewise, still the movement is in some degree upward.

Then we contemplate the singular phenomenon of a gyroscope. Ocean liners have been equipped with powerful ones to stabilize the vessel in stormy voyaging. It is the principle of the spinning top. Its motion, like the swift spiraling of the gods, is so rapid that it can not fall down. So the energic impulsion of the original creative force has enough of the gyrating drive to give the universe its stability.

Then there is another singular mechanical phenomenon that amazingly illustrates one of the more obvious principles of life's *modus operandi*. It is the modern phonographic record. What is analogical here is especially striking. If life is, as the arcane science insisted, an infinite or extended series of cyclings of souls round infinite circles of experience, then both philosophy at large and Aristotle's "entelechy" in particular find their confirmation in the revolving record. As to circularity of movement, it imitates the gods. To the pessimism that bewails the endlessly repeated round of daily life, which allegedly "gets us nowhere," the record registers its positive rebuttal. It does not swing in the same groove, but cuts a new and in some way novel path at each turn; and it does carry its song on to a climax. And how suggestive the thought that the melody of life starts out at the rim, the outer circumference of life, and cycle by cycle takes the movement at each round a perceptible step toward center.

Another physical phenomenon, common in daily observation, perhaps deserves mention for one very salient point of interest. It is that common spectacle of a boy riding a bicycle. This simple exploit, however, on reflection challenges the mind with one of the most perplexing questions, one that matches closely that other debate as to which was first, the hen or the egg. Here it takes the form: Does the bicycle hold up the boy or the boy hold up the machine? In a moment the light of truth flashes and releases a principle of great basic import for philosophy. The fact is that each reciprocally holds up the other. For mental enlightenment, the principle emphasized is that it is only through the conjunct interaction of the two sides of conscious being that anything stands up in the cosmos at all. And what is oracularly revealed to intelligence here is that every living organic entity is composed of a physical instrument housing and implementing an interior conscious intelligence, but controlled by it. When this is fully realized, it may indeed be that in the boy-bicycle situation we have the ultimate key to the philosophy of all existent being. For how can crass materialist philosophy any longer, in the face of such patent dramatization of factual truth, deny the presence and activity of mind and purposive direction in all living action, when it is demonstrated universally that intelligent mind is one half of life's polarity?

CHAPTER TWENTY-TWO

THE LIMITS OF CONSCIOUSNESS

Viewed as a psychological experience, man's life is an adventure in the dual realm of fact and fantasy. By bodily constitution he is inseparably tied to a basis of factuality. An activity necessary for his physical existence demands that he act in relation to what he must consider the material realities of the world in which he finds himself. Abstruse reflection has led philosophers to question whether the objective appearances of the world are themselves "real." Kant contended that at any rate we can not know what they are in their real identity. Others think they exist only in our own area of consciousness and are our own ideal constructions, interior to us, not exterior.

However these questions may be resolved, it is clear that it is the ineluctable experience of all mortals that the environment of man is an objective order, imposing on him the need of acting in relation to them, as if they were completely real things. This is all that needs to be established here as the basis of a summary of our work. It is assumed that in regard to his physical existence, man's life is a contact with physical factuality, the ideal question of its reality being adventitious. It is in any final analysis the actuality of his living experience, and must be accredited as in so far real.

But, as for the rest of his conscious content, a close reading in particular of George Santayana's perceptive insights into the content of our ordinary consciousness, it can not widely miss the truth to say that our existence is passed in a welter of more or less factually grounded fantasies, whimsies and vagaries, capricious flights of imagination and even outright hallucinations. It appears that the moment our minds draw away from the sensory immediacy of contact with concrete pressures of objective things, they tend to fabricate a world of conscious contents, under the impulsion of situations impacting upon them. Minds must react to the challenge of the outer world, and they do so in accordance with their capabilities of analysis, feeling, understanding, knowledge, or the default of these. The character of this digest of individual experience is determined by the degree of evolutionary progress and mastership achieved by the person. It is an inescapable function of the mind thus to make a constant digest of its activities. It engages every soul in deep entanglement in the play of forces which bear him onward to his destiny, with his weal or woe contingent upon his gaining mastery over all the forces prodding him from all sides. His endeavor is to maintain as even a balance as possible between salutary and harmful conditions. The ultimately chief business of mortals, thus committed by their heavenly Father to drift along on the current of life toward a presumably high glory, is to master the *ars vivendi,* to the degree of proficiency requisite to move with the stream in tolerably happy state. It is, of course, the greatest, the consummate art of arts, man's training for divinity. And it embraces and synthesizes all other parts.

In sum this area of our conscious activity is filled with all the feelings, thoughts, imaginations, idle reveries, meditations, day-dreams, all the drift of ideas that float either unbidden and unnoticed; or those generated by the most purposeful and serious thoughtfulness. In a word, the conscious area is filled with all the motions of the mind that sweep through the brain in the course of the day's run of waking awareness. Equally the nature and content of much of this activity of mind can be the emptiest vaporings of the dullard, or the sagest and most elevated visions of truth of the philosopher.

And this is the region in which flourish all the interests and activities of the religious interest of mankind. After that follow philosophy, art, psychology, ethics, education, culture, social life and the drive of intelligent minds for every kind of human uplift. Every motivation of an ideal kind finds play here. But our chief object of study here is the obsession and concern of the human mind with religion.

The issues in this field have been drawn with a severity and even asperity that records perhaps the fiercest and most inhuman savagery of the human race, all the stranger for its exploiting at the same time the most ideal and godlike qualities of the nature of man. In the exercise of the freedom claimed on grounds of the completely inviolable privilege of committing one's mind to any concept of reality, any interpretation or meaning that either wisdom may suggest, earth's people, led in large part by designing priestcraft, has fallen under the dominance of orders and systems of the most tyrannical sort. That this is not merely one writer's biased thought, Dean Milman, in his fine *History of Christianity,* speaks of "the tyranny exercised over the human mind in the name of religion." By the invincible power of traditional subservience, the inertia of the general mind, enhanced by the gullibility of ignorance, the masses have slipped under the force of a victimization that is both pitiable and tragic. The forces of religion have thus exerted their rulership over a vast segment of humanity and virtually provided the masses with their conventional ideas and concepts as to the meaning of the world ordeal.

A catalogue, however, of the run of group persuasions, individual idiosyncrasies, personal obsessions, notions of the operation of exceptional agencies in cases, countless forms of extraordinary beliefs, surrender of reason, credulity as to the manifestation of special acts of Providence, would fill the largest library in the world. All of it has produced a veritable chaos in the ideological life of the race. It has set person against person, group against group, nation against nation, and one half the world against the other. Once attached to or subverted by one or another such form of fixed ideation, the individual tends to become rigidly stultified in his faith, remains obtuse to any enlightenment and with mind closed, becomes the bigot. This would be bad enough, but the force of mental possession tends to fill its victim with the conviction that they are gratuitously authorized by deity to do his will as their impulse dictates. They become slaves driven by one salient idea, for which they may even be willing to sacrifice life itself. If unable to enforce their creed on the public, they indulge in a martyr-like tolerance of sullen character. But if by the contingencies of history, they may ride into power, the suppressed violence of their former restraint breaks out with vindictive ferocity.

But perhaps worst of all in a long perspective is the awesome phenomenon of the development under religious hegemony of what would now be called a cult--the cult of the magical, the miraculous and the supernatural in the religious domain--and from it, permeating the secular mind. This was bound to occur and to be calamitous to an enormous degree, and so it has been. Religion, as hinted, swept into force in history because it was the expression of that content of consciousness that began to function when the mind passes from its dealing with concrete things and begins to speculate on the nature and meaning of the living experience. Religious thought has detached itself from nature and searches in the illimitable areas of feeling, thought, and wonder for what understanding these may yield it. With no guides, checks, clues or competent intelligence to recognize truth, imagination all too readily conjures up wayward, extravagant and strange surmises as to the presence and intervention of forces not naturally operative. The bizarre, the extraordinary, the exceptional, are what these addicts to providentialism come to look for as the product of their devotion and their pleading with deity. Their religion, as a mental support, becomes insipid, uninspiring, unless something in the order of apparently magical phenomenalism comes forth. That God's great benefactions come to them through the normal order of natural law is not ever a matter of interest to them. Religion must yield much in the way of the miraculous, which is interpreted then as certain evidence of God's direct intervention in their favor.

Religion is not the realm of knowledge, or even of thought, but purely of belief, as for the masses. Belief in its efficacy as miracle may be generated by presumptive evidence, the faith and testimony of others, or the lavish promises of the Scriptures for wonder-works in response to faith and prayer. Religion's emphasis on faith, as distinct from knowledge is its charter as a cult of belief. Faith of this sort is always looking for God to produce a marvel. Most of the psychic endeavor that goes with this sort of religion is bent toward the business of cajoling deity, through prayer, into some special demonstration of his beneficent supervision of the world. There are specific ritualisms, or cult practices designed to engage this special attention of deity. Prayer is the most usual resort. Ancient tribes instituted elaborate ceremonials, rituals or customs ostensibly to invoke the favoritism of their god. How far the super-intelligent modern man may be above crudities of the sort, when he still presumes to gain living refreshment and divine grace by eating the essence of the body and drinking the blood of his God may be a question.

The outcome of all this has been one of the most flagrant outflares of the human mind into the wild region of hallucination and delusion ever to obscure man's sanity. It amounts in its most virulent expression to an endless petition ascending continually to God for favors and blessings. Ignoring his natural laws, it amounts to a collective demand that God alter or negate those laws and give attention to unctuous entreaties. The pleas themselves presuppose his willingness to stop the run of his natural order and interpose a miracle for the praying soul. It is a good question whether the cult of prayer, in the crude sense of asking God for favors and blessings is not the most childish infatuation that ever seized the good human mind.

Stress has been laid upon all this religious aberration because it drew the mind and interest of the religious world completely away from nature, and sent it whirling dizzily into the boundless area of the speculative imagination and the unguided realms of the wildest theory. While this run of havoc in the cultural area was most flagrant in the field of religion, it spread widely through all the other ideal interests, tingeing the arts and literature with subtle influences.

One of the most virulent aberrations resulting from the cult of anti-nature has been the exhibition of near masochism throughout the history of religion. The reference is to the cult of asceticism. With the full sweep into Western Christian consciousness of the doctrine of the sinfulness of the flesh, there came the preachment of the evils of the world, the flesh and the devil, giving rise to the practique of self-mortification and brutal suppression of all natural impulses. To indulge the instincts and propensities of the flesh was not only pagan, but the direst sin. Because the body blocked the freer motions of the spirit, it had to be crucified. The spirit was all, the flesh was evil, and the deadly enemy of the immortal soul. The vehemence with which this trend swept the early Church is little dreamed of by those who have not read the record.

Thousands withdrew from the life of the cities and towns of Europe and joined a veritable crusade to the deserts of Assyria, Egypt, Palestine, and Asia Minor to sequester themselves in caves or hovels in order to expiate their succumbing to the "lusts of the flesh, in penance, self-torture and even self-mutilation." Certain seasons of self-denial and self-abasement became established items in the routine of worship, and religious orders were founded to build the spiritual life substantially on the severest of self-disciplines. As the body is an extension of nature into the human system, this special form of pietism had to attack it there where its power over the spirit was most gripping. The devilish power of nature could not be tolerated in such close and dangerous access to the spirit. Great Pan was the deadly enemy. Nature had to be throttled at its source, rooted by original sin in the deepest nooks of man's constitution.

All this chaos in the religious area was attended, accentuated, if not largely inspired by, one of the most staggering phenomena in the history of the race. This was--and is--the presence, power, and influence of a--Book. This momentous tome appears to be a collection of ancient documents, of predominantly hagiographic nature, about which the tradition of their personal authorship by God himself, ostensibly using "holy men of old" as amanuenses for purposes of dictation, has tenaciously clung. It gained the name and renown of being the sole transmission of God's wisdom in literary form to his children on earth. To all intents and purposes, it was regarded as God's manual of instruction, knowledge, wisdom and truth. Under the power of such a persuasion, which spread to virtual universality in the West, this extraordinary volume gained a veritable homage and reverence that would not be erroneously described as the worship of a fetish.

The Book proves to be in many ways undeniably exceptional. It is replete with the maxims of high morality, the soundest incentives to spiritual aspiration and truth and wisdom of unchallengeable authority. But the oldest portion of it purports to record the dealings of God with one particular tribe of early herdsmen in Palestine, whom, for reasons unknown to the rest of humanity, he had chosen to be the special beneficiaries of his favor and his agents for the consummation of his cosmic purposes in the redemption of mankind. The second and smaller portion of the Book is another collation of venerable documents which are claimed to recite chapters of history taking place in Palestine about the beginning of the first Christian century, which are interpreted as being the fulfillment of God's designs for future human history, but in a manner contrary to the expectations of those people he had chosen in the first part of the Book.

The influence of the Book has done nothing to mitigate the virulence of the Western religious bias against nature. Its glorification of the person and function in history of the Son of God has in effect diverted all interest in the religious field away from man's relation to nature.

Having taken a cursory glance at the disastrous outcome for religion and culture of the free mind's efforts to capture truth in the open mental sky looming above nature, it is now our task to examine the activity of more stable-minded and deeply reflective thinkers, who, with better aim and control, have likewise sought out the roads that stretch out in all directions through the vast domain of human psychology. These were not haphazard efforts, but reflection grounded on principle and logic and with an eye never taken completely off the evidence afforded by nature. Here we shall have more balanced and rational consideration of nature. Her testimony will not be scorned. There will be caught also a recognition that nature holds a kind of final jurisdiction in all decisions.

In the use of the free action of the mind in the search for truth, scholars--and one might give outstanding prominence in this respect to George Santayana--have pointed to the way of discovery as running through the region of the imagination. Many speak of the truth-seeking agency of the "literary imagination," and Santayana constantly refers to the broad human effort of the most cultured minds as "literary discourse." By these phrases is connoted that whole cultural enterprise of refined society to carry on the pursuit of knowledge and the refinements of character. Embraced in it are the highest cogitations of philosophers, the most enlightened pronouncements of the clergy, the higher-aiming portion of the output of periodical literature and the finest books of first-grade authors. It represents the most direct effort of a civilization to maintain its most vital relation to the influences of culture.

It is therefore imperative now to trace the possibilities that may be implicit in this liberal but controlled use of the creative imagination, as that implement suggested by learned thinkers as the most eligible pathway to the deepest truth. But what is to distinguish the free use of the imagination here from that same free use of the function that, as we have shown wrought havoc in the realm of religious pietism? This is the big point and the crux of the discussion. In the one case, it was wild license of thought and fancy without restraint of any basic standard of truth or value. In the other it is the play of thought over the ground of reality in a world where the living order itself prescribes the terms of the problem and hints at the answers. All adventuring of the mind in search of truth has had to exercise the power of thought, but the vast difference between some thinking and other consists of the absence or presence of basic principles derived from an authoritative source. So the intellectual quest goes on, with far from futile results. And the aim in this work has been to demonstrate that there is no authoritative source of verity but the world of nature. The human mind may rush into the most active use of its great imaginative powers, but unless it is guided by the principia of a fundamental reality, it runs the risk of wandering astray from truth.

Yet what a strange prospect is unrolled here for our contemplation! What the astute thinkers and writers are saying is that ultimate truth is to be reached by poetic imagination! Not science, not history, not logic, not mathematics lay our path to highest truth, but it is for poets to lead us to truth. Poets, philosophers, romanticists have long used this agency in the enterprise of apprehending truth. But never has this methodology gained any authentic recognition in circles of science or academic authority. In those circles the poetic imagination has been regarded as something undependable, extraneous, outside the pale of either evidence or revelation, amenable to no code of evaluation or judgment. It lay in the sphere of the visionary, the emotional, the fling of fancy. It could not be taken seriously. Now the astutest minds look to it for the clearest perceptions of basic truth. It may be the right road to knowledge, to discovery, to revelation of recondite verity. It can never ignore the basic facts of science, nor can it disregard natural law. But, taking off from there, it can use the faculties of the exploring intellect to envisage inner realities and discern the eternal laws. And why not? The intellectual processes of a poet may be just as keen and subtle as those of the scientist; his logic may be as good, and by nature he may be more discerning of hints and clues to meaning than the scientist. It is the tradition at any rate that the most lucid visions of truth in man's moral-spiritual life have been caught by men who had nothing in the way of science on which to ground their conclusions. The impression still lingers that there is a capability in the as yet unexploited genius of human intellect adequate to pierce to the heart of knowledge. If truth is to be captured, mind must be the agent, whether of the scientist or the poet.

The stage is set finally for the conclusion of our effort. We can go on relying on the faculty which Hindu intelligence has indicated as the one workable tool in the human equipment capable of giving man his deepest and clearest insight into the realities of being. As far as they are apprehensible by man, man can grasp them. Outside of this capability, there is no other road of communication between human consciousness and truth's realizations.

But the ultimate understanding of this transcendent question is to be subsumed under the authoritative principle that links the entire subject with the theme of nature. The vast region of as yet undiscovered truth stretches ahead of man and extends presumably to the heights of the conscious powers of mortals on to the intelligence of minor deities, and on up to the inconceivable summits of the knowledge of archangels and gods, as the Greeks asserted. Into this illimitable field of conscious potential, the mind of man is destined to advance, as his evolving organism develops more sensitive instrumentalities and powers. The road of evolution to higher being beckons man ever onward.

Now the crown of the argument can be put on the whole discussion, with the statement that the human mind may safely and profitably advance into the field of speculative truth if it proceeds with the manual of nature's instruction in hand. Mind has essayed to explore the immense reaches of possible discovery in the area above nature. But to proceed into that terrain without nature's manual as a guide is to risk aberrancy at every turn. Henceforth, investigation must start from nature, and as full and comprehensive a formulation of nature's cardinal principia, her representation of the divine *archai,* as can possibly be outlined and organized in systemic form must be constructed as primary knowledge. Every speculative theory must be held up to nature to see if nature endorses it. Nature must be made the criterion of all judgment and decision. If no analogy or correspondence with a theory can be found in nature, or phenomena contradictory to it are found, it stands discredited. Somewhere in nature will be found a parallel to whatever is true.

The whole problem calls for the intensive cultivation and clever use of what Hindu wisdom called the "sharp and subtle intellect." No powers within reach of a commonplace order of mind can ever discern these analogues. Minds of this caliber look upon nature with no sense of meaning in it whatever. It is, after all, the philosopher, the poet, the mystic, and no less the scientist who may have conditioned his mind to look for the reflection of God's thought in his works, who may be expected to glean a harvest of truth from the cultivation of nature. Thought, divine or human, always precedes and initiates overt action. In every human and divine action, there is implicit the flash of a mental determination.

Nature and spirit together are revelatory of truth. It is the task of spirit to discern truth from the evidences nature presents. As we have seen, nature is the expression of the modes and forms of God's subconscious mind. They are therefore impersonal, immutable products of mind. The child of God who would live his divinely ordained life moving always with the inexorable current of life will be wise to observe the phenomena, study them for discovery of purpose or beneficence, and in the end prudently conform his life to them and the courses they intimate.

THE END.

www.ingramcontent.com/pod-product-compliance
Lightning Source LLC
Chambersburg PA
CBHW042135160426
43200CB00019B/2943